Dialogic Literary Argumentation in High School Language Arts Classrooms

Written by leaders in the field of literacy and language arts education, this volume defines Dialogic Literary Argumentation, outlines its key principles, and provides in-depth analysis of classroom social practices and teacher–student interactions to illustrate the possibilities of a social perspective for a new vision of teaching, reading, and understanding literature.

Dialogic Literary Argumentation builds on the idea of arguing to learn to engage teachers and students in using literature to explore what it means to be human situated in the world at a particular time and place. Dialogic Literary Argumentation fosters deep and complex understandings of literature by engaging students in dialogic social practices that foster dialectical spaces, intertextuality, and an unpacking of taken-for-granted assumptions about rationality and personhood. Dialogic Literary Argumentation offers new ways to engage in argumentation aligned with new ways to read literature in the high school classroom.

Offering theory and analysis to shape the future use of literature in secondary classrooms, this text will be great interest to researchers, graduate and postgraduate students, academics and librarians in the fields of English and language arts education, teacher education, literacy studies, and writing and composition.

David Bloome is EHE Distinguished Professor of Teaching and Learning at The Ohio State University, USA.

George Newell is Professor of English Education at The Ohio State University, USA.

Alan Hirvela is Professor of Teaching and Learning at The Ohio State University, USA.

Tzu-Jung Lin is Associate Professor of Educational Psychology at The Ohio State University, USA.

Routledge Research in Literacy Education

This series provides cutting-edge research relating to the teaching and learning of literacy. Volumes provide coverage of a broad range of topics, theories, and issues from around the world, and contribute to developments in the field.

Recent titles in the series include:

Dialogic Literary Argumentation in High School Language Arts Classrooms
A Social Perspective for Teaching, Learning, and Reading Literature
David Bloome, George Newell, Alan Hirvela, and Tzu-Jung Lin

For a complete list of titles in this series, please visit: https://www.routledge.com/Routledge-Research-in-Literacy-Education/book-series/RRLIT

Dialogic Literary Argumentation in High School Language Arts Classrooms

A Social Perspective for Teaching, Learning, and Reading Literature

David Bloome, George Newell, Alan Hirvela, and Tzu-Jung Lin with John Brady, Seung Yon Ha, Subeom Kwak, Matt Seymour, Eileen Shanahan, Theresa Thanos, Jennifer VanDerHeide, and Allison Wynhoff Olsen

NEW YORK AND LONDON

First published 2020
by Routledge
52 Vanderbilt Avenue, New York, NY 10017

and by Routledge
2 Park Square, Milton Park, Abingdon, Oxon, OX14 4RN

Routledge is an imprint of the Taylor & Francis Group, an informa business

© 2020 Taylor & Francis

The right of David Bloome, George Newell, Alan Hirvela, Tzu-Jung Lin, John Brady, Seung Yon Ha, Subeom Kwak, Matt Seymour, Eileen Shanahan, Theresa Thanos, Jennifer VanDerHeide, and Allison Wynhoff Olsen to be identified as authors of this work has been asserted by them in accordance with sections 77 and 78 of the Copyright, Designs and Patents Act 1988.

All rights reserved. No part of this book may be reprinted or reproduced or utilised in any form or by any electronic, mechanical, or other means, now known or hereafter invented, including photocopying and recording, or in any information storage or retrieval system, without permission in writing from the publishers.

Trademark notice: Product or corporate names may be trademarks or registered trademarks, and are used only for identification and explanation without intent to infringe.

Library of Congress Cataloging-in-Publication Data
Names: Bloome, David, author.
Title: Dialogic literary argumentation in high school language arts classrooms : a social perspective for teaching, learning, and reading literature / David Bloome, George E. Newell, Alan Hirvela, Tzu-Jung Lin ; with John Brady, Seung Yon Ha, Subeom Kwak, Matt Seymour, Eileen Shanahan, Theresa Thanos, Jennifer VanDerHeide, and Allison Wynhoff Olsen.
Description: New York : Routledge, 2019. | Series: Routledge research in literacy education | Includes index.
Identifiers: LCCN 2019028165 (print) | LCCN 2019028166 (ebook) | ISBN 9781138354647 (hardback) | ISBN 9780429424687 (ebook)
Subjects: LCSH: Language arts (Secondary) | Literature—Study and teaching (Secondary) | Interaction analysis in education.
Classification: LCC LB1631 .B66 2019 (print) | LCC LB1631 (ebook) | DDC 428.0071/2—dc23
LC record available at https://lccn.loc.gov/2019028165
LC ebook record available at https://lccn.loc.gov/2019028166

ISBN: 978-1-138-35464-7 (hbk)
ISBN: 978-0-429-42468-7 (ebk)

Typeset in Sabon
by Apex CoVantage, LLC

Contents

	List of Illustrations	vi
	Acknowledgments	vii
	Members of The Ohio State University Argumentative Writing Project	viii
1	Introduction to Dialogic Literary Argumentation	1
2	Toward a Model of Dialogic Literary Argumentation	30
3	Constructing Dialogue and Dialectics in Arguing to Learn in the Teaching, Learning, and Reading of Literature	63
4	Constructing Multiple Perspectives and Rationality in the Teaching, Learning, and Reading of Literature	86
5	Constructing Intertextuality and Indexicality in Dialogic Literary Argumentation	112
6	Constructing Personhood in the Teaching, Learning, and Reading of Literature	134
7	Final Comments: The Possibilities of Dialogic Literary Argumentation in English Language Arts Classrooms	150
	References	170
	Index	182

Illustrations

Tables

2.1	Evolving Definitions of Rationality	44
2.2	Select Functions of the Social Construction of Intertextuality	50
2.3	Select Functions of the Social Construction of Indexicality	52
4.1	Key Features of Role Playing and Process Drama Sessions	98
5.1	Mr. Watson's Literature Evidence Graphic Organizer	118
6.1	Select Nominalizations of Personhood	143
6.2	Narratives of Personhood	144

Diagrams

2.1	Relationship of Theoretical Framings to Model of Dialogic Literary Argumentation	36
2.2	Coming of Age Worksheet	39
2.3	Just Versus Fair Worksheet	39
2.4	Unsub Worksheet	56
3.1	Sources of Evidence for Daisy's Dilemma Generated During the Classroom Event	67
4.1	Student Work Sample MG's Report	104
4.2	Student Work Sample CW's Report	106
5.1	Mr. Watson's "They Say/I Say" Template	117

Acknowledgments

For nine years, we had the great fortune to work with extraordinary English language arts teachers in the central Ohio region. We deeply appreciate all that we have learned from you. Thank you for giving of your time, for your wisdom, for your friendship, for allowing us to "hang out" in your classrooms in most cases for nearly an entire year, for talking with us at length about your teaching and your students, and thank you for thinking with us about the potential of teaching, learning, and reading literature. We hope that this book honors your teaching.

The research reported in this book was funded, in part, by a grant from the U.S. Department of Education, Institute of Education Sciences, through Grant 305A100786 The Ohio State University (Dr. George Newell, principal investigator). We gratefully acknowledge support from the Center for Video Ethnography and Discourse Analysis and the Department of Teaching and Learning both at The Ohio State University, College of Education and Human Ecology. The opinions expressed within this book are those of the authors and do not necessarily represent views of the Institute of Education Sciences, the U.S. Department of Education, or The Ohio State University.

Members of The Ohio State University Argumentative Writing Project

The Ohio State University Argumentative Writing Project (AWP) began in 2010 and is continuing. During that time, the members of the AWP have included faculty members, staff, and doctoral students from The Ohio State University. Some have moved on from The Ohio State University and are now faculty at other universities continuing their scholarship on argumentation, the teaching of literature, literacy, English language arts, and education more generally. In addition to the university-based members of the AWP, there are also the high school teachers. Institutional Review Board policies require that we do not reveal their names or the schools where they teach and, therefore, we have not listed them here.

David Bloome, The Ohio State University
John Brady, The Ohio State University
Jerome D'Agostino, The Ohio State University
Brenton Goff, Ohio University
Seung Yon Ha, The Ohio State University
Alan Hirvela, The Ohio State University
Min-Young Kim, Grand Valley State University
Subeom Kwak, The Ohio State University
Tzu-Jung Lin, The Ohio State University
George Newell, The Ohio State University
Sanghee Ryu, Seoul National University
Matt Seymour, The Ohio State University
Eileen Shanahan, Eastern Kentucky University
Theresa Thanos, The Ohio State University
Jennifer VanDerHeide, Michigan State University
Larkin Weyand, Brigham Young University
Allison Wynhoff Olsen, Montana State University

1 Introduction to Dialogic Literary Argumentation

The primary goal of this book is to define Dialogic Literary Argumentation. For us, Dialogic Literary Argumentation is a framework for the teaching, learning, and reading of literature. We offer this framework at a time when the teaching of literature is facing a crisis of definition and purpose. There have been a series of calls from politicians, business leaders, and some educators to diminish the teaching of literature in favor of information-based texts (for discussions of this debate, see Alsup, 2015; Jago, 2013; Layton, 2012; Schmoker & Jago, 2013). Like Mr. Gradgrind in Charles Dickens's *Hard Times* (1854), the push is for "facts, only facts." It is also the case that too many students are bored and alienated in their secondary schools' literature classes. They find the stories at a distance from their lives and classroom discussions circumscribed by a literary world of which they have no part.

Dialogic Literary Argumentation explicitly holds that the reading of and social interactions around literature are keys to understanding the human condition and the social, cultural, and political conditions of people's lives. Using the construct of argumentation as inquiry and learning (cf., Newell, Bloome, & Hirvela, 2015), Dialogic Literary Argumentation asks students to read literary texts with an open mind and to engage in dialogue with others using the literature they have read to explore what it means to be human and the nature of the human condition within and across particular times, places, and social situations including and perhaps especially the times, places, and social situations in which students and teachers find themselves. The "dialogue" called for in Dialogic Literary Argumentation involves more than simply listening to others and then talking past each other: it eschews competitive argumentation in which one tries to have one's position "win" over others, and it rejects the relativism of disengagement in which people each hold their own views without engaging dialogically and dialectically with each other in crafting either a working consensus or an evolving dialectic that continues to inform. Dialogic Literary Argumentation requires people engaged together in arguing to learn to bring to their dialogues textual evidence that includes the target literary text (the novel, short story, poem, etc.) as well as the texts of instructional conversations then and from previous classes, previously read literary works, texts expressed in other semiotic forms (e.g., paintings, music), and narratives from and about the experiences students have had and those of their communities, among others. As such, Dialogic Literary Argumentation is inherently intertextual at multiple scales and in multiple ways (cf., Bloome & Egan-Robertson, 1993; Hodges, 2018; Tannen, 2006). Metaphorically, the literary text(s) is a prop (cf., Heath & Branscombe, 1986) to foster dialogue that brings together multiple texts (literary and otherwise) and engages people (teachers and students) in ongoing dialogues and conversations about the human condition both in particular situations and beyond. It does so not to fill students' heads with literary knowledge but to engage them in exploring in depth what it means to be human in the world with all of its complexities, contradictions, irrationalities, and incoherencies. Dialogic Literary Argumentation fosters students' engagement in a series of social practices for reading and deliberating about literary texts with others, social practices that are continuously refracted and appropriated for use in other situations and other social contexts.

The framework and model of Dialogic Literary Argumentation evolved from our collaborations with teachers and our long-term ethnographic field work in classrooms.[1] Our ideas developed by moving back and forth between various theories and philosophies (e.g., literary theories, theories of teaching and learning as social, theories of argumentation, theories of languaging in educational settings, social constructionism) and what we were seeing and learning "hanging out" in over 60 high school English language arts classrooms over the past 12 years and from our conversations and collaborations with the teachers of those classrooms. Because what we learned from being there in classrooms is key to the epistemology and ontology of Dialogic Literary Argumentation, we ground our theorizing in the particularities of specific events from the classrooms we studied. We have organized the book to take you on a journey similar to that we took in theorizing Dialogic Literary Argumentation. We looked intensively at classroom events—at the interactions of teachers and students around a novel they were reading—and at student writing with an open mind about the theories we were bringing to our analyses and understandings of those events. We worked back and forth using the analysis of classroom events and student writing to challenge, revise, and remake the theories we had while using those remade theories to challenge the analysis we had done. Thus, throughout the book, we share analyses of classroom events and student writing not so much as illustrations of Dialogic Literary Argumentation (although they do illustrate particular dimensions of Dialogic Literary Argumentation) but rather to share and pull you into how we came to theorize Dialogic Literary Argumentation. We begin our discussion and exploration of Dialogic Literary Argumentation in this chapter, as we do each of the chapters in this book, by discussing one classroom event; for this chapter, it is the teaching, learning, and reading of Hemingway's (1925) short story "Indian Camp" in Ms. Hill's 11th-grade English language arts classroom.[2]

We note here, and throughout the book, that many of the literary texts used in the classrooms we observed concerned issues of race, class, gender, sexuality, and other forms of hierarchy and oppression. And, consequentially, similarly so were many of the classroom discussions we observed. This was not a surprise to us, nor should it be to anyone familiar with the history of literature or the history of the teaching of literature in the United States. Although some scholarly discussions of literary theory and of the teaching, learning, and reading of literature in secondary schools eschew forms of oppression based on race, class, gender, sexuality, ethnicity, and religion, since these and other forms of oppression permeate and define nearly all aspects of daily life in the United States, it would be surprising if the teaching, learning, and reading of literature did not address them. In recognizing the ubiquity of these forms of oppression in the teaching, learning, and reading of literature in high school classrooms in the United States, we have been informed by and have incorporated insights from literary theorists and educational scholars who have theorized the take-up of these and other forms of oppression in high school literature education (e.g., Appleman, 2015; Blackburn, 2019; Lee, 2007; Thomas, 2015).

After discussing the teaching, learning, and reading of "Indian Camp," we then discuss the movement from the current state of the field of teaching and learning literature in secondary classrooms to Dialogic Literary Argumentation. This is followed in this chapter by a brief discussion of key theoretical framings that have guided us in how we are defining Dialogic Literary Argumentation. In subsequent chapters, we explicate key dimensions of a model of Dialogic Literary Argumentation. We also provide a brief overview of the chapters in this book later in this chapter.

It is appropriate at this point that we make clear that we view the discussion of Dialogic Literary Argumentation in this book as a beginning. We look forward to the continuing evolution of our own and others' theorizing (and argumentation) about the teaching, learning, and reading of literature in high school English language arts classrooms and beyond.

Teaching, Learning, and Reading "Indian Camp" in an 11th-Grade English Language Arts Classroom[3]

Ms. Hill told us that she had two related purposes in teaching Hemingway's (1925) short story "Indian Camp": to prepare the students to write a literary argument and to engage them in exploratory talk about the theme of dominance. In the short story "Indian Camp," the first of the Nick Adams series, a country doctor has been summoned to an "Indian" camp to deliver a baby. At the camp, the doctor is forced to perform an emergency caesarean section using a jackknife, with Nick, his son, as

4   *Intro to Dialogic Literary Argumentation*

his assistant. Afterward, the woman's husband is discovered dead, having slit his throat during the operation. Many critics describe "Indian Camp" as a story of initiation—Nick's father exposes his young son to childbirth and unintentionally to violent death (e.g., Defalco, 1963; Strychacz, 2003; Tanselle, 1983). Yet rather than a story of initiation, Ms. Hill frames an analysis of the story using the theme of dominance.

The lesson that day began with 20 minutes of announcements and a summary of the previous class session. Ms. Hill then asked the students to "take out your homework on 'Indian Camp.'" The homework required students to list examples of dominance in "Indian Camp" and to identify evidence, warrants, and backing for each example. She then asked the students to work in groups of four to "come up with the top two examples . . . that you guys can agree on and then we will share out."

The small peer group discussions focused mostly on students telling each other what they did and what examples they found. About 25 minutes into the lesson, Ms. Hill stopped the small peer groups and began a whole class discussion. The participation structure of the whole class discussion was organized by Ms. Hill asking questions or making comments and students responding to her. On occasion, she provided an evaluation—"I agree"—although mostly she repeated, revoiced, or summarized a student response and on occasion juxtaposed it with another student comment that had a different view. She wrote on the white board the terms "evidence," "warrant," and "backing" and throughout the discussion wrote bits from student comments that fit into each category as shown in the following transcribed instructional conversation.[4]

101	T	All right
102		So
103		let's see what you found as far as evidence is concerned
104	Ellen	we agreed that this quote
105		(reads from the story)
106		is strong evidence for the theme
107		the father is ignoring that the woman is pain
108		so rather than serving the people he makes it clear that he is the one with the power
109	T	OK
110		So
111		the woman screams
112		(Ms. Hill writes this on the board under "evidence.")
113		how many of you when you were filling this out were getting confused about what goes in warrants and what goes in backing ↑

114		(looks around room)
115		No ↑
116	Mary	oh
117		Well
118		I have two things
119		I have evidence and I know about rules
120		but I am not sure how to back them up
121	T	OK
122		All right
123		I heard from this group
124		the woman screams and he says they are not important
125		Right ↑
126	Mary	Yes
127	T	(reading from story) "*Oh, daddy, can't you give her something to make her stop screaming,*" asked Nick. "*No, I haven't any anesthetic,*" his father said. "*But her screams are not important.*"
128		So
129		you said
130		(Ms. Hill writes "not important" on board under "evidence")
131		that what↑
132	Mary	(inaudible) xxxxxxxxx
133		said that people who are like subservient have no power
134		my rule was that if there is dominance over someone then one can afford to ignore their feelings
135	T	(Ms. Hill writes student's statement under "warrants" on the board)
136		and I think what you guys were telling me is that / / / there is dominance
137		but what kind of dominance though ↑
138		you think male-woman ↑
139	Ann	Yes
140		in this case
141		but we have another example of evidence
142		there's other dominance
143		like racial dominance
144		there's like other tiny examples that have to do with the word dominance

145	T	there's these other types of dominance but mostly male versus female
146		so
147		and you are telling me also racial right ↑
148		(Ms. Hill writes on board "dominance is male-female" under "warrants")
149	Jane	maybe not in this case
150		but there is racism in this case
151		where she is screaming and he says he has no anesthetic
152		there is not just this male-female ↑
153	T	Amy what do you think ↑
154	Amy	because if she were white she would be in a hospital
155		she would have an anesthetic
156		she would have better resources
157	T	OK
158		I would agree that if she were white
159		Right ↑
160		and have an anesthetic
161		how many of you think. . .
162		OK ↑
163		so if we go into the kind of dominance this might qualify as backing

As the discussion continues, Ms. Hill comments, "I'm hearing good things here. I'm hearing evidence and rules. I like how you are using these [terms] to discuss and to argue about your ideas. You might use these in your paper."

In order to understand what is happening here, it is important to recognize that the theme of dominance is not inherent in the text of the story.[5] Which is merely to say that the story can be read otherwise and indeed many literary critics have read it otherwise, and, in our reading of the story and related literary criticism, there is no evidence that Hemingway intended to foreground the theme of dominance. What Ms. Hill has done is to ask that the students to read the story in a particular way, to read it as a story of dominance and to read it framed as readers making an argument about the meaning of the text. But, as we explain later in this chapter, Ms. Hill has asked the students to do more than read the story as a story of dominance. In both their small peer group conversations and in the whole class conversation, she is asking the students to interactionally construct social relations among themselves, between themselves and the teacher, and between themselves and others (such as the author, literary critics who have otherwise defined the meaning of the story, etc.). Further, Ms. Hill has engaged the students in interactionally defining both the story world and the worlds in which they live, which is merely to say that in order to give a literary text a meaning, the worlds within which that meaning exists must be defined, fashioned, and imagined.[6] It is in this sense that argumentation is a framework for literary analysis in responding to questions such as "How might this text be read?" and "What is the meaning (or meanings) of reading this text with others?"

The discussion of the story continued as Ms. Hill probed the students' reading of the text as a story of social dominance. Much of the discussion to this point involved students sharing their ideas. The students build on each other's ideas, and there is little overt disagreement among them. Many of the students say that there is a theme of male dominance and contribute additional evidence and warrants in support of that claim. Some of the warrants involve premises about individual behavior (e.g., calling a woman a derogatory name), background experiences that the students have had (their experiences with doctors), other stories they have read that are (or could be) related (e.g., other stories by Hemingway), and institutional structures (e.g., the lack of women doctors and what constitutes professional behavior). About 36 minutes into the hour-long lesson, Greg reports that his small peer group questions whether the particular example of the doctor saying that he ignores the woman's screams is evidence of male dominance.

201	Greg	I was just gonna say
202		we were arguing whether or not the first example is really about male dominance over female dominance
203	T	OK
204		tell me why
205	Greg	some of us were saying that he had to push aside screams for the operation rather than
206		"I hate females and I am going to ignore the screams."
207		but that xxxxxx
208	Beth	to concentrate on the operation that he is doing
209		he ignores the screaming because he has to focus so that he doesn't
210		Like
211		poke her in the eye
212	Ss	(laughter from many students)
213	Greg	so we came up with a few counter-examples xxxxxxxx
214	T	So

215		what you are starting to do is listening to others which is great
216		So
217		you are starting to think
218		Uhmm
219		"I don't buy it."
220		and you are giving me examples as proof that you don't buy it
221		right ↑
222		and you mentioned this thing called counter-argument
223		(turns to class)
224		have you guys heard of it ↑
225		all right↑
226		then if you have an argument that you are going to argue against
227		then you need to back it up with something
228		and you're saying that
229		(gestures toward the group)
230		it just a scream
231		and he's a doctor
232		and as doctor you have to block it out
233	Greg	we were just talking about a modern-day example and stuff like that

In this exchange, it becomes evident to everyone there that not all the students agreed with the assumption that "Indian Camp" should be interpreted and critiqued using compassion as a cultural code—or we might say as a warrant for interpreting the doctor's behavior as he tended to the birth. Greg (and at least one other small peer group member) assumed that under the circumstances (attending to a birth), the doctor's actions were both appropriate and necessary. But what is happening here seems to us to be more complex than students disagreeing with each other and offering counter-arguments.

Starting with Greg's comment and continuing to the end of the lesson, the students and Ms. Hill respond to each other's comments by alternatively arguing about the place of male dominance and racial dominance in the events of the story and the strength of the warrants that can be made for these claims. We use the term "alternatively arguing" to characterize what is happening in this instructional conversation rather than counter-argument because the effort does not appear to be one of attempting to convince others that one perspective is correct and another wrong (or less justified) but rather that the students and teacher are exploring the text—how it might be read—adding layers of meaning and insight (also see Kuhn, 1991 on "alternative hypothesis").

During the latter portion of the discussion, Ms. Hill reveals her reading of the story. She states that as there is no evidence in the story that the doctor did not have the proper materials to perform a caesarian birth operation (and that therefore he either did not bring the proper tools with him or otherwise decided not to use them) and instead used a jackknife to perform the operation, that what happens is an example both of male dominance and of racial dominance. What strikes us as telling about the argumentative epistemology at play in this discussion is that even after Ms. Hill states her views and how they are warranted, several students in the classroom publicly present alternative perspectives and warrants. For example, one student notes that in Hemingway's *In Our Time* short story collection, the doctor is described as having a good relationship with the Indians. Another student comments that a particular line in the story could be read as sarcastic, yielding a different interpretation of the whole story and issues of dominance. At the time, the researcher observing the class wrote the following field note: "This line of questioning seems to suggest a rather open-ended approach to the story. Need to ask one of the case study students." Later, when the researcher had an opportunity to talk with Greg about the event, Greg said, "What sort of surprised us was that she [Ms. Hill] was OK with the whole idea of a different view. It's not like other students were wrong or that we are. She just wants us to think things out." Here, the student alludes to the value of Dialogic Literary Argumentation as a means of inquiry that prioritizes multiple perspectives and that this was indeed "surprising" to the students, who may have been accustomed to searching for a preconceived answer determined by the teacher.

It is not easy to engage in the teaching and learning of literary argumentation (or in any subject matter area) as a set of social processes and practices of discovering and exploring complex ideas that values and that respects multiple perspectives. It requires shifting social relationships from being competitive to being a coherency of heteroglossia; it requires redefining knowledge as situated, multiple, and continuously evolving; and it requires redefining oneself as continuously a learner with and among others. It requires prizing an open mind (but not an empty one). It requires understanding argumentation as process and social practice of learning with others through and with literature (see Newell et al., 2015).

From the Current State of the Field of Teaching and Learning Literature in Secondary Classrooms to Dialogic Literary Argumentation

We begin this section by discussing the major literary theories that have been taken up in secondary schools. We then discuss recent trends in the teaching of literature in secondary schools. It is against these two histories—the history of literary theory in secondary schools in the United

States and the history of the teaching of literature in secondary schools in the United States —that we began our study of the teaching and learning of argumentation in high school English language arts classrooms. Our views and understanding of argumentation have evolved since we first began exploring argumentation in high school English language arts classrooms, and our explorations have led us to what we call Dialogic Literary Argumentation. As we see it, Dialogic Literary Argumentation is an approach to (a theorizing of) both reading literature and the teaching of literature. After discussing literary theories in secondary schools and a history of the teaching of literature, we then briefly describe our scholarship on argumentation and on Dialogic Literary Argumentation. Our intent is to share with you how we came to Dialogic Literary Argumentation. This is followed by a brief discussion of key theoretical framings that guided our understanding of Dialogic Literary Argumentation.

Literary Theories in Secondary Schools

Admittedly, what we view as the major literary theories taken up in schools is based in our experiences as former high school English teachers, as teacher educators, from our reading of scholarship, and as researchers of the teaching and learning of literature. We also note a distinction that can be made between theoretical perspectives advocated by leaders and scholars and what we have found to characterize the major literary theories taken up in U.S. high schools (see also Applebee, 1974; Beach & Swiss, 2011).[7] Which is merely to say, first, that others might frame and discuss the major literary theories taken up in secondary schools differently, and second, that we approach the discussion of literary theories in terms of what has been taken up and influenced the teaching and learning of literature in secondary schools (and not, for example, how literary theories have been taken up by literature scholars, at the university level, or how literary theories might be taken up).[8] The discussion here is not intended to be comprehensive but only to set a frame within which to consider Dialogic Literary Argumentation. Here, we focus on three traditions that have shaped, to one degree or another, literature teaching in U.S. secondary schools: New Criticism, reader response, and interpretive communities.

New Criticism

New Criticism's place in the language arts classroom was helped enormously by the fact that it "worked" in classrooms (Graff, 1979). That is, students could be trained to do close readings, and they did not have to spend years examining the life of the author or the historical period of the text to do so. What was important about literature, the New Critics argued, was in the text (Brooks, 1947; Brooks & Warren, 1938). It was there for anyone to read, and almost anyone could be taught to do so. The New Criticism was not just "scientific" (Graff, 1979), it was, in its own way, "democratic" (Rejan, 2017): almost anyone could be taught to do a close reading. Perhaps just as important for its popularity in schools, close reading in the New Criticism tradition was a skill that could be evaluated. Readings could be judged as good, bad, or indifferent by a clear criterion of accuracy by how adequately those readings accounted for the objective reality of the text itself. In a sense, then, the New Criticism mapped so neatly onto some of the conventions of schooling that it almost seemed as if the two had been made for each other. The New Criticism was not just a way of reading literature, it was a way of teaching literature, and, at least through the 1960s, the kinds of procedures proposed by literary scholars and the kinds of instructional procedures practiced by literature teachers shared a set of assumptions that effectively governed the production and consumption of knowledge in literary studies.

Reader Response

Reader-oriented developments in literary theory brought into question many of the premises of the New Criticism. As Mailloux (1982) has argued, reader-oriented critics focus on readers in the act of reading. Some examine individual readers through psychological observations and participation; others discuss reading communities through philosophical speculation and literary intuition. All share the assumption that it is impossible to separate perceiver from perceived, subject from object. Thus, they reject the text's autonomy, its absolute separateness, in favor of its dependence on the reader's creation or participation. Perception is viewed as interpretive; reading is not the discovery of meaning but the creation of it. Reader response criticism replaces examinations of a text in-and-of-itself with discussions of the reading process, the "interaction" of reader and text (Mailloux, 1982, p. 20). By focusing on the reader and the text in transaction (e.g., Rosenblatt, 1976, 1978) rather than on the "text in-and-of-itself," new questions can be raised about how literary texts can be known. The questions address, among others, issues of gender (e.g., Fetterley, 1978), race/ethnicity (e.g., Gates, 2014; Lee, 1993), psychology (e.g., Bleich, 1975; Holland, 1975; Langer, 2011), and culture (e.g., Fish, 1980; Scholes, 1985; Smagorinsky, 2001). If readers are actively involved in the construction of literary meaning, then readers and the contexts surrounding readers are as important to the literary transaction as the texts to which the readers are responding. The most basic critical question in this view is not "What does this text mean?" but "How can this text be read?" and the answer to that question will depend ultimately on who is doing the reading and on what makes up the context of reading.

Interpretive Communities

Fish (1980) argues that the meaning of a text is a product of one's reading strategies operating in specific social contexts. For example, in beginning to teach a class on religious poetry, he found a list of linguists on the blackboard from the previous class. He then asked the students to treat the list as a poem. In their responses, students began attributing religious meanings to the linguists' names. Fish attributes this to the students' membership in an interpretive community accustomed to responding to symbolic meanings of poems. These strategies, Fish argues,

> are finally not our own but have their source in a publicly available system of intelligibility. Insofar as the system (in this case a literary system) constrains us, it also fashions us, furnishing us with categories of understanding, with which we in turn fashion the entities to which we can point.
>
> (Fish, 1980 p. 332)

Thus, the meaning of the transactions is due to neither the reader nor the text but to the "interpretive communities that are responsible for the shape of the reader's activities and for the texts those activities produce"(p. 322). The meanings of Shakespeare's sonnets are not constituted by the text but by the particular kinds of strategies applied to the sonnets.

In our view, recent developments in literary theory have, for the most part, ignored teaching and learning issues; that said, there have been recent efforts to provide teachers with current theory to revitalize their instructional approaches (cf., Appleman, 2015). A key challenge for teachers planning their curriculum and day-to-day instruction is how to move beyond traditional organizational devices such as genre, chronology, and themes. While reader response theory and, to a lesser degree, interpretive communities theory are proffered as a way to foster student involvement and New Criticism approaches as providing techniques for the study of individual texts, these traditions often produce tensions and inconsistencies within the classroom rather than a coherent and integrated approach to the teaching and learning of literature (Applebee, 1993).

A Recent History of the Teaching of Literature in Secondary Schools

For over 50 years, a variety of movements has shaped the teaching of English language arts in general and the teaching of literature in particular. In the teaching of the English language arts in secondary schools, movements have shifted from basic skills and minimal competencies in the 1970s to a reaction to basic skills by a reasserting a return to the traditional values of a liberal, academic curriculum in the 1980s. For example, a report from the NCTE Commission on the English Curriculum (Mandell, 1980) argued for three different models that were reflections and refractions of long-standing traditions: personal growth, cultural heritage, and basic skills. By the end of the 1980s, *The English Coalition Conference: Democracy Through Language* (Lloyd-Jones & Lunsford, 1989) argued from within a firmly constructivist tradition that students as "active learners" would benefit most from "(uniting) skills and content in a dynamic process of practice and assimilation" (xxiii). By the early 1990s, Applebee pointed out that "constructivist approaches have made a large contribution to the theory guiding the teaching of writing and reading, but have a less clearly developed relationship to the teaching of literature" (p. 4). As a response to five "continuing issues" in the teaching of literature, Applebee (1996) proffered his own vision of a constructivist English language arts curriculum in a book titled *Curriculum as Conversation*.

Historically, the teaching of literature has dominated the curriculum of the English language arts classroom; indeed, for many teachers, teaching English language arts has meant the teaching of literature. Yet, their dedication to literature notwithstanding, the recent history of English language arts and the teaching of literature has not been a very happy one, weighted down by what Applebee (1996) describes as "deadly traditions" of book lists, sequencing of "reading" skills, and the study of literature as recitation with students receiving information about literature from teachers. Throughout schooling, students begin with enthusiasm and considerable interest in reading and writing but begin to disengage from "a game they do not want to play," namely figuring out what their teachers would like them to say or write about literature that remains hidden and deeply embedded in the text itself. What is particularly interesting about this state of affairs is that progressive and conservative educators alike have maintained that the study of literature ought to be one of discovery and inquiry building on students' curiosities about the human condition and fostering new ideas and intellectual independence.

Enacting a vision of literature education grounded in discovery and inquiry building on students' curiosities about the human condition has proven a significant challenge, and there is a great deal of evidence that such goals are rarely achieved. During the past 50 years, literature education has remained remarkably stable within Applebee's "deadly traditions" (Applebee, 1996, pp. 21–34). This stability is evident in two series of studies roughly 50 years apart: Smith's analysis of English language arts in the 1930s and 1940s and Applebee's more recent analyses of literature instruction in schools across the United States. Smith's studies (1938, 1941) revealed a rather strong influence of classic texts for study using a typical approach of "question and answer procedures with the teacher in command" (p. 253). Applebee's studies confirmed the sustaining influence of this tradition described by Smith with English department chairs in schools across the United States, reporting that, with only a few exceptions, "the hundreds of selections on the list as whole remained white (98%), male (81%), and Eurocentric (99%), firmly in the tradition established before the turn of century" (1996, p. 28). Perhaps most significant, Applebee found "a continuing emphasis on learning *about*, rather than participating *in*, traditions of literature and criticism" (p. 29). Nystrand and Gamoran's (1991, 1997) observational studies found more evidence for a tradition grounded in teacher-dominated classroom "discussions" of literature: knowledge about texts (agreed upon "author's meaning") dominated most lessons. When Purves (1992) considered the formal assessment of literature, he found that questions posed hardly differed from those that might be asked about expository prose and test items taking the form of multiple-choice rather than more open-ended formats.

The typical lesson remains a mixture of seatwork, in which students focus on "what is happening" in the literature teachers assign, and teacher-led whole class discussion that often seems to blend individual students' understandings into a teacher-sponsored agreed-upon whole. In a pattern that owes much to New Criticism traditions, discussion usually becomes focused on an individual text and the ways in which the text "works" to convey an author's meanings. In some classes, this leads students into thought-provoking engagement with the text and with one another; in many others, it turns literature "into an exercise in puzzle-solving, in which the task for the student is to find the meaning that the teacher sees hidden there" (Applebee, 1993, p. 194).

Another of the legacies of New Criticism's concern with the characteristics of individual texts is a literature curriculum that is dominated by the study of genres. In the United States, in Grades 7, 8, and 9 (and often in Grade 10), the dominance of genre study is overt, with study organized into large units on, for example, the short story, drama, poetry, and so forth. In American, British, and world literature courses (usually in Grades 11 and 12), concern with genre usually resurfaces at the level of subsections within larger units focusing on a chronological period. Instruction in literature in secondary English language arts emerges in these studies as a relatively traditional enterprise, and although 25 years have passed since the most recent status research, there is no reason to believe that the content and teaching of literature has changed dramatically.

Applebee's (1996) alternative vision offers a reassessment of what is meant by literary understanding and knowledge: "The kinds of learning that matter for our schools and colleges represent traditions of knowledge-in-action. These traditions are dynamic and changing, acquired through participation, and oriented toward present and future rather than the past" (p. 20). For Applebee, there is a distinction between such curricular conversations and instructional conversations (specific classroom interactions). Applebee elaborates this thesis as a direction for reform of schooling, as a way to supplant knowledge-out-of-context with its monologic and deadening boredom, with knowledge-in-action entailing student engagement, participation, and "optimal experiences" (cf., Csikszentmihalyi et al., 1993; cited in Applebee, 1996, p. 107).

Recent discussions of academic teaching and learning have focused on academic socialization, the teaching and learning of the practices involved in a particular academic community (e.g., Goldman et al., 2016; Rainey, 2017; Wilder & Wolfe, 2009). Academic socialization is not neutral with regard to cultural, social, and political ideologies that accompany the social practices of reading literary works to which students are being socialized. As such, what is at issue in the teaching and learning of literature from the perspective of academic socialization is (a) access to the community and its social practices (i.e., to the ongoing curricular conversation) and (b) addressing the cultural, social, and political ideologies accompanying those practices with their inherent power relationships and challenges to the social, cultural, gender, sexual, and racial identities and histories of students, teachers, and their communities.

The Common Core State Standards (CCSS) has had a large impact on the teaching of literature at the high school level. Forty-three of the 50 U.S. states, the District of Columbia, four territories, and the Department of Defense schools have adopted the CCSS. The wide-scale adoption of CCSS has impacted the teaching of high school English language arts in three ways: increased emphasis on the use of informational/nonfiction texts, focus on using evidence from text in reading and writing about literature, and a focus on having students engage in "close reading" of complex texts. Positions both in support of and critical of the CCSS for English language arts have largely been focused on the assumed ideology that calls for close analytic reading of canonical texts and the need for evidence when making claims about literature. More problematic is that the CCSS in English language arts make little or no provision for how teachers might develop what Applebee (1996) describes as successful "curricular conversations" with topics worth talking about, appropriate background or specialized knowledge, and an ability to take positions, make arguments, and evaluate evidence in ways appropriate to the discipline.

The Argumentative Writing Project: Twelve Years of Research

Beginning in 2007 and continuing, we have been researching the teaching of argumentation and argumentative writing in secondary English language arts classrooms of teachers, such as Ms. Hill, recommended to us by peers and administrators as outstanding in the teaching of argumentative writing. We have studied 61 classrooms, most of them for the better part of an academic year. Using ethnographic and discourse analysis perspectives and methods, many of the classrooms we studied took up an "arguing to learn" framing to the teaching of literature (see Newell et al., 2015). Although the teachers never labeled their teaching "Dialogic Literary Argumentation," the teachers employed those principles, practices, and perspectives we have come to call Dialogic Literary Argumentation. Perhaps more accurate, as we observed and participated in these classrooms and as we talked with teachers and students, we began to understand that what these teachers and students were doing differed from most widespread approaches to teaching literature in the United States. Indeed, what we call Dialogic Literary Argumentation is less a specific, monolithic framework than a confluence of frameworks, perspectives, and practices that we have learned from the teachers with whom we have collaborated and their students and classrooms. As we spent increasing amounts of time in classrooms, we began to conceptualize Dialogic Literary Argumentation as the social practice of using responsive argumentation to explore the literary in pursuit of understanding the meanings and possibilities of being human in the world.

Dialogic Literary Argumentation builds on recent discussions of argumentation as learning (Newell et al., 2015). Rather than selecting a thesis *a priori* and then seeking evidence to warrant that thesis (or claim) as directed in traditional approaches to argumentation, argumentation as dialogic learning asks students to keep an open mind and allow claims to evolve as they engage with others in dialogue and exploration of a topic, identification and examination of data, and consideration of alternative theses in seeking an understanding of the complexity of human lives. Argumentation as learning asks students to consider more complex and multiple definitions of knowledge and ways of knowing and to recognize that insight into and understanding of the human condition and their own lives are continuously evolving.

Applying argumentation as learning to the teaching and learning of literature, Dialogic Literary Argumentation asks students to treat literary texts as "storied cases" about what it means to be human (here, also referred to as personhood) and about the human condition to be explored with others to gain insight into and understanding of themselves, others, and the worlds in which they live. These storied cases consist not only of the words in the literary text itself but also in its intertextuality—the connections made to past texts and to future texts. Some of these texts are literary texts, some are other forms of written language, some are spoken texts, some are nonverbal texts (e.g., pictures, drawings, dances), and some are conversational texts. Thus, the arguments constructed about personhood and the human condition derive from the exploration of the literary texts themselves, the conversational texts in which students are engaged around the literary texts, the set of intertexts evoked explicitly or implicitly in the conversations about the literary text, the specific, situated experiences and circumstances of the students' lives, and the students' interactions with each other.

The Argumentative Writing Project's initial study of teaching and learning in English language arts classrooms began in 2007 with funding by the Institute of Education Sciences (IES) beginning in 2010. The first phase ended in 2015. During that time, the Argumentative Writing Project collaborated with 31 teachers across a range of school districts in central Ohio. As field researchers employing ethnographic methods, we studied each teacher during a single instructional unit on argumentative writing. Fundamentally, we regarded the teachers as collaborators as we tried to understand what was happening in their classrooms, what they found challenging and compelling about argumentation, and what kinds of instructional conversations and activities supported student learning. In many cases, the collaborating teachers enabled us to understand the current instructional contexts and the significant challenges with which teachers identified and to which they responded. In other cases, experienced and well-informed teachers introduced us to new ways of considering the role of argumentation not as one more instructional unit but as a way to organize and integrate the English language arts curriculum.

One of the more significant intellectual shifts in our thinking about argumentation and argumentative writing was a move from concerns focused largely on structural issues (how can students' argumentative writing be improved with changes in instruction?) to a social practices perspective (how in this classroom is argument defined, understood, and experienced as a set of social constructions and ways of acting, using language, thinking, valuing, and feeling?) (Newell et al., 2015). As we began to realize the situatedness of what counts as argumentative writing, we reframed our work with a social practices perspective to understand what we had previously conceived as cognitive activity within a social setting. We realized that the uniqueness of the social processes of classrooms, like other social contexts, revealed their own shared social beliefs, norms, expectations, and ways of acting and interacting, within which particular social practices are adopted and adapted. We began to understand that what counts as argumentative writing and how teachers and students do argumentative writing within and across the varied social contexts of classrooms were social practices, and this shifted our view of what was to be studied and how.

We also began to understand some of the challenges teachers and students encounter with literature-related argumentative writing. In spite of the fact that the teachers, selected as excellent writing teachers in their respective schools, had a deep commitment to their students' academic learning, they often faced challenges that we were able to explore in the second phase of our research project, beginning in 2014 and continuing (with funding support, in part, from a second IES grant). The teachers we collaborated with in the second study initially had an understanding of argumentation as a set of formal structures focused on claim, evidence, and warrant. For example, although the teachers understood the nature of argumentation in general, they lacked knowledge of literary argumentation and the possible ways that arguing might be a way of knowing literature. That is, they often viewed argumentation as similar to a persuasive argument or as a way to present a fully formulated interpretation rather than as a potential strategy for learning, building consensus, or creating new knowledge. The dominance of teacher presentations about argument as a structure inhibited the epistemology of argumentation as an extended, in-depth, reasoned exchange. As a result, teachers' explanations of argumentation and ways of developing an argument lacked deep and compelling ways of talking with students about their efforts to compose and revise their argumentative writing. This was particularly challenging in the case of literary argumentation in that teachers tended to treat literary texts as sources of information rather than as explorations of experience and new understandings.

As we began the second phase of our study, we made three significant decisions regarding our research agenda. First, we focused on literary argumentation in particular as opposed to argument about broad social, political, or personal topics that we had observed in our earlier study. Second, with a deeper and more complex notion of argumentation, we decided to study each teacher in a single classroom across an entire school year to understand the possible trajectories of teacher change and student learning over time. Third, to work even more collaboratively with teachers, we studied literary argumentation with them during a two-week Summer Workshop and across the school year in monthly teacher meetings to learn a range of approaches to argumentation and to plan an argument-based inquiry approach to English language arts.

Over the 12 years of our research, working with a total of 61 English language arts teachers over that time, we found that teachers enacted instruction with a range of approaches. Beliefs about what literary argumentation is, and in turn, what students should learn about argumentative writing and how they should learn it, tended to privilege differing orientations in the field of English language arts in general and literature instruction in particular. As we talked with and reflected with teachers about what was happening in their classrooms, we all found dynamics in the interactions among teachers and students that surprised us and that led us to reconsider our previous ideas as well as ideas in the field about the teaching of literature, ultimately leading us to explore new ways of theorizing and framing the teaching of literature.

Key Theoretical Framings

In this section, we discuss the broader theoretical framework within which we explored the teaching, learning, and reading of literature in high school classrooms. (In Chapter 2, we discuss the more specific theoretical constructs that constitute a model of Dialogic Literary Argumentation.) We define a theoretical framing as the adoption of an evolving yet coherent set of theoretical constructs that provide interpretations and explanations for what happens in a particular social event. Theoretical framings exist at multiple levels: at a broad social and ideological level (e.g., how might the earlier transcribed event of reading "Indian Camp" be interpreted and explained given the social, cultural, and political ideology of the nation-state?), at an institutional level (e.g., how might the earlier transcribed event of reading "Indian Camp" be interpreted and explained within the ideological context of schooling in the United States?), and, at the local, interactional level (e.g., how might the earlier transcribed event of reading "Indian Camp" be interpreted and explained *in situ* as the teacher and students socially construct meanings for what is happening then and there?).

As we conducted our research on the teaching and learning of argumentative writing and literature, we were constantly interrogating the theoretical frames we brought with us. As our research involved extensive ethnographic engagement in classrooms and conversations and collaborations with teachers, our theoretical framings of the teaching, learning, reading, and writing about literature were constantly challenged and constantly evolving. In general terms, we view our intellectual and theoretical approach to the teaching, learning, reading, and writing about literature in high school classrooms as social practices reflective and projective of social, cultural, and political ideologies associated with social institutions, such as schools, and of more widespread social contexts (such as the ubiquity of individualism and capitalism across domains of everyday life in the United States; cf., Bowles & Gintis, 1986; Giroux, 2011).

The following are four key theoretical framings that have guided our articulation of Dialogic Literary Argumentation:

1. The centrality of the social
2. Learning as a social construction
3. Race, class, gender, and sexuality, as defining social constructions
4. Approaching literature as props to foster dialogue about the human condition

None of these key theoretical framings is new. The discussion of each of these key theoretical framings is necessarily brief given extensive discussions of these framings elsewhere.

Centrality of the Social

The study of social processes and practices in classrooms theorizes and focuses on the work of teachers and students as they construct everyday life in classrooms. Relatedly, a key contribution of empirical work on the social practice of knowledge construction is the shift in focus from the individual student to that of the social (e.g., Baynham & Prinsloo, 2009; Berger & Luckman, 1991; Bloome, Castanheira, Leung, & Rowsell, 2019; Castanheira, Crawford, Green, & Dixon, 2001; Cook-Gumperz, 1986; Gergen, 2001; Green & Dixon, 1993; Heath & Street, 2008; Hymes, 1980; Ivanič, 1998; Schatzki, 1996).[9] This shift suggests the need to examine the social processes shaping what counts as knowledge, to consider a communal understanding of meaning, to evaluate ideas set in historical and public contexts, and to recognize the importance of the assessment of knowledge claims by relevant groups. Such social processes can become routinized and patterned over time becoming social practices. Social practices are the socially organized and interactionally accomplished ways that members of a group propose, communicate, evaluate, and legitimize knowledge claims. Drawing from studies of English language arts classrooms, we argue that social epistemic practices are interactional (constructed among people through concerted activity), contextual (situated in social practices and cultural norms), intertextual (communicated through a history of coherent discourses, signs, and symbols), and consequential (legitimized knowledge instantiates power and culture). While social practices are located in fields (cf., Bourdieu, 1977), in our view, social practices are inherently adapted to, recontextualized, and often refracted in actual social events (e.g., Street, 1993, 1995; Van Leeuwen, 2008; Volosinov, 1929/1973).

For heuristic purposes, we approach the social nature of teaching, learning, and reading literature in classrooms across four broad categories. The first of these is recognition that epistemology and ontology are always socially and culturally realized. It is not just that knowledge and knowing are socially constructed (cf., Gergen, 1999, 2001) but rather that every word is both located in a particularized social and cultural ideological (and sociological) framework and is also responsive to histories of previous actions, languagings, and semiotic assemblages (Agha, 2007; Beach & Bloome, 2019; Latour, 2005; Prior & Olinger, 2019). Epistemology and ontology are not only socially constructed but also situated in specific social events, which is to say that the social practices for constructing knowledge and constructing ways of knowing are not universal or autonomous but are situated social practices that are revised, refracted, and recontextualized in and through each social event. For example, consider Ms. Hill's classroom described at the beginning of this chapter. Ms. Hill is aware of the literary scholarship on the short story "Indian Camp" and the emphasis of that scholarship on the loss of innocence. Yet she ignored that scholarship and focused the students' explorations on the theme of dominance. Thus, she has supplanted authorized literary knowledge (the renderings of literary scholars) with knowledge derived from her own readings of the story which are connected to her history as a biracial woman and her experiences (and her knowledge of others' experiences) of racism. As Ms. Hill orchestrates the discussion of dominance in "Indian Camp," she frames the social construction of knowledge in terms of claim, warrant, evidence, and counter-argument. However, she locates those categories not in traditional argumentative structures used in classrooms but in terms of argumentation as learning (cf., Newell et al., 2015).

The second heuristic category of the social nature of teaching, learning, and reading literature is the social positioning that is inherent in every interactional use of language and related semiotic systems. As there has been extensive discussion of social positioning in and through languaging (e.g., see Anderson, 2009; Davies & Harré, 1990; Holland & Leander, 2004), we do not discuss it at length here. However, we note that social positioning goes beyond social categories. For example, although the way Ms. Hill and her students use language positions them as teacher and students, respectively, what is important about their social positioning is what kinds of teacher and students they are, when, where, and how. It further extends to the subtleties of the social relations they have with each other. In brief, it is not just a matter of the social identities and social positions made available by the social institution of which they are a part but how teachers and students (or other interlocutors) nuance, define, conceptualize, and make complex their social relations among themselves. For example, consider the subtlety involved in how Ms. Hill responds to Ann and the students in that group (lines 127 to 138). She read aloud the text passage they had identified (line 127) and then attributed to them a reasoned connection and warrant (lines 128 to 131) to their claim and wrote it on the board. In so doing, she positioned them as having both epistemological and ontological authority and valorized their voice (line 129). When Ms. Hill says to them, "and I think what you guys were telling me is that (pause) there is dominance" (line 136), there are qualifications (e.g., "I think") and subtle positionings (e.g., "guys") that suggest a different relationship with themselves as readers, with the reading of literature, and with schooling. Further, part of the social action in this social event is to re-position the students in relation to referencing (including how they reference/index) those social practices that count as being engaged in what we are now calling Dialogic Literary Argumentation.

The third heuristic category of the social nature of teaching, learning, and reading literature is related to the second as it involves social relationships. However, what is at play in this third category is the inherent nature of social relations. For example, consider Buber's (1976) discussion of social relationships. For Buber, the concept of the "I" is a non-sequitur; there is only "I-thou" and "I-it." The first of these, "I-thou," is defined as authentic realization and state of being human that can occur only within the minimal unit of a social relationship. The "I-it" state references being as objects. Objects are not just non-human entities but anything, including people, that are defined as objects. Thus, an "I-it" state can refer to people and even oneself when defined as objects (for further discussion of Buber's philosophy, see Biemann, 2002; Friedman, 2003). What is at issue is not taking on Buber's philosophy *per se*, or the philosophy articulated by any particular other philosopher, but rather recognizing and foregrounding debates about the nature of human relations as inherent to the human condition as inclusive of spirituality, alienation, authenticity, consciousness, labor, work, history, agency, love, voice, and so forth (e.g., Arendt, 1959; Dillard, 2012; Dussel, 2013; Freire, 1970). Whatever labels are used or philosophical frameworks adopted, these states are part of the human condition inseparable from human relations (both that represented in literature and that experienced by teachers and students). What seems key to us is not adherence to one philosophical framing of human relations versus another, but rather using philosophical frameworks to raise questions and issues for how we might understand the social nature of everyday life in classrooms and in particular in those social events in which teachers and students are teaching, learning, and reading literature. To rephrase a sound-bite associated with Arendt (1977/2000), it is the banality of everyday life (including everyday life in literature classrooms) that we need to see through in order to understand what it means to be human with others in a particular place, time, and social event.

Learning as a Social Construction

Our view of Dialogic Literary Argumentation as a social construction is based on a sociolinguistic view of language derived primarily from the work of Bakhtin (1935/1981, 1984, 1953/1986), Volosinov (1929/1973), Gumperz (1982), and Hymes (1974). On the basis of our reading of the research on the teaching of argumentation and argumentative writing, that research has been primarily conducted from cognitive and structural perspectives (e.g., Kuhn, Hemberger, & Khait, 2016) and from rhetoric and composition perspectives (e.g., Graff, 2001; Graff & Birkenstein, 2018; Lunsford, Ruszkiewicz, & Walters, 2004). Although we incorporate insights from those perspectives, our theoretical framework is grounded in social constructionist perspectives, emphasizing how people jointly construct definitions through languaging of their activities, of themselves, of social relationships, and of experiences (for a more detailed discussion of our social constructionist approach to argumentation, see Newell, Beach, Smith, & VanDerHeide, 2011; Newell et al., 2015). In our research, we employ a microethnographic approach to discourse analysis (Bloome et al., 2005), identifying key events, transcribing them from video recordings, and analyzing each line (utterance) with regard to how it builds upon previous utterances, how it implies social relations among people including the reader and the author, indexes particular kinds of evidence, constructs opportunities for engagement with others, shifts between the substance of an argument (content) and the structure of an argument (form), references previous and future events, and links to various social contexts.

Bloome and Egan-Robertson (1993) describe social construction as including five related constructs:

> First basic analytic unit is not the action of an individual but the interaction of a group of people, people are the context for each other (Erickson & Shultz, 1977). This does not mean that there must be two or more people present in order for there to be an event. People are sometimes by themselves. However, whether with others or alone, a person is acting and reacting in response to other people, what they have done, what they are doing, and what they will do. Second, people act. That is, they are strategic in what they do, acting on the/their situation. Third, people react. People react to actions immediately previous, to actions that occurred sometime earlier, and to sets, groups, and patterns of action. People also react to future actions. Any action, including a reaction, inherently includes within it a concept of consequence. Consequences presume future actions either by others or by oneself. A "nonaction" can be a reaction. Fourth, the actions and reactions people take to each other are not necessarily linear and they are not necessarily contiguous. People may act together, and actions and reactions may occur simultaneously, or they may be separated by time and distance. Fifth, people may act and react to each other through sequences of actions and not just through a single act.
>
> (pp. 308–309)

Race, Class, Gender, and Sexuality, as Defining Social Constructions

As we noted previously, many of the literary texts taught, learned, and read in the high school classrooms we observed involved issues of race, class, gender, and/or sexuality. However, issues of race, class, gender, and sexuality were not limited to the literary texts selected for study in those classrooms but were issues that permeated nearly all aspects of the English language arts classroom including who the students were in each class, how students related to each other (and to the teacher), the arguments made, and the nature of the classroom discussions. Scholarship on race, class, gender, and sexuality has made clear that each of these is a social construction rather than an inherently given human condition (e.g., Blackburn & Schultz, 2015; Isenberg, 2016; Painter, 2010). Yet they are powerful social constructions that are materially enacted, with histories, shaping ideologies that have hierarchically structured power relations. The pain, suffering, and indignities that have been promulgated by the social constructions of race, class, gender, and sexuality are not abstractions to most students (nor to their teachers) but constitute much of their experiences in and outside of school.

As we discussed earlier, the major literary theories taken up in high school English language arts classrooms in the United States are defined in ways that eschew recognition of the ubiquity of the social constructions of race, class, gender, and sexuality. These theories may treat race, class, gender, and sexuality as aspects of plot, character, or theme (objectifying and distancing them), but they are not constitutive of the literary theories themselves or of the pedagogies taking up these literary theories. This is not to say that there are not literary theories in which the social constructions of race, class, gender, and/or sexuality are constitutive (e.g., Fetterley, 1978; Gates, 2014; Morrison, 1992) nor that there are not high school classrooms that have taken up such theories in the teaching, learning, and reading of literature (e.g., Greene & Abt-Perkins, 2003), but rather that, as our experiences in classrooms have suggested to us and as research suggests, at the high school level, such literary theories are mostly either not taken up or are rare and isolated (Applebee, 1993).

At issue here is how recognition of the ubiquity of the social constructions of race, class, gender, and sexuality defines Dialogic Literary Argumentation. Let's begin by considering Ms. Hill's framing of the reading of "Indian Camp" in terms of "dominance" (e.g., line 137). As we noted earlier, Hemingway's Nick Adams series, of which "Indian Camp" is a part, has traditionally been framed as stories of "initiation." What Ms. Hill has done, we would argue, is to (a) offer the possibilities of a counter-narrative interpretation for "Indian Camp" based on the recognition of racialized and gendered power relations, (b) undermine the authority of the literary establishment in setting interpretive frames available for interpreting stories that eschew power relations, and (c) relocate interpretive framing in the dialogic interactions of readers with each other (i.e., in the discussion among the students) such that they are encouraged to consider the social construction of power relations related to race, class, gender, and sexuality in a space (the high school English classroom) in which such framings are rare (see Rogers & Soter, 1997). She has also framed the process of interpretation as an interactional process of arguing to learn where evidence and warrants are derived from multiple sources including the students' own experiences. As the discussion of "Indian Camp" continues, the students employ textual evidence in their arguments about male power over women (e.g., lines 107–108) and white dominance over non-white (e.g., line 151) and generate warrants that are logical as they define logic and they generate warrants based on their own experiences (e.g., see line 134 for a warrant of male dominance over females; lines 154–156 for a warrant of white dominance over non-white dominance).

A close analysis of the transcribed conversation earlier regarding "Indian Camp" raises a series of grounded theoretical constructs and questions regarding the social construction of race, class, gender, and sexuality in that event. Although it may seem obvious, one of the grounded theoretical constructs raised is that the dynamics of dominance are material, painful, and particular. In line 103, Ms. Hill asks for evidence and Ellen provides evidence in lines 104 to 115 and then provides a low-level interpretation of that textual evidence as materially revealing power (dominance) and pain (the woman's pain) that is ignored. Although the characters are fictional, they are treated in the classroom discussion as real people (i.e., no one in the classroom says anything like "the evidence should be discounted because the people are fictional characters and not real ones"). In line 111, Ms. Hill validates the evidence and at the same time validates the particularity and materiality of dominance, hierarchy, misogyny, and pain.

There is a change of tone in the discussion of warrants that begins on line 113 and continues through line 148. The tone is one that we associate more so with doing school as opposed to expressing outrage at how the woman was being treated. This raises a question about how schooling—not defined here as a general institutional context but rather as a situated "key" (cf., Beauchemin, 2019), a particular and *in situ* manner of people relating to each other—distances the intimacy, particularity, and painful nature of dominance and hierarchy. That said, it is not necessarily the case that such distance is not tactical; that is, as this classroom event evolves, the students and teacher move back and forth between the "key" of schooling and the "key" of *in situ* outrage. That back-and-forth movement, constituting a particular social practice of reading and discussing literature, may be allowing students and the teacher in this particular situation to explore dominance in ways that adherence to only one key might not facilitate. Amy's comments in lines 154 to 156 are uttered in a tone that signals outrage, an outrage that is validated by Ms. Hill in lines 158 and 159, themselves uttered in a tone mirroring Amy's.

In brief, then, a microethnographic discourse analysis of the brief classroom discussion transcribed earlier raises issues and questions for further exploration and theorizing. In addition to foregrounding how classroom conversations about literature have the potential to define hierarchy, dominance, and oppression related to race, class, gender, sexuality, and so forth as material, intimate, and painful, defenestrating the distancing of a schooling key, questions are raised—both theoretical and empirical—about how tone (as part of the key of a socially constructed interaction) constitutes a metadiscursive level. This metadiscursive level may be—and we emphasize that this is an open theoretical question (also known as a grounded hypothesis), not a conclusion—what frames at least part of the socialization of students both with regard to how they understand dominance related to race, class, gender, sexuality, and so forth but also how they take it on as something distanced or as something material, particular and intimately painful.

Approaching Literature as Props to Foster Dialogue About the Human Condition

As was discussed previously, the study of literature in school has from the start been marked by tensions concerning the kinds of conventions that ought to prevail and about the kinds of literary knowledge teachers ought to foster. This tension has been most dramatically presented in the New Criticism concern with the teaching of literature that emphasizes literature's formal, objective characteristics and that de-emphasized the importance of both the author and the reader and Rosenblatt's concern with an exploration, a process, an experience in which readers draw upon their own histories, their own emotions, in order to, quite literally, make sense of the text. Although Dialogic Literary Argumentation recognizes the value of both text and reader, it does so by arguing for the dialogic that is socially constructed within instructional conversations; that is, by the literacy event as a bounded system of actions and reactions during which teacher and students respond to one another. By implication, this social dynamic shifts the meaning making process from the text itself and from the transaction of reader and text to the social construction of meaning that unfolds during talk and social interactions around literary texts. This shift also alters the role of the reader and text in a rather dramatic way: what counts as "text" is not just the print text of, say, "Indian Camp," but also the social practices of discussion, then, as well as the texts from previous classes, previous read literary works, texts expressed in other semiotic forms (e.g., paintings, music), narratives from and about the experiences students have had and those of their communities, among others. Metaphorically, the literary text is a prop to foster dialogue that brings together multiple texts and engages people (teachers and students) in ongoing dialogue and conversation about the human condition in the world (cf., Heath & Branscombe, 1986). It does so not to fill students' heads with literary knowledge but to engage them in exploring, in depth, the human condition in world with all of its complexities and contradictions.

Recall Ms. Hill, and her 11th-grade students as they discussed "Indian Camp." In an interview with Ms. Hill about the instructional conversation on "Indian Camp," she pointed out that "this is the first time I really saw the value of warranting an argument. Now I see that this is getting at the hidden areas of the story—what I want them to talk about but they never do." This comment brings us to what we understand as a key element of literary argumentation: how students might read and understand a text are shaped by the teacher's willingness to explore the warrants and backing for the interpretations proffered during instructional conversations that are not just text based or grounded in canonical literary interpretations but in the students' and teacher's own lived experiences and in their engagement with each other. For instance, when another group of students raised an alternative explanation for the doctor's seemingly callous behavior toward the mother in terms of how doctors need to act during a dangerous medical procedure, rather than rejecting this claim as irrelevant to the assumption of his domineering behavior, Ms. Hill asked the students to unpack their warrants:

> Then if you have an argument that you are going to argue against, then you need to back it up with something. And you're saying that . . . (gestures toward the group) it is just a scream, and he's a doctor, and as doctor you have to block it out.

We understand the move captured in the phrase "And you're saying" as a revoicing that signals the value of offering new ideas that opens a space for what Barnes (1976) calls "exploratory talk." We can also see in Ms. Hill's languaging of warranting the initiation and validation of a key of conversation in which dominance, hierarchy, and oppression related to race, class, gender, sexuality, and so forth, is made material, particular, painful, and intimate. What becomes clear in conversations such as the one in Ms. Hill's class is that exploring the literary text is subordinate to exploring the human condition.

Final Comments

In this chapter, we have introduced the concept of Dialogic Literary Argumentation. We emphasized that the concept of Dialogic Literary Argumentation evolved from our interactions with high school English language arts teachers and their students over a long period of time. We were fortunate to be able to spend so much time in their classrooms, and we are grateful that the teachers gave up so much of their time to struggle with us over how the teaching of literature might be conceptualized so that arguing to learn was at the center of the teaching, learning, and reading. In this chapter, we shared one event from Ms. Hill's classroom. For us, the events of Ms. Hill's classroom, and the other classroom events from other teachers and schools that we will share in subsequent chapters, are not just illustrations of Dialogic Literary Argumentation but rather they (and the corpus of events collected over the past nine years of research in over 61 classrooms) are the ontological basis for Dialogic Literary Argumentation. We also shared in this chapter four key theoretical framings that guided how we approached the teaching, learning, and reading of literature in high school classrooms. We emphasized in the presentation of these four theoretical framings that as educational researchers and as educators, we did not view ourselves as needing to be bound by the strictures of these theoretical framings. Rather, we viewed ourselves (inclusive of those of us at the university and those in high school classrooms) as being informed by and invited into the debates and discussions indexed by those theoretical framings. In the next chapter, we discuss movement toward a model of Dialogic Literary Argumentation. We emphasize that it is a movement "toward," not so much because it is incomplete—such models of teaching, learning, reading, and classroom life are always incomplete—but rather because we view Dialogic Literary Argumentation as inherently always evolving, always being recontextualized, reconstructed, and refracted.

Notes

1. Our research on the teaching, learning, and reading of literature took place in high school classrooms in the United States. Whenever we mention classrooms or teaching in this book, we are referring to classrooms in the United States. As such, we recognize the limitations of our research being located solely in the United States. We caution readers to be careful in assuming that the findings, concepts, and theorizings here can be unproblematically extended to the teaching, learning, and reading of literature elsewhere.
2. All names of people, schools, and places are pseudonyms. We note that the research reported here was conducted with approval of The Ohio State University Institutional Review Board and was consistent with all policies and conditions thereof.
3. Throughout the book, we present transcripts and descriptions of brief moments from high school classrooms. We caution readers that it is unfair to judge a teacher, students, a classroom, or a school from a few bits of classroom data. We have great respect for all of the teachers with whom we worked. They were chosen for participation in the study because they had reputations among colleagues, administrators, and students as excellent teachers, and, through our observations of their teaching and our conversations with them, we also viewed them as excellent.
4. We use transcription conventions derived from Green and Wallat (1981) and from Bloome, Carter, Christian, Otto, and Shuart-Faris (2005). In brief, each line is a message unit (similar to an utterance) determined by prosodic contour constituting a minimal unit of conversational meaning. With regard to symbols, / indicates a pause; xxxx indicates inaudible conversation, ↑ indicates a rising intonation pattern (such as often occurs in English in signaling a question); ↓ indicates a falling intonation; + indicates an elongated vowel. Descriptions inside parentheses indicate nonverbal behavior. Italics indicate written text and print that is being read aloud. A word in uppercase letters indicates emphasis.
5. While we do not take up the issue in this book, we take the position it is not just interpretations of a literary-text that are socially constructed but the events of the story as well (what Kintsch & van Dijk, 1978 have called the situation-model and the text-base, respectively; see Agha, 2007 for a discussion of the sociological nature of denotational language). The position we take is not one of relativism but rather a position that places the social, the sociological, and the social interactional at the core of the process of languaging whether that languaging involves spoken or written language (for further discussion of this

issue, see Street, 1995; Lysaker & Wessel-Powell, 2019; Popova, 2019; among others).
6. We use the terms "defined, fashioned, and imagined" not to suggest that the teacher and students engage in a relativistic exercise of creating imagined worlds unconnected to the material realities of the worlds in which they live but rather to emphasize that every understanding of a world (e.g., the world of "Indian Camp" and the local world in which the students live) is a constructed one (and in the case of classroom lessons, a necessarily socially constructed one).
7. Beach and Swiss (2011, p. 145) write, "An analysis of two states' literary standards found that these standards [the theory of literary analysis promulgated by high school teachers] reflect either a 'cultural heritage model' (Applebee, 1974) valuing historical knowledge about literature reflecting neoconservative notions of schooling imparting traditional values versus a New Criticism model of close reading of the autonomous text, reading strategies that can be assessed on standardized reading tests that reflect a neo-liberal, auditing model of schooling (Caughlan, 2007)."
8. In our view, it is not necessarily the case that a particular approach to the teaching of literature is incompatible with Dialogic Literary Argumentation. Depending on how an approach is taken up by teachers and teacher educators, we view approaches such as Appleman's (2015) critical encounters and Lee's (2007) cultural modeling as compatible with and a potential layering of Dialogic Literary Argumentation.
9. The shift to the social we refer to here does not deny a cognitive dimension to the teaching, learning, and reading of literature, but rather argues for a more complex approach to cognitive dimensions that acknowledges the social as permeating (and not just contextualing) the teaching, learning, and reading of literature.

2 Toward a Model of Dialogic Literary Argumentation

Dialogic Literary Argumentation is more than a shift in instructional methods for teaching literature and argument: it is a shift in the underlying conception and philosophy of teaching, learning, and reading literature. This shift begins, as noted in the discussion of the framings in Chapter 1, with recognition that there is no separation of the reader's interaction with a literary text and the social event of the reading (including the history of social events of which any particular reading event is a part and of the network of related social events). Once it is recognized that there is no separation of the reader's interaction with a literary text and the social event of the reading, the question "What meaning does this text have?" is supplanted with the question: *How are the people in the event socially constructing "meaning" with this literary text in this social event at this historical time?*

"Meaning" in the question above refers to:

- The socially constructed ideation assigned to the literary text;
- The ideation of the exchanges between and among interlocutors (both those physically present and those at a distance in space and time);
- Constructed social significance (e.g., social relations, social positionings, social identities); and
- Constructed cultural import, including the following:
  o Those social practices for socially constructing ideation
  o Those social practices for socially constructing both imagined story worlds and imagined future worlds within which interlocutors might be located
  o Those social practices for interactionally adopting, adapting, refracting, and languaging ideation, social significance, and social systems of meanings, significations, feelings, thinking, beliefs, actions, and personhood

Also noteworthy in the aforementioned question is that "people" refers not only to the people who are face-to-face with each other but also to all the people involved in a non-trivial way in the event regardless of spatial and temporal distance and regardless of whether they are named or name-able.

In this chapter, we present a model of Dialogic Literary Argumentation. That is, this chapter takes up the definition of Dialogic Literary Argumentation and the discussion of key theoretical framings in Chapter 1, the aforementioned question, and articulates what we view as a set of dimensions that need to be considered in theorizing a model of Dialogic Literary Argumentation. As we define them, models exist halfway between abstracted theorizing on one hand, and enactments of a social practice on the other; halfway between the abstract theorizing of the teaching, learning, and reading of literature and the specific, unique events in which teachers and students are interacting with each other and with literary texts. We use the term, "model" as similar to what Geertz (1983) and Bazerman (2008) describe as mid-level theory.

In generating dimensions of a model of Dialogic Literary Argumentation, we have worked back and forth between theorizing on one hand, and on the other hand, detailed, thick microethnographic discourse analytic descriptions (cf., Bloome et al., 2005) of actual and particular social events in which teachers and students were engaged in Dialogic Literary Argumentation. Because our process of theorizing involves constant movement back and forth between theories and classrooms, constantly revising our understanding and ways of articulating what we learn from being in classrooms and how we are theorizing Dialogic Literary Argumentation, we begin this chapter with a brief description of a classroom literature lesson that we will use in articulating a model of Dialogic Literary Argumentation in the rest of the chapter.

Teaching, Learning, and Reading *To Kill a Mockingbird* in a Tenth-Grade Honors English Language Arts Classroom

The students in Ms. Field's tenth-grade honors classroom were assigned to read Harper Lee's (1960) novel *To Kill a Mockingbird* over the summer. According to Macaluso (2017), *To Kill a Mockingbird* is widely read in U.S. high schools. On the first day of class and throughout the school year, Ms. Field told the class that they would be writing more complex argumentative essays than they had in ninth grade. She had informed us that in ninth grade, all of the students in the school had been taught what was called the "three-prong" essay (consisting of a claim, three bits of supporting evidence, and a conclusion; elsewhere this has been called the five-paragraph theme; cf., Johnson, Thompson, Smagorinsky, & Fry, 2003). Following the framework of arguing to learn (cf., Newell et al., 2015) that Ms. Field had learned during a two-week Argumentative Writing Project summer program, she announced to her students that their writing assignments would require them to think more deeply and to consider multiple perspectives. They would be expected to listen to the views of other students, consider alternative perspectives, and build their claims after considering all the evidence and discussing what ideas might be therefore claimed and how. They were to view the making of an argument not so much as taking and defending a position as an exploration of how one might understand a literary text or a set of literary texts in dialogue with others who might bring to the dialogue other experiences and perspectives.

During the first few days of the school year they began discussion of *To Kill a Mockingbird* by considering the plot and some of the characters, both major characters and minor ones. During one set of lessons, Ms. Field focused attention on the role of the minor characters in the novel, highlighting their importance to themes that might be constructed from reading and talking about the novel. One of the teacher-designed activities the students did in class and for homework was titled the "Unsub" worksheet that required students to first work by themselves and then in groups identifying claims, evidence, and warrants about a minor character. We will examine one response to that activity later in this chapter.

Two days before the following transcribed classroom events, they discussed Gladwell's (2009) essay that is critical of Atticus Finch, the protagonist of *To Kill a Mockingbird*.[1] At issue is the question of whether Atticus Finch should be considered a hero. The reading and discussion of Gladwell's essay were followed the next day by a homework assignment that was completed the night before the following transcribed event. The homework assignment was to read Chotiner's (2009) critique of Gladwell's essay.[2] The following transcribed event begins after Ms. Field has asked the students what their reactions were to Chotiner's critique of Gladwell. As the discussion evolves, Ms. Field notes that both Gladwell and Chotiner are using the same passage from *To Kill a Mockingbird* as evidence for their arguments.

301	T	Here they [Gladwell and Chotiner] are fighting a battle with the same textual evidence
302		Marsha
303		What do you think about that?
304	Marsha	thought I thought Gladwell's (two-second pause, waving hands in front of herself)
305		whole | ummm |
306		article was more constructive
307		like it made you question a lot more
308		I don't know more meaningful
309		while I might not have agreed with all of it

310	T	OK
311	Marsha	I don't know if I agreed more I Malcolm I I mean Chotiner
312		it was bashing Gladwell
313		it did not bring up any
314		I felt it did not bring up any real tangible content itself
315		he just bashed it in a sense
316	T	So even though you might not have sided with Gladwell
317		it
318		he made you think more
319		it he had more constructive content

The classroom conversation continues with Ms. Field asking other students what they thought about Chotiner's essay. There are few responses. What responses are made express a positive view of Atticus Finch. None of the responses take up what we interpreted as a move by Ms. Field (in line 301) to highlight a key aspect of argumentation. That is, the relationship between a bit of textual evidence and a claim is mediated by how the warrant for a claim is constructed, and that evidence does not inherently support or undermine a claim.

Marsha re-enters the classroom conversation later by reading a quote from the novel (see line 401 in the following transcript). Part of what is interesting to us about this utterance is that she is introducing a different conversational structure. So far in classroom conversations involving what the students have read (either the novel or an essay), Ms. Field has asked the students to identify and read from the text to provide evidence in support of a claim they have made. But, in our view, Marsha is not using the text she is quoting as evidence but as a site of exploration for contesting how a reader might ethically contextualize and evaluate what is happening in the novel.

401	Marsha	[Reading from the novel] *To my way of think' Mr. Finch taking the one man who's done you and this town a great service an' draggin him with his shy ways into the limelight— to me that's a sin.*
402		And he is talking about Mr. Owl
403		Owl Well I don't know
404		Umm
405		So Heck Tate who is speaking to Atticus about Boo Radley who killed Mr. Owl
406	T	Yes
407		[nonverbally gives student a thumbs up]

34 A Model of Dialogic Literary Argumentation

408	Marsha	and
409	T	It's early I decided to help you out I've read it a few more times than you have
410	Marsha	Mr. Owl was trying...
411	T	Ewell
412	Marsha	Ewell
413	T	It's OK, Mr. E
414	Marsha	Mr. E was trying to kill Scout and Jem
415		Right ↑
416	T	Right
417	Marsha	Umm but the
418		Mr. Heck Tate is that how you say it
419	T	Uh hum he's the sheriff
420	Marsha	He's trying to convince Atticus that you know he did a great service
421		But what it brought up to me was
422		What about Tom Robinson ↑
423		Like he didn't even do anything
424		And he was a good man
425		And he was brought into the limelight and accused him of something he didn't do
426		And that's why I don't think Finch is an actual hero because
427		When it comes to standing up for what he really believes in
428		He really shies away from that

Before discussing this bit of classroom life, it is important to locate this interaction between Ms. Field and Marsha in a broader community and school context. Of the 21 students in the class, two were male and the rest female, and all of the students were white. The ethnographic research we conducted on the community and school as part of the discourse analysis (cf., Bloome et al., 2005) noted that the communities served by the school were overwhelmingly white. Part of the school catchment area included housing developments and neighborhoods characterizable as middle-class and suburban, whereas other areas in the school district were rural and much less affluent. At the time of the study, there was a lot of housing growth in the area, with housing developments aimed at a range of household income levels from modest means to affluent. The catchment area served by the high school was approximately 30 miles distant from a major urban area.

Most of the students at this rural high school had attended the school from kindergarten, although there was a growing population of students who had recently moved into the area. Politically and culturally, the community was solidly conservative, and we were told that parents and others often asserted their culturally and politically conservative views by attempting to intervene in the school. Indeed, during the year of the study, one parent in another class and with another English language arts teacher complained about what the parent perceived as the teacher's liberal bias, which resulted in a formal hearing. Although the hearing found that the teacher acted professionally and that there was no indication of any inappropriate actions, the ordeal had an effect both on that teacher and more broadly in the school. All of the aforementioned observations we gathered through the ethnographic component of our research were confirmed by the teachers and by students.

Thus, in many ways, the cultural and social context for engaging in Dialogic Literary Argumentation in Ms. Field's class was very different from that of Ms. Hill's class (in Chapter 1). In our view, these contextual differences are important to note in how the languaging (cf., Beach & Bloome, 2019) of teachers and students is to be interpreted. That said, the influence of these differing contexts on what happens in a classroom and what meanings are constructed *in situ* are not given, but socially constructed, and the obligation for researchers is to warrant empirically and materially how contextual aspects are brought into and influence what happens.

Four Dimensions Toward a Model of Dialogic Literary Argumentation

In Chapter 1, we discussed four key theoretical framings. These four key theoretical framings provide the broader theoretical context within which we discuss a model of Dialogic Literary Argumentation in this chapter (see Diagram 2.1).

In the title of this chapter, we use the modifier "Toward"—*Toward* a Model of Dialogic Literary Argumentation—to emphasize that models are always dynamic, continuously evolving, part of a dialogic and dialectic process. Here, we briefly discuss what we believe are four key dimensions of a model of Dialogic Literary Argumentation. (Subsequent chapters each take up one of the following dimensions and provide more detailed discussion.) Please note that we separate out each of the four dimensions for heuristic purposes; in practice and in researching, they are inseparable.

1. Constructing Dialogue and Dialectics in Arguing to Learn in the Teaching, Learning, and Reading of Literature
2. Constructing Multiple Perspectives and Rationality in the Teaching, Learning, and Reading of Literature
3. Constructing Intertextuality and Indexicality in Dialogic Literary Argumentation
4. Constructing Personhood in the Teaching, Learning, and Reading of Literature

36 *A Model of Dialogic Literary Argumentation*

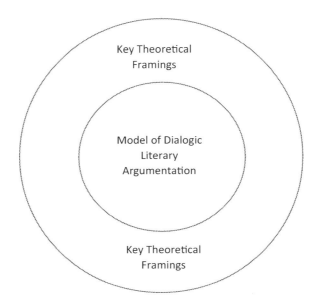

Diagram 2.1 Relationship of Theoretical Framings to Model of Dialogic Literary Argumentation

Constructing Dialogue and Dialectics in Arguing to Learn in the Teaching, Learning, and Reading of Literature

As we noted in Chapter 1, we began our research in 2007 focusing on the teaching and learning of argumentation, and our research led us to the conception of "arguing to learn," which we have contrasted with "learning to argue" (Newell et al., 2015). Typically, argumentation is taught in high school English language arts classrooms as a structure consisting of a claim, evidence, and warrants (occasionally structural components are added such as counter-argument and backing; cf., Toulmin, 2003). Most of what we observed in our initial study did not involve literature; teachers often had students read an essay and then asked their students to write an essay in response by composing a claim supported by evidence and warrants.

Among the talented teachers we had the privilege to work with, there was a subset who eschewed the five-paragraph essay. Although most of the subset said that they taught traditional argumentative structure, in fact what we observed and what became evident in our conversations with them was that they focused the students on considering all of the evidence and all points of view, on engaging their students in dialogue with one another, and only then on crafting their claims and warrants.

The process of writing an essay was neither competitive nor linear but recursive and collaborative, requiring revision and reconceptualizing at every point toward building a shared argument.[3] We called this "arguing to learn" (see Newell et al., 2015).

The recognition of the power of "arguing to learn" in exploration of a topic—how it opens minds and leads to more complex, deep, and nuanced arguments and understandings and how it brings people together (including people who had widely differing views in the beginning)—led us to ask how "arguing to learn" might be employed in the teaching, learning, and reading of literature. We knew from our own experiences and from research that English language arts teachers mostly used approaches grounded in the New Criticism (cf., Brooks & Warren, 1938), in reader response (cf., Levine & Horton, 2013; Probst, 2004), or to a lesser degree in critical theory (cf., Lewis & Ferretti, 2011; Mellor, O'Neill & Patterson, 1991), or some combination thereof (cf., Appleman, 2015). Yet our observations showed us that many teachers encouraged and valued what the students had to say about their own lives and the nature of the worlds in which they lived prompted by the literature being read. Specifically, it seemed as if the teachers wanted the students to use the literary text to explore with one another what it meant to be human among others in the world together (what we have called personhood, discussed in Chapter 6).

Beginning in summer 2014, with some of the teachers in the project, we organized a series of summer workshops to explore among ourselves and with teachers new to the Argumentative Writing Project what it might mean to use "arguing to learn" (cf., Newell et al., 2015) in the teaching, learning, and reading of literature in their classrooms. We did not expect that how the teachers would use "arguing to learn" in teaching literature would be similar to each other. We expected a lot of diversity, and indeed there was. But as we spent time in their classrooms and spoke with the teachers and their students, there were a number of commonalities (which we have encapsulated as four dimensions of the model of Dialogic Literary Argumentation, as listed earlier).

Most obvious across the classrooms was that there was a lot of student engagement in dialogue with each other and the teacher. Whether the teachers used Socratic Circles, small group discussion, whole group discussion, or some other conversational structure, the teachers focused students on responding to each other (not just necessarily to contradict but also to complement, clarify, offer potential alternatives, etc.). They sought to create dialogue among the students and between themselves and the students, and on occasion they imagined dialogues between the students and the author or a literary character. We need to pause here to note that philosophers (e.g., Buber, 1966, 1976) and scholars (e.g., Bakhtin, 1981) have differentiated between what might be called superficial and substantive dialogues. In superficial dialogues, the participants go through the motions and structures of dialogue as an interactional genre without substantively engaging each other in mutuality and reciprocity, with the authority for the ideation of the dialogue located in the person (or source) in a power hierarchy. Substantive dialogues are "internally persuasive" (cf., Bakhtin, 1981) and are presaged by the participants having open minds and engaging each other in ways that create a spiritual connection (a co-joined stance) such that the participants are better characterized as an inseparable partnership seeking together to explore an aspect of the world in which they jointly live (cf., Buber, 1966, 1976) rather than as two (or more) distinct individuals.

Ms. Field was one of the teachers who participated in a summer workshop on Dialogic Literary Argumentation and who explored using "arguing to learn" as a framework in her classroom for teaching, learning, and reading literature. As Ms. Field and nearly every teacher we worked with would say, teaching "arguing to learn" takes a long time—at least a year if not multiple years. And, we would add that teaching students how to engage in substantive dialogue also takes a long time.

As the students in Ms. Field's class discussed Chotiner's and Gladwell's essays (see the earlier transcript), Ms. Field orchestrated a dialogue among them about whether Atticus Finch is a hero. One of the reasons this particular classroom event is useful to examine is that it occurred at the beginning of the year and because the students had been taught the three-prong essay the year before. As such, Ms. Field had to address a number of hurdles in engaging her students in Dialogic Literary Argumentation and its emphases on "arguing to learn," substantive dialogue, and exploring personhood.

Before returning to the transcript, it is useful to look at the tasks Ms. Field had given the students previously. One task asked the students to bridge between some of what was happening in the novel (see Diagram 2.2) and their own lives (thematically, "Coming of Age" issues).

A second task asked the students to compare the difference between "just" and "fair" (see Diagram 2.3).

The second task set up a dialectic between "just" and "fair," and Ms. Field pushed the students to struggle with that dialectic by challenging superficial responses. Both of these tasks engaged the students in the kind of classroom conversational practices that align with Dialogic Literary Argumentation.

A few days later, as homework, Ms. Field assigns Gladwell's essay in which he argues that Atticus Finch is not a hero. They discuss the essay in class. Then, Ms. Field gives the students Chotiner's essay to read in which he rebuts Gladwell's arguments. In class, Ms. Field pushes the students to argue whether they agree with Gladwell or Chotiner. Ms. Field notes that Gladwell and Chotiner are using the same evidence (lines 301–302), foregrounding the importance of warranting. Marsha provides one response that, in some regards, is similar to the responses other students make and

English 10

1. What does it mean to "come of age"? (For a fancier term use bildungsroman).

2. What do you expect of yourself as you transition into the "real world"? How are these expectation between children and adults?

3. Who or what is responsible for how your life turns out?

Diagram 2.2 Coming of Age Worksheet

1. Please define justice versus fairness.

2. What is the connotation of the above words? What is your connotation based on?

3. Please give an example of something from your life, through firsthand experience or secondary experience (reading or witnessing), that was just but not fair or fair but not just. Explain. How does this relate to the moral or ethical code?

Diagram 2.3 Just Versus Fair Worksheet

that Ms. Field makes. But Marsha does not take up the issue of warranting and instead provides a more global response characterizing Chotiner as merely bashing Gladwell without providing substance (lines 312–315), which is validated by Ms. Field in her revoicing (lines 316–319). We note especially that Marsha hedges her response, "while I might not have agreed with all of it" (line 309). Our analysis of the conversations in this class is that often the students will hedge their responses. We view the hedging as directed both to their interactions with other students (avoiding disagreements and "face" confrontations with others; cf., Goffman, 1963) and to the teacher (avoiding an assertively wrong answer).

Part of what is at issue, based on our long-term ethnographic participation in the class, is that the students want to do well in class and want to provide Ms. Field with the responses they believe she wants. However, Ms. Field rarely reveals either directly or indirectly what particular responses she wants. For example, in the previous lesson she asks the students, "What do you think? Do you think Atticus Finch was a hero? Do you agree with Chotiner or Gladwell? Do you agree with the statement made by a particular student in the class?" Although she accepted all responses, noting when students agreed or disagreed with other students, this should not be viewed as engendering a relativistic ideology of response. Almost always, Ms. Field asks the students for the basis for their views (evidence and warrants) and probes how what they have said is similar to or different from others' comments. One of the students said that while Atticus Finch might not be considered a hero now, back then he was. Thereafter, many of the student responses take up the same refrain. Perhaps the students were attempting to provide a more "complex" response that brings together both sides of the debate (something that Ms. Field had noted at the beginning of the school year and that she reminded the students of frequently). Or perhaps the students who repeated the trope did so to signal social cohesion and an avoidance of conflict with other students—a value that we identified from our long-term ethnographic observations and interviews with students. Regardless, substantively the argument that Atticus Finch would not be a hero now but was "back then" characterizes the racialized past as somehow morally distinct from a present that is more racially and morally enlightened,[4] embracing a temporal relativity.

In sum, what happened in Ms. Field's class at the beginning of the year was an initial engagement in "arguing to learn" in response to a literary text, an initial foray into dialogue and the crafting of a dialectic. That there was only some uptake on key aspects of Dialogic Literary Argumentation is most likely due to it being the beginning of the academic year and the fact that the students had learned (and learned quite well) a different definition and social practice for engaging in argumentation and writing arguments. They had learned to avoid public disagreements (both in school and elsewhere) especially with authority figures like teachers, and, previously, they had not been confronted with the complex and unresolved nature of dialectical questions.

Constructing Multiple Perspectives and Rationality in the Teaching, Learning, and Reading of Literature

In our experiences working with English language arts teachers, while it may not be widespread, it is not unusual for teachers to organize a unit or the school year's curriculum around applying different perspectives of literary texts. As occurred in one of the classrooms we observed, one instructional unit might focus on a psychoanalytic perspective, a second on a feminist perspective, a third on a critical/Marxist sociological perspective, a fourth on a perspective from marginalized racial and ethnic groups, and so on. While we view such a curriculum as valuable, it is not how we define "multiple perspectives" within Dialogic Literary Argumentation. As we define it, a multiple perspectives framing of the teaching, learning, and reading of literature involves a complex, dynamic, and evolving dialectic, a chronotopic complexity with implications for the social construction of meaning, cultural import, and social significance over time and space. That is, we eschew the relativism that often frames the envisionment and enactment of multiple perspectives and foreground the construction of and wrestling with tensions among the perspectives in producing new insights, conceptions, perspectives, frames (cf., Tannen, 1993), and stances.[5] The movement toward such a view of multiple perspectives requires students and teachers to embrace complexity and to view themselves framed by a chronotope in which they and the worlds they envision (i.e., personhood) are continuously evolving.

Underlying our view of multiple perspectives and of complexity is a view of rationality as dialogic.[6] Our view of rationality builds on discussions by Habermas (1984), Gadamer (1976), and Flyvbjerg (2000), among others, in which rationality is located and defined within the complexities, contradictions, ambiguities, and power dynamics of specific social situations in which people, often with diverse perspectives, goals, and intentions, must work together in constructing a working consensus about what is happening, what meanings the event and situation have, who they are in relation to each other, and what its import is for future events and for the relationships of people to each other. Our view of rationality also builds on discussions of language by Volosinov (1929/1973) and Bakhtin (1981) and the centrality of dialogic interaction in everyday life and in meaning construction.

That is, for our purposes, rationality refers to how people together interactionally define what's reasonable and what's not reasonable. We should clarify that what we mean by "how people define what's reasonable" is not their adoption of a formal logic or an abstract, decontextualized definition of rationality but rather an interactional enactment of situated rationality. That is, mostly people do not explicitly reflect on rationality and what is reasonable. As they interact with others, they enact a rationality that they assume is reasonable and implicitly they assume others hold the same rationality. Only when there is a glitch or misunderstanding in an event might they pay explicit attention to rationality.

The way we see it, heuristically, there are two major categories of rationality: (a) decontextualized rationality and (b) contextualized rationality. Decontextualized rationality begins with the assumption that what's rational does not depend on the context or situation. What's true is true, always. The earth revolves around the sun, all the astronomical evidence supports this truth, and this has been so and will be so for as long as there is a sun and an earth, and it is irrational to consider it otherwise (such as the sun revolving around the earth). One could, of course, acknowledge that there was a time when overwhelmingly people viewed the sun as revolving around the earth and to consider it otherwise was considered irrational (and dangerous; see Wooten, 2015). But, for the sake of discussion, let's consider the earth revolving around the sun a warranted universalist and decontextualized rational argument. That is, even if one concedes that the rationality of the astronomical world is a decontextualized and universalist rationality, it is not possible to make such decontextualized, universalist statements when the subject matter involves human beings and how they write and read literature.[7] As Geertz (1983) argues:

> [Social scientists are] looking less for the sort of thing that connects planets and pendulums and more for the sort that connects chrysanthemums and swords[8] [p. 165]. . . . The instruments of reasoning are changing and society is less and less represented as an elaborate machine or a quasi-organism than as a serious game, a sidewalk drama, or a behavioral text.
>
> (p. 168)

More simply stated, in discussing the meaning, cultural import, and social significance of reading literature in the context of teaching and learning, we need to consider how teachers and students implicitly invoke and enact a rationality as they argue with each other.

We use the term "dialogic rationality" to refer to an enacted process in which people dialogue with each other and come to understand each other's perspectives, including the nature of the rationalities that underlie both their perspectives and their interactions with others. Through their interaction, they recognize that different people might see the "truth" differently and work with each other in moving toward an intersubjective understanding. We need to be clear, as we see it, an intersubjective understanding is not a negotiated agreement or consensus on the meaning, cultural import, and social significance of the teaching, learning, and reading of literature in a specific classroom event but rather consists of

A Model of Dialogic Literary Argumentation 43

the coming to a shared stance of recognizing diverse rationalities that are themselves refracting and evolving.

Consider, for example, Marsha's response to Ms. Field's question, "What do you think about that?" (line 303).[9]

304	Marsha	thought I thought Gladwell's (two-second pause, waving hands in front of herself)
305		whole I ummm I
306		article was more constructive
307		like it made you question a lot more
308		I don't know more meaningful
309		while I might not have agreed with all of it
310	T	OK
311	Marsha	I don't know if I agreed more I Malcolm I I mean Chotiner
312		it was bashing Gladwell
313		it did not bring up any
314		I felt it did not bring up any real tangible content itself
315		he just bashed it in a sense
316	T	So even though you might not have sided with Gladwell
317		it
318		he made you think more
319		it he had more constructive content

We have "mapped" (cf., Bloome et al., 2005; Green & Wallat, 1981) an analysis of their social construction of definitions of rationality (see Table 2.1).

The mapping shows that although Ms. Field initiated the interaction with Marsha by invoking a definition of rationality as a "battle" over the Truth (line 301), Marsha did not take that up (lines 304–315). She responded by invoking a framing of rationality as subjective (line 304), in part with rationality as singular (lines 308 and 312), in part with rationality as defined by a binary moral good (line 306), and in part with rationality as ideational (line 314). As shown in the mapping of these layers of defining rationality as indicated by the recurrent themes of "I think" (lines 304, 308, 309, 311, 314, 316, 318), agreeing with one side (lines 304, 306, 307, 316), being constructive versus bashing (lines 306, 307, 312, 315, 319), and content (lines 314, 319), Marsha also frames her response to Ms. Field's question as one of how the essays position her as reader of the essays. In line 307 Marsha states, "like it made you question a lot more." Although the emphasis in that utterance is on "question

Table 2.1 Evolving Definitions of Rationality

			Definition of Rationality	Contextualized/ Decontextualized Definition of Rationality	Contextualization Cues Used to Infer Implicit Definition of Rationality
301	T	Here they are fighting a battle with the same textual evidence	Different but unspecified systems of rationality (Gladwell versus Chotiner) yielding different warranting processes: argument defined as "battle" over Truth grounded in rationality as singular Truth	Decontextualized	Here = quotation from *TKAM* "Same textual evidence" is emphasized to foreground an issue in the relationship of evidence to claim
302		Marsha			
303		What do you think about that?	Opens up the possibility to question definition of rationality as a singular Truth, implies the potential for multiple definitions of rationality	Contextualized	Emphasis on "that" foregrounding the use of the same textual evidence across the two essays
304	M	thought I thought Gladwell's (two-second pause, waving hands in front of herself)	Rationality is subjective, located in the mind of the individual	Contextualized	The repetition of "thought" with a stressed and inserted "I" emphasizing a metadiscursive characterization of ensuing comments as a subjective framing
305		whole l ummm l			
306		article was more constructive	Rationality is a moral stance of good/constructive versus bad/unconstructive	Decontextualized	The prosody of "constructive" suggests a positive quality

307		like it made you question a lot more	Rationality is the creation of a positive reader response, rationality is thoughtful and ideational (not emotional; see line 314 that clarifies meaning of "question" here)	Decontextualized	Emphasis on "question a lot more" (elongated vowel in "more")
308		I don't know more meaningful	Rationality as layered: one level focused on the logic of the "meaning" of the text and another as subjectively experienced by the reader related to "questioning" (from line 307)	Decontextualized	Stress on "meaningful" suggesting an emphasis on ideation in the text
309		while I might not have agreed with all of it		Contextualized	"while I" references individual subjectivity as base rationality "might" hedges stance toward Marsha's evaluation of Gladwell essay
310	T	OK			
311	M	I don't know if I agreed more I Malcolm I I mean Chotiner	Rationality as "better" or "correct" reasoning	Decontextualized	Prosodic rendering change from "I don't know" to "more" with emphasis on "more"
312		it was bashing Gladwell	Rationality as logical ideation and poor quality argument is grounded in immoral behavior of "bashing"	Decontextualized	Emphasis on "bashing," "bashing" register suggests "fight" metaphor for argumentation
313		it did not bring up any	Rationality requires content	Decontextualized	
314		I felt it did not bring up any real tangible content itself	And the eschewing of emotional relationships		"felt" = reader response "real tangible content" = rationality linked to empirical ideation

(Continued)

Table 2.1 (Continued)

		Definition of Rationality	Contextualized/ Decontextualized Definition of Rationality	Contextualization Cues Used to Infer Implicit Definition of Rationality
315		he just bashed it in a sense	Decontextualized	"in a sense" = hedge that references teacher authority that could evaluate the adequacy of Marsha's response
316	T	So even though you might not have sided with Gladwell	Contextualized	"even though" emphasizes individualized subjective stance
317		it	Rationality as textual	
318		he made you think more	Contextualized	"he made you think" highlights the relational aspect through "he" and "you"
319		it he had more constructive content	Contextualized	"constructive content" references line 306 and the definitions of rationality evoked there

Note for row 316: Definition of Rationality = "Rationality as being convinced by a 'side' (rationality as a subjective response to whether the ideation of a text was sufficient to support it)"

Note for row 315: Definition of Rationality = "Repeat of line 312 with a hedge ('in a sense')"

Note for row 318: Definition of Rationality = "Rationality as interpersonal"

Note for row 319: Definition of Rationality = "Rationality as a moral stance" a lot more," "like" frames the response as similar to other events and texts that similarly make one think more and thus "to make one think a lot more" is a shared, public, and established category of text. This suggests also a different kind of definition of rationality that is less about the reasonableness of the ideation in the text but more so about how the text positions readers in relationship to established categories of text. We note that in lines 316 through 319, Ms. Field validates Marsha's response and that validation includes the *in situ* definition of rationality as positioning the reader within an established category of text response.

Constructing Intertextuality and Indexicality in the Teaching, Learning, and Reading of Literature

Simply stated, intertextuality is the juxtaposition of two of more texts. The texts may be co-present or located in different events, locations, times, and social contexts; they may be juxtaposed at various levels from the level of words to genres. For some scholars, intertextuality and indexicality are overlapping concepts (e.g., Agha & Wortham, 2005; Prior, 2001). Indexicality can be simply defined as a sign that points to something outside of the event. Hanks (1999) defines indexicality as follows:

> The term *indexicality* refers to the pervasive context-dependency of natural language utterances, including such varied phenomena as regional accent (indexing speaker's identity), indicators of verbal etiquette (marking deference and demeanor), the referential use of pronouns (I, you, we, he, etc.), demonstratives (this, that), and tense . . . what indexicals encode are the relations between objects and contexts.
>
> (p. 124)

There is increasing recognition in literary studies and in studies of literacy education that intertextuality and indexicality are inherent in any act of reading or writing (see Bazerman, 2004a, 2004b; Shuart-Faris & Bloome, 2004).[10] We concur but do not view the nature, meaningfulness, social significance, or cultural import of intertextuality and indexicality as inherent in a decontextualized word, utterance, sign, or text. Rather, the approach we take here conceptualizes intertextuality and indexicality as socially and interactionally constructed (cf., Bloome & Egan-Robertson, 1993). The social construction of intertextuality and indexicality are part of how people, teachers and students, construct classroom events characterizable as Dialogic Literary Argumentation.

One place to begin examining the nature of the social construction of intertextuality and indexicality that contributes to crafting Dialogic Literary Argumentation is by listing the texts (written, spoken, and otherwise) Ms. Field and her students have been using in their discussion of *To Kill a Mockingbird*. These written texts include worksheets, literary essays (such as those written by Gladwell and Chotiner), PowerPoint slides and other LCD projections, teacher writing on the whiteboard, notes students are taking in their notebooks, and the marginalia the students have written in their copies of *To Kill a Mockingbird*. Beyond written texts are the conversations the teacher and students have had both in the classroom and beyond it. With regard to the conversational texts, students are held accountable for juxtaposing what is said in class with what they write at home, for what is said on Monday for the discussion later in the week, for what is said in class with how they render an interpretation of a literary text or essay, and so forth. There are also electronic texts as the students look up topics on their smartphones (both during and after class) and text each other and friends (both during and after class). Also not to be overlooked is the movie *To Kill a Mockingbird* (Mulligan, 1962), which the students and the teacher may have watched online or elsewhere. Each of these texts is interactionally referenced (noted by at least one person and then taken up or otherwise validated by another) at one time or another by the teacher or the students in their classroom conversations such that we have evidence that these texts are indeed substantive parts of their classroom events. That is, while one might speculate on other possible texts that might be related to *To Kill a Mockingbird*, in our view, there must be material evidence that a text is indeed substantively a part of the classroom event and this material evidence must show that a text is publicly recognized as part of the event (and not just located invisibly in the mind of an individual).[11]

In addition to an analysis based on the texts that are juxtaposed, there are times when, from an emic perspective, it is pertinent to analyze the absence of a text or related set of texts. For example, in the classroom discussions in Ms. Field's class, there is no explicit discussion of the brutality of the Jim Crow South toward people of African heritage (although Ms. Field may have assumed shared knowledge of the brutality of the Jim Crow South). Ms. Field does not provide the students with historical texts related to the lynching of African Americans or the anti-lynching speeches of leaders such as Ida B. Wells and Mary Burnett Talbert. While it is impossible to predict the specific effect the inclusion such texts might have had on classroom conversations and on what students wrote, it is reasonable to suspect that there would be some kind of socially constructed effect. That is, inclusion of such texts might have resulted in differently socially constructing the meaningfulness, social significance, and cultural import of *To Kill a Mockingbird* and the response to the question, "Was Atticus Finch a hero?" We want to be clear that this is not a criticism of Ms. Field and how she orchestrated the instructional conversation and the set of texts available for intertextual juxtaposition. It was the beginning of the school year, there is only so much time, and how a teacher orchestrates an instructional conversation must be pegged both to the instructional goals (e.g., beginning to engage students in Dialogic Literary Argumentation, setting norms for participation, beginning to engage students in multiple perspectives, officially established educational standards) and especially at the beginning of the year with establishing an appropriate classroom climate and rapport.

While important, listing the texts that are juxtaposed does not get us answers to the questions, What are the students and the teacher using intertextuality and indexicality to do? How are they using intertextuality and indexicality to construct classroom events characterizable as Dialogic Literary Argumentation? To illustrate how a teacher and students might use intertextuality to interactionally construct a social event characterizable as Dialogic Literary Argumentation, Table 2.2 provides a beginning analysis of what the students and teacher accomplished through their uses of intertextuality in lines 301 to 311.

Part of what we find interesting in exploring the functions of intertextuality in lines 301 to 311 is the reframing of the teacher's question in lines 301 to 303. The teacher juxtaposes the Gladwell and Chotiner essays that inherently are juxtaposed with *To Kill a Mockingbird*. There is also a juxtaposition to instructional conversations the class has had about argumentation that serves as the frame for the proposed juxtaposition in line 301. But Marsha does not take up the proposed framing of the intertextuality Ms. Field has proposed. Instead, she juxtaposes the Gladwell and Chotiner essays within a framework of a reader response theory (line 304) and uses the criterion of being "constructive" as evaluation (line 306). As such, part of what we learn about the social construction of intertextuality in classroom discussions of literature is that the meaningfulness of the intertextuality is in the framing that accompanies the juxtaposition. That framing can evolve over the course of social interaction in a social event (or across social events). We can also take from the analysis of the social construction of intertextuality in lines 301 to 311 that also at stake are social relations including social positionings. Marsha is negotiating her relationship with the teacher through how she frames the meaningfulness of the intertextual relation of the Chotiner and Gladwell essays. Marsha is positioning herself as a particular kind of student and person: one who read and did the assignment and as a person focused on substance and reason, eschewing "bashing." In sum, pertinent to the question of how the teacher and students are using the social construction of intertextuality to construct a social event characterizable as Dialogic Literary Argumentation is the negotiation over framing that occurred in lines 301 to 311. Inasmuch as Dialogic Literary Argumentation is more than procedural display (cf., Bloome, Puro, & Theodorou, 1989), it is critical for Ms. Field and her students to establish a shared frame for how they are to value, language, conceptualize, act and react, feel, believe, rationalize, and give meaning to what they are reading and discussing. But establishing such a shared frame requires more than

Table 2.2 Select Functions of the Social Construction of Intertextuality

		Texts Referenced	Uptake	Functions	Comments
301	T Here they are fighting a battle with the same textual evidence	• Gladwell's essay • Chotiner's essay • *TKAM* • Classroom conversations on argumentation		Proposing a problematic focused on differential warranting	
302	Marsha				
303	What do you think about that?	"that" connects to 301		Initiating a discussion with a student on the topic (problematic) raised in 301	"that" = *TKAM*, Gladwell essay, Chotiner essay, and instructional conversations from previous classes about differing ways of warranting and reasoning
304	M thought I thought Gladwell's (two-second pause, waving hands in front of herself)	Response to 301 and 303	"Gladwell" takes up "they" in 301 and "that" in 303 (but not "textual evidence" from *TKAM* in 301)	Comparing Gladwell and Chotiner essays framed as reader response (indicated by "I thought")	Classroom conversations on argumentation not taken up and thus that intertextual proposal is dropped
305	whole I ummm I				
306	article was more constructive	"more" connects to "they" in 301	Uptake on 301	Providing a criterion for comparison of texts while also responding to teacher question while also indicating that the student read both essays	

307		like it made you question a lot more	"more" connects to "they" in 301 and to juxtaposition of Gladwell and Chotiner	"Question" is uptake on "classroom conversation" in 301 but not classroom conversation on argumentation	Construct a proposed student identity (as one who thinks and questions); re-states criterion of comparison	Shifts framing of intertextual connection between response to essays and classroom conversation to nature and quality of individual student response
308		I don't know more meaningful		"more" continues uptake on 301	Qualifies response	"more meaningful" juxtaposes the Gladwell and Chotiner essays
309		while I might not have agreed with all of it			Frames self in relation to response to the criterion for juxtapositions	
310	T	OK		Uptake on 304, 307, and 311	Validates Marsha's responses	Validates social consequence of intertextuality in lines 304-309
311	M	I don't know if I agreed more I Malcolm I I mean Chotiner		Uptake on 309	Continued qualification of response as in 309	"more" juxtaposes Gladwell and Chotiner essays

Ms. Field simply announcing it. It requires her ongoing interaction with her students and the constant negotiation and re-negotiation of a shared framing of how they read, learn, understand, talk, and write about literature; and they accomplish this in part through how they socially construct intertextuality.

Part of the dynamics of establishing a shared framing for Dialogic Literary Argumentation involves constructing an ideology for teaching, learning, and reading literature. The teaching of literature has been dominated by four literary ideological frameworks: New Criticism, reader response, interpretive communities (these three briefly discussed in Chapter 1), and critical theory (see Appleman, 2015). We refer to these frameworks as ideological because they involve more than procedures for assigning meaning to a literary text. They also network particular definitions of knowledge, knowing, social relationships, power relations, social identities, and more. In Table 2.3, we explore how Ms. Field and her students used indexicality to construct an ideological framing.

Table 2.3 Select Functions of the Social Construction of Indexicality

			Select Indexical References
301	T	Here they are fighting a battle with the same textual evidence	"Fighting a battle" = traditional three-prong essay from last year seeking to support a claim against others' claims "evidence" indexes the series of classroom conversations in that class and in previous years to argumentation
302		Marsha	
303		What do you think about that?	"that" refers to both "same textual evidence" and indirectly to having done the homework the night before to read Chotiner essay. The question indexes a classroom conversation in which the teacher has the right to call upon students who have the obligation to respond. As this is the beginning of the year, there is no particular pattern on which the students can rely to assess whether they need to produce a response that is content wise what the teacher is expecting.
304	M	thought I thought Gladwell's	"I thought" indexes instructional conversations used in previous classroom conversations about an approach to reading literature grounded in reader response theory; a particular ideology of reading literature linked to particular teacher education programs and literary theories.
305		whole ǀ ummm ǀ	

Table 2.3 (Continued)

		Select Indexical References
306		article was more constructive	"Constructive" indexes a binary of constructive versus not constructive and a schooling ideology of good placed on being "constructive."
307		like it made you question a lot more	"like" indexes a youth generation as it is a term associated with the talk of students (as opposed to teachers and adults); "question a lot more" indexes a broadly shared educational moral good.
308		I don't know more meaningful	
309		while I might not have agreed with all of it	indexes a reflective positionality associated with being intellectual
310	T	OK	
311	M	I don't know if I agreed more | Malcolm | I mean Chotiner	
312		it was bashing Gladwell	"bashing" indexes an ideology of good versus evil, with "bashing" defined as a shared moral evil
313		it did not bring up any	indexes an ideology that places value on content; while also indexing an ideology of reader response
314		I felt it did not bring up any real tangible content itself	

When Ms. Field uses the metaphor of "fighting a battle" (line 301), she is asking her students to rise above the ideology of Truth through "battle," with its positioning of people engaged in argumentation as opposing combatants. Ms. Field can also be viewed as referencing the three-prong essay structure that the students had learned the previous year as that argumentative structure had been framed as one of opposing claims (rather than the dialogic exploration of a literary text for shared understandings). However, Marsha does not take up the "battle" indexical ideological. That is, Marsha takes up "what do you think" but does not take up "that" ("Marsha, what do you think about that?" lines 302 and 303). Marsha offers an ideology of reader response and more particularly the ideology of good as being constructive and substantive and bad as bashing and lacking substance (lines 306 to 308 and 312 to 314). At issue also are the opportunities that ideology provides Marsha for socially positioning herself and others (line 309).

Of course, teachers and students are always indexing ideologies of reading and other domains all the time, and they do so in all classes and not just in those classrooms where teachers are engaging their students in Dialogic Literary Argumentation. One of the reasons we identify indexicality as a dimension of a model of Dialogic Literary Argumentation is that our research suggested that underlying the move to Dialogic Literary Argumentation are changes in the ideological foundations for what counts as knowledge and knowing and for framing how to read a literary text. Earlier we have only focused on a small bit of the indexing of social and cultural ideologies in the classroom event. There are many other dimensions of indexing ideology that might be considered, such as ideologies of personhood which we address in the next section and in Chapter 6.

Constructing Personhood in the Teaching, Learning, and Reading of Literature

Many literary theorists and scholars have argued for approaching literature as an exploration of the human condition, even if they differ in how they define "the human condition" (for examples of differing stances on the human condition in literature see: Eagleton, 2003; Fuentes, 2007; Gates, 2014; Holloway, 2013; Langer, 1995; McEwan, 2005; Schrijvers, Janssen, Fiahlo, & Rijlaarsdam, 2018). While we do not feel a need to be loyal to only one definition of or stance toward the human condition in reading literature, we find Greene's (1968) discussion compelling:

> What is the function of imaginative literature in the lives of men [sic]? What do we take "human understanding" to mean? If we enable young people to engage with awareness and appreciation in the illusioned worlds created by literary artists, will they emerge with heightened knowledge about the world in which they live? Will they be better equipped to make enlightened value judgments? Will they have learned more about themselves as human beings—more about human condition at this particular moment of time? (p. 11). . . . The notion that the understanding (if any) to be gained is of some ideal dimension of reality does not appear to be tenable. Neither does the notion that literature adds to our factual knowledge. . . . A reader encounters—when he [sic] involves himself [sic] with a poem or a novel—a patterning of sounds, a play of images, a structure of intricately organized meanings with the power to address his [sic] senses, feelings, and intelligence at one and the same time. They may enable him [sic] to become conscious of a kind of message which cannot be

paraphrased, which does not even exist except at the moment when the reader is actively engaged with the work. It need not be "true" in any empirical sense. . . . It need not be translatable in any way at all. But it is a message, nonetheless, about the human condition. It is an expressive rendering of what it is to be alive at a particular moment of time.

(p. 14)

Part of what we take away from Greene's articulation of literature and the human condition is, first, ambiguity about whether readers will indeed "benefit" from literature. Doubts about whether readers—and most particularly teachers and students—benefit from reading literature compels us to ask in what social situations, under what conditions, when, where, and how might it be of "benefit" (and correspondingly not of benefit) to teachers and students? And what might be meant by "benefit"? From whose perspective? Second, Greene's argument about the nature of the literary text, that it is untranslatable into another form (such as an essay or expository text), propels us to consider how a reader's experience reading literature might be defined, remembering that all reading is the enactment of social practices in social events, implicating other people and other texts both present and at a distance in time and space, responsive, reflective, and refracted (cf., Bakhtin, 1981; Bloome & Egan-Robertson, 1993; Kristeva, 1986: Volosinov, 1973). In other words, both in classrooms and beyond, reading literature is a social encounter (dialogue) among people with a set of texts, socially constructing explorations of the human condition.

An essential part of that social exploration of the human condition (an essence of those explorations) is personhood. Following Egan-Robertson (1998, p. 453), personhood can be defined as "a dynamic, cultural construct about who is and what is considered a person, what attributes and rights are constructed as inherent to being a person, and what social positions are available within the construct of being a person." (See also definitions of personhood by Butler, 1990/2007; Fowler, 2004; Geertz, 1973, 1979; Gergen & Davis, 1985.) The exploration of personhood is promulgated in part because any use of language involves a definition of personhood (cf., Rorty, 1992). The words, phrases, and discourses used as people act and react to each other always implicate a social positioning of the speaker, the interlocutors, and of others including those implicitly or explicitly referenced in the world involved in the dialogue as well as those involved in the world imagined in the literary text. The set of social positionings invoked and the distribution of characteristics, qualities, and rights and privileges, aligned across those social positionings, implicitly construct an ideology of personhood. More simply stated, both in their conversations about a literary text (or more accurately, a set of texts) and in the literary text(s) itself, teachers and students together

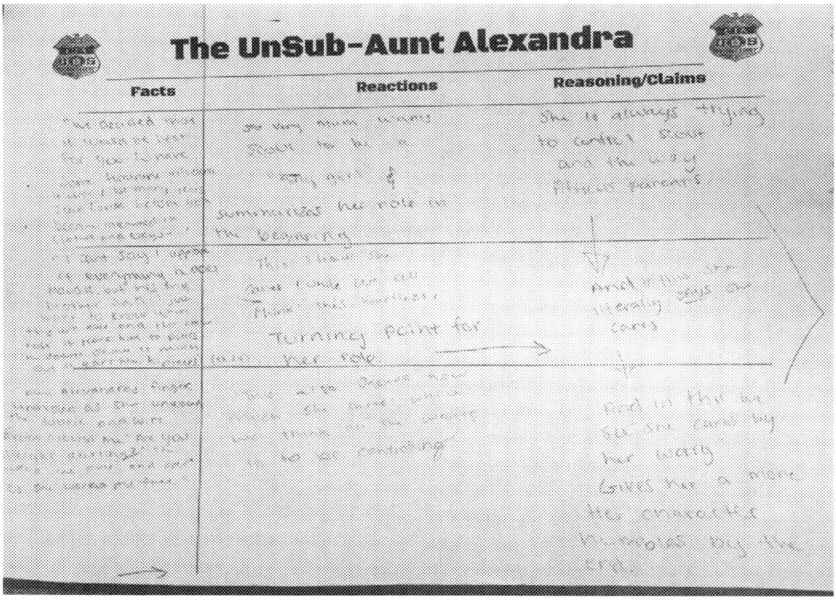

56   A Model of Dialogic Literary Argumentation

Diagram 2.4 Unsub Worksheet

are always negotiating what it means be human, when, where, how, and with what consequences.

For example, consider how one group of students in Ms. Field's class completed the worksheet task labeled "Unsub" (see Diagram 2.4).

The "Unsub" task asked the students to examine the role of minor characters in the novel. The students were formed into groups of four to six students and given a character to examine. Each group had to complete its own worksheet and then report on it to the class. The design of the instructional task required the students to work together in class to complete the worksheet and to explore together the evidence and potential warrants prior to making their claims about the role of the minor character in the novel. They had to listen to each other, then come together in expressing how the evidence and warrants they had found yielded a claim (a framework for argumentation aligned with "arguing to learn," cf., Newell et al., 2015). As the students completed the task, they wrote on the back of the worksheet (the front of which is shown in Diagram 2.4), "Aunt Alexandra reminds us of what's happening with the rest of the town. Other people's thoughts/stance vs Jem, Scout & Atticus who think different." We read the phrase "rest of the town" as referring to the white people in the town. Yet in our reading of the novel, the town includes a substantial number of Black people.

But they do not appear to be included in "rest of the town" because of the subsequent modifier ("Other people's thoughts/stance vs Jem, Scout & Atticus who think different"). Unfortunately, we did not ask the students what they intended by "rest of the town," so we can only infer. If our inference is correct, there is an erasure of Black people from the town and from consideration. This is a matter of personhood, as it is a specification of who exists. All this suggests that the personhood issues in that particular event at that time concern who gets to be in the "unmarked" case (the naturalized situation) and who needs to be the "marked" case. We can further speculate about various contextualizing issues that might have been at play. For example, perhaps the nearly all-white context of the school and of the community fostered a naturalization of defining the "rest of the town" as white. Perhaps if this classroom task and topic had been located in a mostly Black high school in a mostly Black community, the students there would have explicitly noted the Black people in the town and perhaps both Black and white would have been "marked" cases.

In a subsequent classroom discussion revolving around the question of whether Atticus Finch is a hero, Marsha also raises questions about who is visible and who is invisible. Marsha begins by retelling a scene from the book, and her retelling is confirmed by Ms. Field.

405	Marsha	So Heck Tate who is speaking to Atticus about Boo Radley who killed Mr. Ewell
406	T	Yes
407		[nonverbally gives student a thumbs up]
408	Marsha	and
409	T	It's early I decided to help you out I've read it a few more times than you have
410	Marsha	Mr. Owl was trying
411	T	Ewell
412	Marsha	Ewell
413	T	It's OK, Mr. E

After the teacher and Marsha agree on a pronunciation for Mr. Ewell's name (lines 410 to 413), Marsha asks for confirmation about the action in the novel. She asks:

414	Marsha	Mr. E was trying to kill Scout and Jem
415		Right ↑
416	T	Right

58 *A Model of Dialogic Literary Argumentation*

Once she gets confirmation that her version of what happens is an approved version, she then compares the evaluation that Mr. Tate gives of Atticus to what happens to Tom Robinson.

417	Marsha	Umm but the
418		Mr. Hecate is that how you say it
419	T	Uh hum he's the sheriff
420	Marsha	He's trying to convince Atticus that you know he did a great service
421		But what it brought up to me was
422		What about Tom Robinson ↑
423		Like he didn't even do anything
424		And he was a good man
425		And he was brought into the limelight and accused him of something he didn't do
426		And that's why I don't think Finch is an actual hero because
427		When it comes to standing up for what he really believes in
428		He really shies away from that

Marsha uses the comparison to warrant her claim that Atticus is not a hero (lines 426 to 428), but there is more being interactionally constructed here than a response to that question.

Looking more closely at what happens in that classroom event, Marsha begins by reading from the novel. In doing so, she is responding to Ms. Field's call for textual evidence. But notice lines 402 and 403 where Marsha mispronounces Bob Ewell's name. Marsha seems to be aware that she mispronounces Ewell's name and then moves on. She is corrected by Ms. Field in lines 409 and 411. Marsha pronounces it correctly in line 412 but then Ms. Field shortens it to "Mr. E" in line 413.

The dynamic of doing oral reading in school and reading each word accurately is a social practice that occurs in most school reading programs, which is merely to note that the ideological model of literacy (cf., Street, 1985) students acquire for reading in school is one of word-by-word accuracy. There is a deep debate among scholars of reading and learning to read whether such a school practice is beneficial or detrimental to learning to read, comprehend, and understand. Some argue that there is a hidden curriculum in that social practice about there being one way to read (e.g., Bernstein, 1975, 1990). For a student to err in that social practice would be to leave one vulnerable to being labeled and positioned as a non-reader or a less capable reader. There seems to be some evidence to suggest that such an ideological framing is being indexed. Ms. Field tells Marsha, "It's early [in the morning and in the school year] I decided to help you out/I've read it a few more times than you have" (line 409) just before she corrects Marsha (line 411). There is a politeness and face-saving dimension in "It's early," referring to the early morning hour. Although softening the correction, the face-saving dimension indicates that the content could threaten the social positioning and social identity of Marsha. As such, it can be reasonably inferred that the social practice of correctly rendering written text and its accompanying social significance is being indexed at that moment. The exactness and authoritative discourse of the teacher (cf., Bakhtin's, 1981) is similarly referenced when Marsha asks Ms. Field if she is correctly rendering the plot and Ms. Field confirms that she is (lines 415 and 416) and when Ms. Field confirms the pronunciation of Sheriff Tate's name. What is at stake here, we speculate, is the epistemological context for engaging in Dialogic Literary Argumentation and relatedly exploring issues of personhood. That is, people cannot substantively engage in dialogue if the epistemological context is one of authoritative discourse (cf., Bakhtin, 1981).

After clarifying the plot and characters at the particular point in the novel to which Marsha was referring, she then presents a comparison between the characterization of Boo Radley and Tom Robinson as both being brought into the "limelight" (line 425) and being "a good man" (line 424). Marsha builds her comparison on textual evidence countering the erasure of Tom Robinson from that scene in the book and from the classroom discussion of the question of whether Atticus Finch is a hero. It is also to call into question Harper Lee's construction of personhood and Harper Lee's use of Tom Robinson.

Part of what is at issue at this point is that Marsha is offering an interpretation that could be viewed as contrary to dominant interpretations of Atticus Finch as a hero. She is examining a range of textual evidence and crafting a claim that can account for all of the textual evidence (similar to the social practice of "arguing to learn," cf., Newell et al., 2015) as opposed to selecting only that evidence that supports an *a priori* selected claim. She makes clear that this is her interpretation (line 421) as opposed to being *the* interpretation. Marsha does not ask Ms. Field if her interpretation is correct (Ms. Field does not correct her argument about why Atticus Finch is not a hero) and smiled at her before moving on to ask other students the same question. Marsha appears to be indexing what might be called "internally persuasive" discourse (cf., Bakhtin, 1981) that is foundational to "arguing to learn" (Newell et al., 2015). Although there is little dialogue in the class discussion (dialogue in the sense of people listening to each other and building on each other's ideas in an effort to reach deeper understandings), in these few lines (401 to 428) we have a layering of ideologies of literacy: the first associated with correctness and authoritative discourse related to written language and the second associated with "arguing to learn" and internally persuasive discourse—different ways of using written language to construct meaning, social significance, and cultural import. Placed into an educational context, two key questions to ask are (a) "How does this moment index different ideologies of teaching, learning, and reading literature?" and (b) "How does the construction of personhood evolve over time in the classroom?" That is, over time, is there change or stability in the ideologies of reading and personhood that are indexed? We have evidence from our year-long ethnographic study in Ms. Field's classroom, that indeed there is an evolution of the ideologies of reading and personhood that are indexed. Across the year, as the students read and discuss literature including *Of Mice and Men* (Steinbeck, 1937), *Lord of the Flies* (Golding, 1954), *Hamlet* (Shakespeare, 1603), *Looking for Alaska* (Green, 2006), among others, the ideologies of reading and personhood they index do change and evolve—more of the students more frequently engage in "arguing to learn" (as opposed to the three-prong argument framework), they increasingly engage each other in substantive dialogue, and they increasingly explore issues of personhood.

Final Comments

Both in our research and in our conversations with teachers, it is clear that the teaching and learning of Dialogic Literary Argumentation (and more generally, the teaching and learning of argumentation) does not occur in a single lesson or even an instructional unit; it is a year-long and multi-year process. Indeed, when we had first approached teachers about observing an instructional unit on writing arguments, they informed us that they taught argument all year long, and in some of the schools in which we conducted research, the teachers had organized themselves so that the students were learning to write arguments over two or three years. Both with Dialogic Literary Argumentation and with learning to use argumentation as a way to learn and explore the world (cf., Newell et al., 2015), it is our view that the length of time needed is not just a matter of the teaching and learning being hard but that students must unlearn previous understandings of argumentation and of reading and learning literature also, and perhaps more important, they are learning new ways of being in the world.

For example, in Ms. Field's school, we had the pleasure of working with and studying four teachers who were interested in shifting how they taught the writing of arguments about literature from a structural view (students producing an essay with a claim, warrant, evidence, and perhaps a counter-argument) to Dialogic Literary Argumentation. For more than a decade, the ninth-grade teachers in that school had taught the students what they called the "three-prong" essay (elsewhere sometimes called the five-paragraph theme—thesis statement, three supporting facts, and concluding paragraph). The tenth-, 11th-, and 12th-grade teachers had previously reinforced that structure in their assignments and in their evaluations. The change that the teachers wanted to make—from a structuralist view to Dialogic Literary Argumentation—had to push against what had become part of the school culture and part of what the community of language arts teachers had established for themselves as a core social practice. Further, some of the students who had been successful with the three-prong essay found it difficult to give it up and shift how they were conceptualizing the writing of arguments about literature. Throughout the year, the teachers framed the shift as not just a shift in the writing, not just additional knowledge about how to write arguments, but as also a shift in who the students were. They were told that they were now (because they were older and experienced with writing at the high school level) better able to handle complexity and contradictions, to learn from each other, to eschew predetermined structures and vary the structures they used to help them explain their now more complex views, and to keep an open mind. Interviews with students suggested that some welcomed such changes both in the writing and in who they were being asked to be, but others were confused. The students had done well with the three-prong essay and they struggled with what they viewed as the ambiguity of Dialogic Literary Argumentation. Yet as the teachers provided learning opportunities and contexts that facilitated the students' engagement in using argumentation to learn, in keeping an open mind, in listening to others, and in addressing complexity and contradiction without needing to necessarily resolve complexity and contradiction, over the course of the year even those students who were resistant at the beginning of the year were able to engage in Dialogic Literary Argumentation with at least some success. All of which is merely to say that it is not just time that is needed in shifting to Dialogic Literary Argumentation, it is also a different chronotope (to use Bakhtin's, 1981, terminology) and a different set of ideologies for conceptualizing reading literature and personhood: a new vision of who teachers and students are as readers of and meaning-makers with literature as they make their way through time and space.

Notes

1. Malcolm Gladwell's essay can be found at <www.newyorker.com/magazine/2009/08/10/the-courthouse-ring>
2. Chotiner's (2009) critique of Gladwell's essay can be found at <https://newrepublic.com/article/51326/what-malcolm-gladwell-talking-about>
3. By "toward building a shared argument," we do not mean that the students all came to the same argument or all agreed on a particular argument but rather they pursued consensus and, in the pursuit, crafted more complex and nuanced arguments and understandings oriented not to a competition of positions but rather to learning and holistic sensemaking (see Newell et al., 2015).

4. We find the use of this trope curious as, on the basis of one-on-one interviews, materially the students were very much aware of the lack of racial diversity in their school and community and which many expressed as a negative. We speculate that they have frequently heard this trope of then versus now elsewhere and took it up as a way to address the problem of agreeing with both sides of the argument of whether Atticus Finch is a hero. We do not know whether the trope was merely part of a cultural context held at a surface level or whether it was a substantive part of a cultural ideology they held with others.
5. Earlier we cited Appleman (2015) as one scholar who promotes the use of multiple perspectives in the teaching of literature. We note that Appleman frames the use of multiple perspectives as a way to "read the world" (2015, p. 142), allowing students to access layers of meaning beyond a hegemonic ideology. Thus, although we view her approach to multiple perspectives as different from ours, we would not characterize her discussion of multiple perspectives as a surface-level relativistic perspective.
6. Many of the concepts in this section are derived from the scholarship of Allison Wynhoff Olsen (2018; Wynhoff Olsen, VanDerHeide, Goff, & Dunn, 2018) and Sanghee Ryu (2016, 2017).
7. Since in this book we are focusing on Dialogic Literary Argumentation and not on philosophies of rationality, we do not provide an in-depth discussion of debates about differing philosophies of rationality and the nature of being human. It may be helpful to know that we take the position that implicitly everyone explicitly or implicitly holds a philosophy of rationality, although that philosophy may vary across social situations, over time, and operate less as a guide to action and more as a *post hoc* explanation of behavior. And, as such, philosophies of rationality may more so be veneers in the social construction of a world that "makes sense" in the understanding of social and ethical behavior, an effort to explain the unexplainable, make sense of the senseless, and project an ethics on a universe in which ethics is a non-sequitur. Moreover, it is our view that the attempt to philosophize rationality takes on all of the complexities and uncertainties of language and is implicated in power relations among people, institutions, the state, and social and cultural ideologies.
8. The phrase "chrysanthemums and swords" would appear to be a reference to Ruth Benedict's book *The Chrysanthemum and the Sword: Patterns of Japanese Culture* originally published in 1946.
9. Marsha's response does not appear to address directly the content of the question Ms. Field asked but rather a different question, "What did Marsha think about the essays by Gladwell and Chotiner?"
10. In our discussion of intertextuality and indexicality, even if not explicitly named, we include the concepts of interdiscursivity (e.g., Ketter and Lewis (2004), intercontextuality (e.g., Bloome, Beierle, Grigorenko, & Goldman, 2009), interpellation (e.g., Althusser, 1970), and other similar efforts to conceptualize how relationships among events and social and cultural contexts are languaged. Further, we recognize that some scholars would argue that intertextuality and indexicality are conceptually indistinguishable, whereas others view them as distinct. Here, we sidestep that discussion as it is not pertinent to our purpose of explicating and exploring Dialogic Literary Argumentation.
11. Since there are several discussions of intertextuality as given versus socially constructed (see Hodges, 2015), we do not repeat those discussions here.

3 Constructing Dialogue and Dialectics in Arguing to Learn in the Teaching, Learning, and Reading of Literature

> A definition of language is always, implicitly or explicitly, a definition of human beings in the world. The received categories—"world", "reality", "nature", "human"—may be counter posed or related to the category "language", but it is now commonplace to observe that all categories, including the category "language" are themselves constructions in language and can thus only with an effort, and within a particular system of thought, be separated from language for relational inquiry. Such efforts and such systems, nevertheless, constitute a major part of the history of thought.
>
> (Williams, 1977, p. 21)

We begin with the opening quotation from Raymond Williams because there is no getting away from the fact that teaching, learning, reading literature, talking and writing about literature, and arguing are all essentially done through languaging. Further, there is no getting away from the fact that any use of language (what some scholars have called "languaging"; Beach & Bloome, 2019; Beach & Beauchemin, 2019; Becker, 1991; Jorgensen, 2004; Madsen, Karrebæk, & Møller, 2015), implicates definitions of personhood, of social relations, and of connections among specific events (such as a classroom conversation) and other events and diverse social, cultural, and historical ideologies. Once we acknowledge that languaging is the essence of teaching, learning, and reading literature, then we can begin to ask questions about that languaging.

There is a series of terms that linguists, postmodern theorists, poststructuralists, discourse analysts, critical theorists, and others have used to describe the exploration of language and languaging in order to focus attention on meaning, social significance, and cultural import beyond the surface level. These terms include "unpacking" (e.g., Carter, 2007; Halliday, 1998), "deconstructing" (e.g., Derrida, 1967/2016), "problematizing" (e.g., Foucault, 1961), "critical discourse analysis" (e.g., Rogers, 2004), "defamiliarization" (Miall & Kuiken, 1994; Richardson, 1987; Stacy, 1977), among others. While there are important theoretical and practical differences among the perspectives indexed by different terms, for our purposes we treat these terms collectively as an approach to dialoguing about literature. That is, for the most part, the analysis of "received categories" (cf., Williams, 1977, p. 21) has been an endeavor of scholars and researchers; however, high school teachers and students can no less engage in such analyses.

The analysis of "received categories" by teachers and students is a key dimension of Dialogic Literary Argumentation, which is merely to say that when teachers engage students in Dialogic Literary Argumentation, an essential aspect of their interactions (whether conversational or in writing) is the unpacking of "received categories" in the language and languaging of a novel, in the literary theories that underlie their interpretations of the literary texts, of classroom conversations, and of their own writing. One of the reasons that the unpacking of "received categories" is key to Dialogic Literary Argumentation is that the dialoguing in which teachers and students engage is not simply structural—an exchange of turns at talk, an allowance of extended turns at talk by students, and students taking up the content of other students' and the teacher's utterances—nor is the dialogue simply a conversational movement toward consensus based on a simplistic notion of a compromise of diverse or opposing positions. Rather, part of the essence of dialoguing within Dialogic Literary Argumentation is the creation of a dialectical space in classroom conversations, where students and teachers engage in languaging to take hold of these "received categories," converse upon the tensions present, and refract them for the inquiry at hand.

There are many definitions of "dialectic(s)." One of the definitions offered by *Merriam-Webster* comes close to what we mean by our use of dialectic:

> any systematic reasoning, exposition . . . or argument that juxtaposes opposed or contradictory ideas and usually seeks to resolve their conflict: a method of examining and discussing opposing ideas in order to find the truth . . . the dialectical tension or opposition between two interacting forces or elements.
> (*Merriam-Webster Dictionary*, www.merriam-webster.com/dictionary/dialectic, on May 3, 2019)

While we are aware of diverse philosophical discussions of dialectics (e.g., Hegel, 1812/2010; Marx, 1868/2004; Plato [in Hamilton, Cairns, & Cooper, 1961]; see van Eemeren & Houtlosser, 2013, for an overview of dialectics and argumentation), our focus here is on neither a particular system of reasoning *per se* nor a resolution of an opposing thesis and anti-thesis. Rather, our focus is on the interactional construction of dialogic spaces in which interlocutors can explore how the tensions between opposing theses can provide additional insight and depth into the complexities of the human condition and personhood.

When we first began exploring argumentation in high school classrooms, we did not appreciate the centrality and essential nature of constructing a dialectic in arguing to learn. As we further explored classroom conversations in detail, we began to understand the importance of constructing a dialectic. Thus, as with other chapters, we begin this chapter with a transcript of a classroom conversation. The classroom conversation comes from an 11th-grade college preparation English language arts class in which the students were reading and discussing F. Scott Fitzgerald's *The Great Gatsby* (1925). As we noted in Chapter 1, we use the transcripts and descriptions of the classroom conversations not as illustration of Dialogic Literary Argumentation *per se* (although they do illustrate some dimensions of a model of Dialogic Literary Argumentation) but rather to share at least in part the process we employed that led us to theorize a model of Dialogic Literary Argumentation as a way to share and discuss dimensions of Dialogic Literary Argumentation.

Teaching, Learning, and Reading *The Great Gatsby* in an 11th-Grade College Preparation English Language Arts Classroom

Mr. Mosley had taught high school English language arts for 11 years at the time of our observations. The high school is located in a suburban school district in the midwestern United States. The school is highly ranked academically. There were 22 students in Mr. Mosley's class: 20 white and two Asian American students. Mr. Mosley is white. Most students come from middle-class or upper middle-class families. Some of these students learned basic concepts of argumentation in the ninth or tenth grades.

Mr. Mosley has a local reputation for excellence as a writing teacher, with eight years of teaching argumentation and argumentative writing in his high school's College Preparatory English 11 course and Advanced Placement Language and Composition course. For his College Preparatory English 11 course, he developed an approach to argumentation and argumentative writing that he taught across an entire school year. The year-long curriculum begins with teaching argumentative writing with concern for both structural and topical knowledge—what the Argumentative Writing Project calls "learning to argue" (cf., Newell et al., 2015). Mr. Mosley's initial consideration of argument focused on the Toulmin model (2003), with elements such as claim, evidence, and warrant. Then, for the rest of the school year, he shifted to "arguing to learn" (cf., Newell et al., 2015), an approach that primarily uses argumentation as a heuristic for understanding and engaging with literature while helping students to develop their ideas about argument and argumentative writing.

Mr. Mosley had attended a summer workshop offered by the Argumentative Writing Project on arguing to learn and had participated in a previous study with researchers from the Argumentative Writing Project.

The following transcribed classroom event comes from Mr. Mosley's classroom at that point in the school year when he was engaging his students in making the transition from learning to argue to arguing to learn. The curriculum of the course was focused on American Literature, and throughout the year, Mr. Mosley organized instructional units to explore a particular cultural ideology often associated with the United States. One instructional unit focused on the American dream. As part of that instructional unit, the class was reading and discussing Fitzgerald's (1925) *The Great Gatsby*. The novel includes characters living in the fictional towns of West Egg and East Egg on Long Island, New York, in 1922. The story primarily concerns Jay Gatsby and Daisy Buchanan. Gatsby attempts to convince Daisy to leave her husband, Tom Buchanan. The novel explores a range of literary themes and creates a portrait of the so-called Roaring Twenties (the 1920s) that is often characterized by literary critics as a cautionary tale about the American Dream (e.g., Bewley, 1954; Callahan, 1996; Pearson, 1970; Roberts, 2006). The following event focused on Daisy and her relationship with Tom Buchanan and Jay Gatsby. The class had reached that point in the novel where Daisy has to choose between Tom and Gatsby.

Mr. Mosley used a graphic organizer to guide the organization of the classroom event (see Diagram 3.1). The day before the following classroom event transcribed, Mr. Mosley asked the students to complete a graphic organizer "to consider the evidence so far [in the novel] that they can use to predict what Daisy's decision might be—who do you think Daisy is going to end up with and why?" So students were expected to come prepared to discuss textual evidence they had chosen and thought about rather than "on-the-spot thinking" (from interview with Mr. Mosley).

The graphic organizer has three columns: "Evidence in favor of Gatsby," "Evidence in favor of Tom," and "What Are the Key Issues in Tension for Daisy?" The class begins with Mr. Mosley dividing the students into two groups: (a) those providing "Evidence in favor of Gatsby" and (b) those providing "Evidence in favor of Tom." The first part of the following transcript captures a part of the class discussion when each group is providing evidence for its side. As such, the class is enacting an "arguing for their side" stance to argumentation (marshaling evidence and warrants to persuade others of their claim/thesis) as opposed to an "arguing to learn" stance (cf., Newell et al., 2015). After generating a list of "Evidence in favor of Gatsby" and "Evidence in favor of Tom," Mr. Mosley turns the class's attention to the middle column. As such, the students need to explore the evidence in both the "Evidence in favor of Gatsby" column and the "Evidence in favor

Tom or Gatsby? What's at Stake for Daisy?

Evidence in favor of Gatsby	WHAT ARE THE KEY ISSUES IN TENSION FOR DAISY?	Evidence in favor of Tom
Daisy risks going over to Gatsby's party with Tom to be with Gatsby (105) "Her throat [...] told of her unexpected joy" (89) - Never experiences joy with Tom "Beautiful little fool" (76-77) - Daisy got drunk on the night before her wedding—"Say Daisy's change her mind" - holding onto Gatsby's letter—suggests she knows she's making a mistake. "At least they're more important than the people we know" (108) - Daisy to Tom at Gatsby's party—hints she's intrigued by Gatsby's lifestyle 108—Gatsby's party contains romance "absent from her world" 103 Tom—"Women run around all too much these days. They meet all kinds of crazy fish" - Tom has not been a husband figure Daisy's reaction to Gatsby's shirts "They're such beautiful shirts"—sobbing Shows she's all about the $$$ "This is your house?" -- surprised that he has such a house. (77) "Can't repeat the past...why of course you can!" - Shows his determination...he will stop at nothing to get Daisy back - Go back to Louisville and get married—wipe out the past and free her from Tom	Daisy is a mother and has a duty to her child to provide stable life. Daisy's reputation (super important to her...not wanting to get judged) Stability (Tom) vs. Happiness (Gatsby) The past vs. the present True love and happiness Trust and care	"I'd never seen a girl so mad about her husband. It was touching to see them together" (76) - Jordan's idea about Daisy after her wedding She wouldn't get mad if she didn't care "They moved with a fast crowd [...] but she came out with a perfect reputation" - Reputation matters HUGE to Daisy... - Gatsby is a bootlegger...would ruin it - Everything Gatsby does is based on a lie Daisy's behavior with letter suggests she is letting go. - Mood changes after she "lets letter go" - "The next day she married Tom without so much a shiver" Tom is "the guy you marry" vs. Gatsby is "the guy you date" What else will Gatsby lie about to Daisy, besides how he got his $$? She is not pulling at him...it's all Gatsby doing the work. Daisy has a child...it's impossible to wipe out the past five years - Gatsby wants Daisy to tell Tom she never loved him—is that possible?

Diagram 3.1 Sources of Evidence for Daisy's Dilemma Generated During the Classroom Event

of Tom" column not to construct a synthesis or a consensus but to identify and explore the tensions that exist around Daisy's decisions. About the graphic organizer, Mr. Mosley notes, "With the middle column of the graphic organizer—is my attempt to push [the students] beyond that mode of arguing [arguing for your side] to more complex and less binary understandings."[1] Just before the classroom discussion began, Mr. Mosley reminds the students that he was not expecting a debate and that he was not looking for a consensus of opinion. Mr. Mosley began the discussion by directing the students' attention to a chart on a screen in front of the classroom.

> I did not want this to turn into a competitive win the debate situation. . . . I reminded them [the students] that I really wanted them to use it as a way to unpack ideas. So, as the lesson started, I stepped back and simply took notes on this chart (see Diagram 3.1). I wanted them to walk out of class not feeling like "I won" but "now I have a lot of good ideas."
>
> (interview with Mr. Mosley)

501	T	What is the evidence suggesting to us ↑
502	Carrie	I feel like Daisy
503		something that xxxxxx if she leaves Tom
504		But on account of her reputation
505		It says on page 77 "they moved with a fast crowd all of them young and rich and wild, but she came out with an absolutely perfect reputation."
506		And in that time period it wasn't necessarily like normal to divorce your husband
507		especially when guys have problems you just work it out
508		And I think that like what she liked about being with Tom is that she had a good reputation and that she was young and rich and it kind of had that reputation
509	Lena	If I can add to that
510	T	So
511		yeah
512		You can add
513		Keep talking
514	Lena	When //
515		it's on page 108
516		To add
517		it goes off the back of that where it says "at least they're more interesting than people we know"

Constructing Dialogue and Dialectics

518		and um Daisy was saying this to Tom when he didn't seem to like the party and everything.
519		I think that she kinda had /
520		over the past couple of years a change of heart.
521		Having that //
522		wanting that good reputation
523		and now she's more interested in hinting that she's interested in Gatsby //
524		xxxx Tom without him realizing what's going on
525	T	Anything else in that passage in 76 and 77 that seems to xxxxxx
526	Jack	I think where she says /
527		say Daisy changed her mind /
528		That's a big part because that's the day of her wedding and she doesn't want to marry Tom /
529		She wants to marry Gatsby /
530		Usually you do want to marry the person that you're having a relationship with
531	T	What happened that brought this on ↑
532	Rex	Gatsby sent a letter to her
533	T	So that letter
534		Is that what we're inferring here ↑
535		Is that the inference we're making //
536		that this letter came from Gatsby ↑
537		What in the text suggest that to us ↑
538	Rex	said that on page 76 "She wouldn't let go of the letter and took it into the tub with her and squeezed it up into a wet ball, and only let me leave it in the soap dish when she saw it was coming to pieces like snow."
539		She was holding on to it as tight as she could and was feeling like she made a mistake by wanting to marry Tom
540	Megan	In a way that went just as that /
541		It kind of symbolizes letting go of the past because the letter she /
542		The past is the past /
543		You can always remember it but you have to be able to move on from it /
544		And so she kinda saw what was ahead of her and the fact that she has her relationship with Tom ahead of her /
545		But that note like when she set it down it was kind of resembling the fact that she's gonna let Gatsby go /

546		Like it had to happen
547	T	What is our evidence then "Tom people" ↑
548		What is our evidence that she lets Gatsby go in this scene ↑
549	Ss	She marries Tom
550	Megan	Like she stops crying
551		Everything just stops
552	T	Look how this is presented in the text
553		Besides just marrying Tom
554	Megan	All of a sudden her mood just kind of changes and I think that she.
555		The whole bathtub scene is kinda when she comes to the realization that she has to make a choice
556		It's either you go and proceed ahead or you stay back and remorse and stuff about the past
557	T	Is there anything else Tom people that
558		yes Justin ↑
559	Justin	It says "The next day at five o'clock she married Tom Buchanan without so much as a shiver and started off on a three months' trip to the South Seas."
560		So /
561		she kind of by then already knew that she made up her mind
562	Ashley	On the bottom of page 108 it says "After all, in the very casualness of Gatsby's party there were romantic possibilities totally absent from her world."
563		And the way I took that is that inside that party there was so much romance and love and all this stuff
564		And she just doesn't have that with Tom
565		So.
566	Ben	She is married xxxxxx to Tom so she could end the marriage
567		and because he said xxxxx yesterday about /
568		It wasn't really a common thing but it can happen /
569		So /
570		she could have and if she wanted to that badly /
571		So I think she still loves Tom a lot and she wants to stay with him
572	Carrie	I also think on page 103 when Gatsby brings out he knows Daisy /

Constructing Dialogue and Dialectics 71

573		Tom responds and says "I wonder where in the devil he met Daisy, by God. I may be old-fashioned in my ideas but women run around too much these days to suit me. They meet all kinds of crazy fish."
574		And I think that's kind of a problem for Daisy because she doesn't know how to act because Tom hasn't really acted in that husband figure kind of way to her/
575		But she also wants to be with him the way that a husband should be like /
576		And I think that Tom is just xxxxx
578	Megan	I feel like we all know
579		especially with girls like /
580		we all know we want the bad boy and everything like that /
581		And in a way Gatsby kind of represents that
582		He pushes the norms in a way
583		Where her relationship with him is exciting
584		But it's the fact that she's ready at that point to settle down and Tom /
585		I guess in a way is. We all know the guy that you date versus the guy that you marry or the girl
586		that you date versus the girl that you marry
587		They're completely different people /
588		I just feel like she sees with Tom is the guy that you're supposed to marry whereas Gatsby who is just that fling that she had /
589	Vick	So then why does he [Tom] have a mistress now ↑
590	Charles	That's what I thought /
591	Vick	If he really wants to get things back together with Daisy then why does he still have a mistress ↑
592	Carrie	Yeah
593	T	So what you're saying Vick is that
594		as a rule
595		the guy that you marry usually isn't the guy who has a mistress ↑
596	Vick	I'm just saying because right now
597		I don't like Tom that much
598		I'm gonna say that honestly from my opinion because if you marry somebody you're not going to have a mistress off the street
599		At least I'm not

600		I didn't mean it like that but I don't think that that's /
601	Avery	And Gatsby's just as rich as Tom /
602		so I don't understand if Daisy wants to be someone like //
603		and you're supposed to be with not just date
604		Like Gatsby got his life //
605		well not his life together
606		But he left his family got money and got a house right across the bay from her
607	Megan	But that's just it.
608		Everything Gatsby does is based on a lie.
609	Avery	I know but
610	Megan	How is Daisy going to feel about that though when she finds out anything
611	Avery	I don't think Tom lets her and Tom cheats on her.
612	Megan	Yeah but she knows about Tom's lies
613		She doesn't know about Gatsby's lie
614		Gatsby is a complete fake
615	Lena	At least Gatsby isn't lying about hooking up with another girl
616	Vick	I mean come on are you gonna have
617	Avery	I mean,
618		if he lied about how he got his money
619		All she cares about is money anyway
620		She doesn't care how he got it
621	Vick	Are you gonna have somebody that's gonna risk everything for you
622		Risk money everything just to be with you?
623		Or do you want to have somebody your husband or your wife cheating on you with somebody in New York or whatever
624	Charles	I think /
625		like on page 9 when she says, "They're such beautiful shirts. She sobbed. Her voice muffled in the thick folds. It makes me sad because I've never seen such beautiful shirts before."
626		I think she's all in it for just the money /
627		She really doesn't care about the love or what they do for each other /
628		It's all about the money /

Constructing Dialogue and Dialectics 73

629		So /
630		I think that /
631		this is my counter-argument /
632		that since she's sobbing over these beautiful shirts that she might actually go for Gatsby
633	T	You want me to put that on the other side [of figure 1] Charles ↑
634	Charles	Either way
635	T	well which side should I put that on ↑
636		I thought you were going to do something with that and talk about why
637		Or it's Tom
638	Charles	That was xxxxx
639	Megan	I'll back that up /
640		Tom is the fact that
641		yeah he has money
642		But wouldn't she be doing the same thing with Gatsby ↑
643		She could be playing Gatsby for all of his money too
644		And then what's gonna happen when she finds out all that money's fake and it could all go away in like two seconds
645	Steve	She doesn't care
646		She only cares about the money

A bit later, Mr. Mosley directed the students to the column on the graphic organizer labeled "What Are the Key Issues in Tension for Daisy?"

701	T	Can we kind a focus on the middle box now ↑
702		We're not going to so much be about who's right /
703		who's wrong /
704		but now kind of work together /
705		This is the pool of evidence that you guys kind of pulled up here /
706		Can we identify the forces that are in tension regarding Daisy's choice ↑
707		So /
708		we're kind of unpacking her motivation here /

709		What the issues are /
710		Take all of this and let's characterize them as issues /
711	T	so what are some of the issues in tension related to her choice ↑
712	Eric	The child it feels like is a really good xxxxx
713	T	OK
714		Why ↑
715	Eric	Because.
716		I feel like as a mom she wants her child to have a steady family and be able to have a mother and a father figure in her life
717		So really that's a big reason why she is so torn between these two people
718	Ashley	And I think it's because her reputation /
719		because like she would literally be leaving one guy for another /
720		it's kind of like hopping from one guy to another and she's known as like /
721		Like they said after their honeymoon /
722		she had a perfect reputation and they said /
723		maybe it's because she doesn't drink /
724		She doesn't seem to do anything bad /
725		So /
726		leaving one guy and getting married to another is really bad
727		with a child
728	T	And is there any other evidence up there on the chart that we could put under reputation ↑
729		The idea of reputation being really important to her ↑
730	S1	Money
731	T	Hmm ↑
732	S1	Just money /
733		just from the other guys /
734		she only wants money
735	Megan	The fact that if she does go with Gatsby /
736		he's known for being in the drugs /
737		or the bootlegging and all that stuff with all the alcohol /
738		But that would make her look bad because it makes her look involved /

Constructing Dialogue and Dialectics

739	T	Anything else ↑
740	Carrie	I think her reputation is definitely important to her or else /
741		I think that's partially why she got married to Tom /
742		because she knew he was gonna have money for a long time because xxxxx inherited it /
743		and so I think that's a good reputation for her because people think of her as always going to be rich /
744		always going to have that life /
745		and power over other people
746	T	So /
747		can I do that ↑
748		Stability versus happiness ↑
749		Like true stability versus true happiness ↑
750		Yeah↑
751	Ben	I think another big issue is if she leaves for Gatsby
752		I think xxxx
753		I think she'll get judged a lot by everyone
754		and because they'll think that she's just leaving Tom for Gatsby for more money
755		so she'll get judged by people
756	T	What other issues are at stake for Daisy here?
757		What else?
758	Megan	I want to say something about the past
759		like her feelings for Gatsby versus the present
760		her feelings for Tom
761	T	Anything else ↑
762		A lot of our tensions here are things that seem like they favor Tom.
763		So /
764		what are the issues that are in favor of Gatsby?
765	Jasper	Her happiness
766	T	And why ↑
767		Can you talk about that
768		Jasper ↑
769	Jasper	Well /
770		whoever she has the better time with
771		like at the party

772		she danced with Gatsby instead of Tom while Tom remained the polo player
773	T	Mm-hmm
774		Gatsby did that intentionally
775		(One second pause)
776		kept referring to Tom as the polo player during the party ↑
778		Totally doing that on purpose to get under his skin.
779		What else ↑
780		Anything else ↑
781	Lena	So /
782		like
783		xxxxxxxxxx
784		why she wouldn't want to stay with Tom is because then she would totally like
785		knowing even though she cheated /
786		he's cheated on her all the time and hasn't really cared about it

Re-Locating Authority

When we interviewed Mr. Mosley about the lesson, he commented:

> Really what this activity is doing is putting Daisy at the center of the exploration and really unpacking. And what I really liked about it is we did this right before the chapter where they go to New York and everything happens. So, this is a way to kind of crystalize the first six chapters into one discussion and really lay out all of the complex dimensions that are going on so that when they read the Chapter 7 the reading is informed by all of these sorts of things.

It is worth noting that this is not a typical approach to understanding characterization in Fitzgerald's novel since the concern is typically on Gatsby's motives rather than how Daisy might be understood on the basis of her experiences with Tom and Gatsby. Indeed, Mr. Mosley and his students had spent a great deal of time in prior lessons focused on Gatsby's character and motivation. About the shift to focusing on Daisy's perspective, Mr. Mosley noted, "framing the question around Daisy's perspective offers a fresh way to extend these discussions [about the American dream and Gatsby's character and motivation] while also putting them into conversation with the complex dynamics of Daisy and Tom's relationship revealed throughout the novel."[2] One of the key questions to ask here is, "Who has the authority and what does it mean to shift the focus from those characters that have traditionally received the focus of attention in literary criticism to other characters?" One could interpret this move in Mr. Mosley's classroom as reflecting a feminist orientation that seeks to move women characters from the margins and from being objects whose primary purpose is to highlight aspects of the male protagonists and that seeks to examine the limitations of (usually male) authors' framing of women characters.[3] On the basis of our many conversations with Mr. Mosley, it is reasonable to believe that this was part of his orientation. That said, we notice that focusing on characters other than those typically targeted also occurred in Ms. Field's classroom in their discussion of *To Kill a Mockingbird* (see Chapter 2) and such an instructional move also occurred in the literary discussions in many of the other classrooms in our study.

At issue here is who has the authority to place a character in a novel as central to the discussion of the novel. Mr. Mosley, Ms. Field, and the other teachers may have taken that authority perhaps as a function of their pedagogical responsibilities. If so, we could theorize that the location of authority for centralizing particular characters in a novel is an institutional authority (the teachers have such authority because they are representatives of the institution of schooling). But while not denying that such a location would seem reasonable at least in part in the case of Mr. Mosley, Ms. Field, and the other teachers, it is not sufficiently a sole location. While it is true that the teachers have authority as a function of being representatives of the institution of schooling, that institution also constrains how they exercise that authority through holding the teachers accountable for student test scores (on standardized tests and Advanced Placement examinations that reflect mainstream framings of novels and their characters) and accountable for teaching in ways that are recognizable as acceptable within the field of English language arts education. Simply put, if any of the teachers taught literature in a way that students, parents, or others viewed as aberrant, they would be corrected by the institution. The centralizing of characters and perspectives not typically centralized in the teaching of canonical novels may not place the teachers in serious trouble with their school institutions, but they know they have varied from the mainstream; thus, the question to ask about authority is whether authority beyond institutional authority may be located with the teacher.

From the perspective of Dialogic Literary Argumentation, the authority for focusing on any particular character or on any particular event in a novel is not a function of a teacher *per se*, but rather is a function of its use in engaging others in a dialogue. That is, Mr. Mosley can centralize Daisy only if his students agree with him doing so. That is, the authority lies not with Mr. Mosley nor with the students *per se*, but in their interactions (their negotiations) with each other; which is merely to say that what is at issue is not simply the taking of a feminist perspective or any other perspective of *The Great Gatsby* (or of *To Kill a Mockingbird* or a Hemingway short story) but also the re-location of authority for exploring the meaning, social significance, and cultural import of the reading of a literary text(s). Instead of locating that authority in a person, such as a teacher (or a student), regardless of how enlightened or knowledgeable that person might be, authority is relocated to what Bertau (2014) calls the "in-between" space among those dialoguing, or more simply stated, the authority for framing the exploration of the meaning, social significance, and cultural import of the reading of a literary text is located in the evolving conversation that was prompted by the reading of the literary text.

In an interview with Mr. Mosley about the instructional conversation on "Daisy's dilemma," he pointed out that, "this use of the chart (see Diagram 3.1) and me recording allows for all of us to see [through the use of an LCD projector] what ideas we're making." By making the ideas public and visible, the ideas no longer belong to a particular person but are available for anyone to take up, and as such, they exist not in any one person but in the "in-between" space of the classroom conversation.

This shift in the location of authority from a person to the "in-between spaces" in dialogic interaction is key to moving from a stance of arguing for one's claim (i.e., traditionally defined argumentation) to a stance of dialogic rationality in which the power for constructing meaning, social significance, and cultural import is a "power with" rather than a "power over" (cf., Kriesberg, 1991; Noddings, 1992). A close look at the transcript earlier shows subtle conversational moves that Mr. Mosley makes to shift the authority from himself to the "in-between" spaces of the dialoguing, to a stance of "power with." For example, consider lines 501 to 513. Notice that in line 501 ("What is the evidence suggesting to us?") Mr. Mosley uses "us" instead of "you" and instead of a generic universalistic ellipsis. Authority for reasonableness of an evidence- and warrant-based claim is located in the collective, not the individual. As such, both an individualized reader response framing and a top-down New Criticism framing are defenestrated.

Also consider how Mr. Mosley responds to Lena after Carrie makes her argument about reputation (lines 502 to 508). Lena asks "If I can add to that" (line 509). It is not just that Mr. Mosley approves but also how he approves of Lena's building on Carrie's argument. "You can add | keep talking" (lines 512 and 513). These lines are addressed to Lena specifically and to the class as a whole to build on what others have said and keep the conversation going. In simple terms it is to value the give and take of the classroom conversation; in more technical and theoretical terms, it is to locate the authority for meaning, social significance, and cultural import in the "in-between" spaces of social interaction. There are important details also to consider in the lines that immediately precede Mr. Mosley's approval of Lena taking a turn at talk. First, in line 509, Lena has "usurped" Mr. Mosley's authority to assign turns at talk. Lena's politeness form "If I can . . ." makes clear that she is not confronting Mr. Mosley about authority for assigning turn-taking but rather at one and the same time Lena acknowledges Mr. Mosley's authority while also publicly acknowledging that the hierarchical social relationship in how the conversation unfolds has shifted. Mr. Mosley's "So" (line 510) appears to be connected to Carrie's contribution to the conversation as if he is going to respond more fully to Carrie, but then Mr. Mosley shifts to addressing Lena with the next utterance "yeah" (line 511). He could have stopped there, but he continues with "You can add | Keep talking" (lines 512 and 513), not just clarifying that she can take a turn at talk (which was clarified in the previous utterance) but also valuing it and then making a metadiscursive comment about the importance of keeping the conversation going in exploration of Daisy's dilemma, which is all simply to say that the ideational aspect of their classroom conversation is intimate with regards to the social relations aspect of their conversation (with their assigning of roles, positionalities, social relations, and authorities, etc., to each other).

Another example can be found in lines 631 to 640. Charles is making what he calls a counter-argument (line 631). Mr. Mosley asks in which column on the graphic organizer he should put that counter-argument (line 633). But Charles appears to have eschewed the graphic organizer and its columns (line 634) and is instead engaged in responding to others' comments in exploring how Daisy's situation might be understood, which is merely to say that he is engrossed in the conversation such that he appears to have transcended the instructional task frame. Indeed, Mr. Mosley notes that he "valued the fact that Charles is thinking about the question from multiple perspectives."[4] Mr. Mosley brings Charles and the class back to the instructional task (line 635 to 637), but Megan (line 639) subtly sets aside Mr. Mosley's effort to come back to the instructional task and graphic organizer by continuing Charles's focus on the meaning, social significance, and cultural import of the instructional conversation (as opposed to the instructional task, completing the graphic organizer). Note that once Megan takes up Charles's comments, Mr. Mosley does not interject further. Megan's take-up of Charles's comments is consistent with Mr. Mosley's efforts to promote "shared ownership" of the conversation and authority for interpretation, what he calls "a give-and-take of classroom authority."[5] What Charles and Megan contribute to the dialogue about Daisy's choosing does not fit in any of the columns; yet, because the authority for determining what counts as worthwhile lies in the in-between spaces (the give-and-take interactional spaces) among Mr. Mosley and the students, Charles's and Megan's interactional construction of a quality of Daisy's character has importance within the classroom conversation.

Also telling about the location of authority being shifted to the in-between spaces are lines 702 through 704:

702	T	We're not going to so much be about who's right /
703		who's wrong /
704		but now kind of work together /

Mr. Mosley is initiating the shift from arguing for a position to exploring the tensions within which Daisy finds herself. Gone is the framing of who is right and who is wrong (or even the notion of right and wrong) as it is supplanted by working together to explore tensions related to Daisy's choice (lines 706, 708, 710, and 711).

Although we have highlighted only a few of the places in the transcribed conversation in Mr. Mosley's class, we can observe that the shift in authority from the teacher to the "in-between" spaces is thematic across the instructional conversation. In addition to the conversational interactions discussed earlier, we can also point to Mr. Mosley's contributions to this theme of shifting authority by Mr. Mosley's pronoun usage across this classroom conversation (e.g., lines 534, 537, 547, 701, 702, 728) and by how Mr. Mosley encourages students to expand their responses (e.g., framing student responses as building on and extending previous ones and as being something to which others need to be accountable; e.g., lines 635 to 637, 731, 739, lines 766 to 768).

Exploration of Warrants and Backing

Beyond the thematic of relocating authority, we can also observe how Mr. Mosley is engaging the students in a key element of Dialogic Literary Argumentation: the exploration of the warrants and backing for the interpretations proffered during instructional conversations to allow for an open and public consideration.

As students offer warrants for their views, for example, "Usually you do want to marry the person that you're having a relationship with" (line 530), they ground their understanding of Daisy's dilemma in their understandings of human relationships but also remain open to other's values and beliefs. Megan provides a warrant that raises questions about what it means to claim that someone engages in warranting on the basis of their experiences. Megan seems to position herself as a kind of spokesperson

Constructing Dialogue and Dialectics 81

for her gender: "I feel like we all know | especially with girls like, we all know we want the bad boy and everything like that | And in a way Gatsby kind of represents that | He pushes the norms in a way" (lines 578 to 582). Megan assumes the role of "spokesperson" for her gender "we all know we want the bad boy" (line 580). It is not clear that Megan has actually had the experience of wanting the "bad boy" that is "exciting" (line 583) nor is it clear on what basis she has decided that she has the authority to speak for her gender. So the basis of her warranting is not experience *per* se but the presentation of experience and the presentation of authority to speak for others whether one has indeed had the experience or the authority. Of course, Megan could be challenged on these grounds, but she is not and thus the warranting is validated by how others take it up. Indeed, Megan's warranting marks a turning point in the discussion as Megan has described how, in her judgment, Daisy's decision not to marry Gatsby is an easy interpretation of Daisy as superficial and perhaps representative of a female stereotype. However, Vick is not satisfied with this comment and raises the issue of Tom's infidelity and in so doing complicates the warranting.

Mr. Mosley revoices the warrant (as he does with many other warrants), "So, what you're saying Vick is that | as a rule | the guy that you marry usually isn't the guy who has a mistress?" (line 593 to 595). We understand the move captured in the phrase, "So, what you're saying" as a revoicing that signals the value of offering new ideas that opens a space for what Barnes (1976) calls "exploratory talk." Part of what is key to warranting and exploratory talk within Dialogic Literary Argumentation is that students listen to each other and build on what each other offers. For instance, when Eric suggests that Daisy may want Tom as a husband to have a steady home for her children (line 716), Ashley reminds Eric and the other students of Tom's lies and infidelities (line 612). Rather than rejecting Eric's warrant (and related claim), Ashley builds on it making the argument more complex and mediated.

Building a Dialectical Space

As we noted earlier, Mr. Mosley used a graphic organizer with three columns (see Diagram 3.1) to organize the classroom lesson, part of which is transcribed earlier. The left and right columns had spaces for recording evidence in support of Daisy choosing Tom or Gatsby. Mr. Mosley divided the students into two groups: (a) the "Tom" group and (b) the "Gatsby" group, with each group providing evidence in support of its person (we note that the students had been assigned for homework the previous evening to search for evidence to use in support of their group). Mr. Mosley explicitly told the students before the discussion began that he would sit back at his computer and that he wanted the students to tell him what to put on the chart displayed via projector. He positioned himself as both a facilitator and a recorder of the evidence and warrants that the students generated. Thus, the class began with students providing evidence in favor of one side or the other (that Daisy would choose Tom Buchanan or that she would choose Jay Gatsby). With the question, "Can we identify the forces that are in tension regarding Daisy's choice?" (line 706), Mr. Mosley engaged the students in deconstructing the dichotomous framework that had organized the previous discussion in the class. They were now to "work together" (line 704) to identify the complexities around Daisy's choosing. Mr. Mosley's orchestration of the instructional conversation around the column labeled "What Are the Key Issues in Tension for Daisy?" focused on identifying tensions and providing a dialectic space for students to engage in dialogue. In this sense, students' discussion of the key issues around Daisy's decision seems to allow space for the teacher and students to produce utterances that are not exclusively representing one side over the other. The discussion about key issues (the middle column) is where these voices are entering into a relationship in a way that formulates more general issues, resulting in an exploration of Daisy's situation. These issues the students raised included the following:

- "Daisy is a mother, and has a duty to her child to provide stable life" (line 716)
- Daisy's "reputation" (lines 718 to 745)
- "Stability [Tom] versus happiness [Gatsby]" (lines 748 to 750)
- "The past versus the present" (lines 758 to 760)
- True love and "happiness" (lines 765 to 772)
- Trust and care (lines 784 to 796)

These responses that were articulated by students (occasionally revoiced by Mr. Mosley) required the students to warrant the tensions articulated by reference to what they took as evidence of personhood: mothers inherently care for their children (line 716), a two-parent family is best for children (line 716), people care about their reputations (line 718, line 740), money is important to people (line 734), caring is a quality people desire (to be cared for; line 786).

What we are interested in here is how Mr. Mosley and his students constructed that dialectical space. The graphic organizer Mr. Mosley created (see Diagram 3.1) provides a visual representation of the creation of a dialectic; the arrows suggesting that the ideas from the two different positions come together in the middle column in creating a tension. Mr. Mosley continuously asks the students in which column he should place their comments, thereby asking them to consider the difference between arguing for one's side (the columns labeled "Evidence in favor of Gatsby" and "Evidence in favor of Tom") versus arguing to explore (the column labeled "What Are the Key Issues in Tension for Daisy?"). Notice that the middle column is framed as a question that is ideationally different from the other columns and that also requires a different set of social relations than the other columns. Ideationally, the items in the middle column do not require a resolution but rather contribute to the understanding that Daisy exists in unresolvable tension, and it is in recognition that the tensions are unresolvable that the students gain insight into the human condition and a glimpse into the *in situ* nature of personhood. In terms of social relations, left and right columns required the students to advocate for their own positions and engage in competitive relationships with others. Although they did not become competitive (indeed, they tended to build on each other's comments), the scheme of the graphic organizer framed their social relations in a competitive manner. The middle column requires a different set of social relations. Students need to listen to each other and cooperatively build on each other's ideas such that differences do not index isolation, competition, or individualism but rather index dialogic relations that allow continuous evolution of ideas without necessarily coming to consensus. Ideationally, the items in the middle column involve the compression of opposing forces. For example, consider the first item in the middle column. Daisy is a mother and has a duty to provide for her child as opposed to her desire to pursue love, happiness, and the realization of herself. This tension is compressed by the urgency of needing to make a choice between two men, in part because of how her personhood as a woman is conceptualized in the novel.

In part, the construction of the dialectical space involves languaging. Mr. Mosley provides the students with a way to language their exploration of the tensions within which they locate Daisy and more generally how they language engagement in Dialogic Literary Argumentation. Part of that languaging involves explicitly naming the relationship the students should have with the claims and warrants they make. Mr. Mosley tells them, "We're not going to so much be about who's right | who's wrong | but now kind of work together | . . . Can we identify the forces that are in tension regarding Daisy's choice? | So | we're kind of unpacking her motivation here" (lines 701 to 708). Here, Mr. Mosley is providing the students with language to use in exploring the dialectics that contextualize the lives of the fictional characters in *The Great Gatsby*, most notably in the syntax of "not . . . be about who's right, who's wrong" (lines 702 and 703), identify tensions (line 706), and "unpacking" (line 708). Later in the classroom conversation, Mr. Mosley provides additional language for engaging in the classroom conversation about the dialectics within which the characters in the novel live their lives. He models language for the search for further insight and evidence (e.g., "What is the evidence suggesting to us?" line 501; "What other issues are at stake for Daisy here?" line 756; "Anything else?" line 761) and the languaging of the intellectual processes at play, what Kim (2018) has called languaging thinking (e.g., "Is that what we're inferring here? | Is that the inference we're making?" lines 534 to 535; "as a rule," line 594; "we're kind of unpacking . . ." line 708; the grammatical construction of _____ versus _____, lines 748 and 749). In our view, providing the class (both teacher and students) with a language for engaging in Dialogic Literary Argumentation may not have been a deliberate plan by Mr. Mosley or any of the other teachers but nonetheless it is a necessary element for moving to Dialogic Literary Argumentation both because it shifts the location of authority for constructing meaning, social significance, and cultural import and because it makes it possible for the students and teacher to construct a dialectic framing of the meaning, social significance, and cultural import of the novel.

Also at stake in constructing a dialectical space as part of Dialogic Literary Argumentation are power relations. There are power relations in the relationships of the characters in the novel and discussion of these power relations may provide insight into the power relations that exist in the lives of students, teachers, their families, their communities, and others beyond. The power relations that the students explore cover a wide range of situations: there are power relations related to gender, money, sex, law and crime, class, and so forth. Identifying power relations is only one aspect, however. It is recognizing that power relations often exist in ways that make it difficult to take agency. For example, consider the students' discussion of Daisy's reputation (lines 718 to 744). We notice that their use of reputation concerns her moral reputation (lines 718 to 727), involvement in criminal activity (lines 735 to 738), and her reputation related to money (line 742 and 743), all of which are placed in compressed opposition to her happiness (line 765 and lines 770 to 772). And similarly so, she needs to marry Tom, Carrie argues (lines 740 to 745), in order to have the money to have "power over other people" (line 745), but marrying Tom (or Gatsby for that matter) is a consequence of her disempowered status as a desired woman they both want to have.

The discussion of the tensions has turned to the "hard reality" of "the overarching power relations, growing social inequalities and increasing commoditization of all aspects of human life and experience" (Dafermos, 2018, p. A13). That is, the discussion explores the moral and ethical bases of the characters: both Gatsby and Tom are lying to Daisy, and maybe Daisy is "in it for the money." The students are not just exchanging different interpretations but also actively considering one another's differing opinions to get to deeper understandings of what Daisy has to consider in her choice between Tom and Gatsby, neither of which is a clear choice. In brief, the construction of a dialectical space in the classroom conversation considered here in Mr. Mosley's classroom involves a graphic conceptualization, a language for use in exploring the unresolvable tensions in which characters in the novel exist, and attention to the power relations among the characters in the novel.

Notes

1. Quotation taken from comment Mr. Mosley wrote in response to an earlier version of this chapter on May 12, 2019.
2. Quotation taken from comment Mr. Mosley wrote in response to an earlier version of this chapter on May 12, 2019.
3. Mr. Mosley confirmed this interpretation of the shift he initiated to focusing on Daisy's perspective in a response he wrote to an earlier version of this chapter on May 12, 2019.
4. Quotation taken from comment Mr. Mosley wrote in response to an earlier version of this chapter on May 12, 2019.
5. Quotation taken from comment Mr. Mosley wrote in response to an earlier version of this chapter on May 12, 2019.

4 Constructing Multiple Perspectives and Rationality in the Teaching, Learning, and Reading of Literature

In the previous chapter, we discussed one of the dimensions of a model of Dialogic Literary Argumentation, the social construction of dialectical space in classrooms for teaching, learning, and reading literature. The particular dialectical space socially constructed in Mr. Mosley's class (from Chapter 3) involved unpacking and problematizing tensions that contextualized a decision that one of the characters in a novel had to make. As students discussed and analyzed the choice that Daisy had to make (in *The Great Gatsby*), they had to grapple with the complexities of the tensions in which Daisy found herself. Some of these tensions reflected a hierarchically gendered and class context that the teacher made visible by foregrounding Daisy as a decision-maker (rather than as solely an object for which two men were competing). The situation in which Daisy found herself was such that neither choice nor direction was unconflicted or unproblematic. Although the focus is on a character's situation, exploring such a dialectical space may provide teachers and students with insights into the tensions within the worlds in which they live. That is one kind of dialectical space, a compression of unresolvable opposing elements and forces contextualizing the actions, thoughts, decisions, feelings, and understandings of characters in a novel. In this chapter, we explore another kind of dialectical space, one in which the tensions to be unpacked and critically analyzed are defined by the juxtaposition of multiple perspectives and rationalities.

Although the teaching of multiple perspectives of a literary text is commonplace in high school English language arts classrooms, the term "multiple perspectives" typically has one of two meanings. It may refer to the use of personal experiences and cultural backgrounds in interpreting a literary text. Given different personal experiences and cultural backgrounds, there are likely to be different interpretations. Alternatively, multiple perspectives may refer to the use of various literary perspectives: reader response, New Criticism, feminist, Marxist, psychoanalytical, postcolonial, critical race theory, and so forth, with each perspective offering a different interpretation and way of constructing meaning, social significance, and cultural import.

From our observations of classrooms and our reading of the scholarship on the teaching, learning, and reading of literature, the use of multiple literary perspectives is often a goal in and of itself. It is taken as a worthy goal to expose students to the notion that there exist multiple perspectives and that they can bring them to bear upon their reading and understanding of a literary work. While we acknowledge that depending upon the circumstance, the teaching of multiple perspectives regardless of how defined can be a worthy goal in and of itself, it is a limited goal. Metaphorically, such an approach to multiple perspectives is like receiving a menu and choosing an item from it. Different people will select different items on the menu depending on their taste preferences or their nutritional and health needs. Abstractly, the choice of one item on the menu as legitimate and as good as the next.

Here, we problematize the use of multiple perspectives by insisting that regardless of how defined, multiple perspectives always exist in an ideological context. Even when teachers and students do not recognize the ideological contexts, nonetheless there are ideological contexts. For example, consider a classroom in which the teacher and students employed multiple perspectives foregrounding how their own diverse experiences, values, and personalities yield diverse interpretations for a literary text. We can imagine several ideological contexts that are framing the use of multiple perspectives by the teacher and the students: a shift from an empiricist philosophical ideology to a phenomenological one, an individualist ideology that valorizes individual choice and a free market consumerism (of ideas as merchandise), and perhaps a social institutional ideology of schooling in which the teaching and learning of multiple perspectives is preparation for participation in future educational institutions. What is at issue here, in part, is that even when teachers and students are unaware of the ideological contexts they are there nonetheless. That said, the ideological contexts of the teaching, learning, and reading of literature are not given but are socially constructed and situated. Simply stated, the question to ask is not "Are there ideological contexts for the use of multiple perspectives in the teaching, learning and reading of literature?" but rather "What are the ideological contexts?" and "How did these particular ideological contexts come to be at this time and place with these people? How are they evolving?"

In this chapter, we begin an exploration of the use of multiple perspectives in the teaching, learning, and reading of literature by taking a close look at Ms. Nelson's 11th-grade English language arts classroom and an instructional unit focused on reading Chinua Achebe's *Things Fall Apart* (1958). Ms. Nelson designed the unit around the use of multiple perspectives, what she called "ways of seeing." While Ms. Nelson encouraged her students to develop multiple ways of seeing *Things Fall Apart* and other literary texts, there are subtleties and complexities in how Ms. Nelson frames multiple ways of seeing that create a dialectical space that redefines multiple ways of seeing. The dialectical space that Ms. Nelson and her students construct involves the juxtaposition of diverse rationalities. While Ms. Nelson may not have labeled it as such, as we observed in her classroom, talked with her and her students about what was happening in her classroom, carefully analyzed video recordings of classroom conversations and student writings, and read what Ms. Nelson wrote about her teaching of argumentation and literature, we began to understand that part of the dialectical space they socially constructed for teaching, learning, and reading literature involved tensions among diverse rationalities. Although the issue of rationality/rationalities in argumentation had been raised in our studies of argumentation previously (see Newell et al., 2015), what we learned from Ms. Nelson's class was the potential of centralizing, unpacking, and problematizing rationality/rationalities for constructing meaning, social significance, and cultural impact in the teaching, learning, and reading of literature.

Thus, as we began to conceptualize and define Dialogic Literary Argumentation, we recognized that the dynamics of multiple perspectives and rationalities needed to be linked and be viewed as part of the ideological context(s) of teaching, learning, and reading literature. More simply stated, if one defines multiple perspectives as an engagement across rationalities, then the question to ask is, "How might the enactment of multiple perspectives constitute an engagement of diverse rationalities?" With regard to Dialogic Literary Argumentation, we are interested in those engagements of rationalities that might be characterized as dialogic. We view dialogic rationalities (cf., Gadamer, 1976, 1989) as creating dialectical spaces within which students and teachers can grapple with complexity, ambiguities, uncertainty, tensions, and oppositions that may or may not be resolvable—and in so doing, come to deeper and more complex understandings of personhood and the human condition. Thus, while teachers and students could treat multiple perspectives on a surface level, in our view, the teaching, learning, and reading of literature linking multiple perspectives with diverse rationalities creates potentials for deeper explorations and understandings of what it means to be human.

Teaching, Learning, and Reading *Things Fall Apart* in an 11th-Grade English Language Arts Classroom

Ms. Nelson had 18 years of teaching experience at the time of data collection in her classroom. She is highly regarded by her peers, especially for her analytic writing instruction that she has developed collaboratively with other teachers in her high school English department. The school in which Ms. Nelson teaches is located in a suburban community in an affluent area of a large city in the Midwestern United States. The year during which we observed Ms. Nelson's classroom, she was teaching 11th-grade Advanced Placement "Language and Composition." The class comprised

29 students. While Ms. Nelson's classroom had diverse students in regard to gender, culture, and religion, it was predominantly white and upper-middle class. This make-up reflects the high school more generally. The expectations for students are high with regard to the quality of work, college preparations, and professional aspirations.

Ms. Nelson participated in the Argumentative Writing Project beginning with a two-week summer workshop in the summer of 2014 and then attended monthly teacher meetings during the 2014–2015 school year. During that time, she had begun to work collaboratively with her colleagues to develop their entire Advanced Placement Language and Composition curriculum around argumentation and the development of argumentative practices. She felt that argumentation was important to the teaching and learning of writing and to developing learning practices in general. Indeed, the students in this high school studied argumentation and wrote argumentative essays during all four years of high school. In ninth grade, the students were introduced to analytic writing grounded in the practice of making an argument about a literary interpretation. Across all subject areas, according to Ms. Nelson, the teachers in the school recognized "the value of argument and reasoning as keys to academic success, and access to prestigious schools and a professional career."

Ms. Nelson engaged her students in an instructional unit on *Things Fall Apart* in the second semester of the 2014–2015 school year. While we focus on the teaching, learning, and reading about *Things Fall Apart* in her class, an understanding of what occurred in the instructional unit around *Things Fall Apart* requires an examination of how Ms. Nelson began the school year.

Ms. Nelson began the school year with an instructional unit on "ways of seeing." About that school year, she wrote:

> By the start of this leg of our journey in argumentation, my eleventh-grade language and composition students have already studied elements of voice, the ways that purpose and audience shift voice, cultural critical theories, elements of rhetoric, and the relationships between and among speaker, audience, and subject matter. Thematically, students have begun to explore the politics of language, focusing now on the ways in which language challenges and reinforces power and culture.[1]

Ms. Nelson laid the groundwork for ways of seeing during the first month of the school year, when she also taught literary criticism, focusing mainly on critical theories: Marxism, feminism, and critical race theory. As Ms. Nelson's previous statement shows, she believed that these ways of seeing could help students recognize that there are perspectives that differ greatly from their own that are valid and worthwhile to explore and integrate into

90 *Constructing Perspectives and Rationality*

their understandings of the world. To do so, she had students read articles and stories through the lenses of race, class, and gender.

There were several class sessions at the beginning of the school year that introduced students to "ways of seeing." This framing offered a kind of perspective-taking grounded in the idea that the knower requires empathy and critical awareness of one's own intellectual limitations. Using Plato's "Allegory of the Cave," Ms. Nelson introduced the "ways of seeing" unit to students by explaining what they might experience and what they might take from it.

801	T	what does he mean when you're looking at the sun ↑
802		if you fully can stand there without hurting your eyes and looking at the sun /
803		then you can fully comprehend a truth ///
804		about something /
805		you can completely understand ///
806		something /
807		right ↑
808		you have full comprehension of something important /
809		and Plato says that's good /
810		that's where the goodness is ///
811		now you think about that /
812		if you've ever had any suffering in your life /
813		and I know that some of you have /
814		initially when you go through that suffering /
815		when we're coming up out of the cave /
816		you know /
817		it's denial /
818		right ↑
819		you don't /
820		I wish this didn't happen /
821		I wish I could back to not knowing /
822		right ↑
823		that's /
824		that's what we feel like /
825		but if we're able to come through these sufferings /
826		all the way to the end /

Constructing Perspectives and Rationality 91

827		learn about ourselves /
828		get all the way to the end /
829		so that we feel whole /
830		we feel complete
831		and we can truly understand and acknowledge everything that happened /
832		most likely people who do that /
833		don't want to go back to not knowing /
834		they don't want to go back to ignorance because they've learned something /
835		right ↑
836		they gained something
837		that can fully look at the sun /
838		they can fully xxxxxxxx /
839		so /
840		we're going to be talking about some different /
841		some very different things this week
842		and I think for you /
843		for all of us /
844		it's going to make us squint /
845		it's going to make us feel like
846		wow
847		I can't just look right at that /
848		I need to go in stages
849		I need to gradually turn my body toward understanding that /
850		I need to try it on /
851		step by step /
852		and think about it /

Part of what we find interesting about Ms. Nelson's framing of "ways of seeing" is that it is not a relativist ideological framing. She is juxtaposing ignorance (lines 834 and 821) with "a truth" (line 803), "understanding" (lines 805, 831, and 849), and "knowing" (lines 821 and 833). The process of moving from "not knowing" to "understanding" is mediated by suffering (lines 812 to 814, and 825) and by difficult, reflexive processes (lines 842 to 847, 850 to 852). The movement Ms. Nelson is referring to is one in which the students are going to need to understand that others may legitimately view and understand the world in ways that the students do not, and such understandings may be uncomfortable or even painful and require a decentering of themselves.

Starting at the beginning of the school year and then throughout, Ms. Nelson selected multicultural texts for students to read and framed them in ways that fit into the theme of "ways of seeing." While we focus on the texts related to *Things Fall Apart*, there were also many other texts prior to and after this unit that explicitly addressed gender, sexuality, class, and the intersections of these critical perspectives. The texts explicitly connected to *Things Fall Apart* included a Christian Children's Fund commercial and the song "Do They Know It's Christmas?" These texts provided the opportunity to build and expand on previous themes and issues introduced earlier in the school year as she asked her students to draw on their experiences with race, class, and gender while also integrating new constructs such as power, colonialism, and cultural values.

To frame their instructional conversations with a critical perspective, Ms. Nelson asked, "What is a text's subtext? How is it [subtext] working on you? How does language work to challenge and reinforce cultural power?" The students returned repeatedly to these questions.

About three days before the students began reading *Things Fall Apart*, Ms. Nelson organized a small group activity that introduced her students to reading for and talking about hidden subtexts. After showing the commercial produced by Christian Children's Fund featuring a video of a woman in an impoverished country asking for money for poor children, Ms. Nelson asked her students to "look for the subtexts and jot notes down with observations of everything you saw and heard in the video." She then gave students some time to write silently followed by the small group activity, asking them to notice two features of the video: (a) the physical and historical context of the video's setting suggestive of the director's intentions and (b) the video's possible intended audience that should lead the students to the subtexts of the commercial.

901	T	Please don't forget thought about two important things /
902		One is about context
903		Two /
904		so context you might think about /
905		And /
906		This is the 1980s /
907		but how is this commercial
908		how would the directors achieve /
909		Or /
910		what is their purpose and how would they achieve it ↑
911		They know some things about society

Constructing Perspectives and Rationality

912		they made some choices because of the context in which this is happening /
913		and then audience /
914		Don't forget about audience
915		You were the audience just now to this ad
916		What did you feel ↑
917		did it work on you or not ↑
918		Yo /
919		OK /
920		so have all those conversations and those conversations should lead you to those subtexts

After that introduction and framing, the students worked in small peer groups. Following is one of the small peer group discussions.

1001	Pat	You have this abundance in society and these people have nothing
1002		and all it takes is 70 cents a day to give someone life /
1003		Like it literally says life sale 70 cents
1004	Taylor	The audience is like middle and upper class who can give 70 cents a day /
1005		which doesn't seem like a lot but when you think about it /
1006		70 cents times 365
1007		[laughs]
1008		I don't know $300 /
1009		So
1010		I guess by putting her in those clothes it's like kind of appealing
1011	Chris	Yeah
1012	Taylor	But still
1013	Chris	And there's like no color at the beginning
1014		and then as soon as she like says you can get medicine into a dying little body and food into a child you see like all this color [rubs her fingers together]
1015	Taylor	Yeah /
1016		The kids start to smile and like /
1017	Pat	Yeah and like make noise that isn't crying
1018		I think the most impactful part is the life //
1019		70 cents

1020		Like that's well worded /
1021		Like that's like loaded language /
1022		Like they're saying you can like [save] someone a life for less than a dollar /
1023		To us like 70 cents is nothing
1024	Taylor	Yeah
1025	Alex	Literally
1026	Pat	Like 70 cents and change I would like leave it on this table
1027	Ss	[laughter from some students]
1028	Taylor	I think like the best part of the commercial is when she's [host] not in it /
1029		Like when they're just showing the kids
1030	Ss	[laughter from some students]
1031	Taylor	That's the part I enjoyed. [Looks down at paper]
1032		I mean obviously it has an emotional appeal when she tries to draw emotion by saying like
1033		"having a heart" /
1034	Alex	Yeah /
1035		Guys what's the context for this ↑
1036	Pat	Where is she ↑
1037	Alex	It doesn't even say /
1038		It's a random impoverished location
1039	Pat	Like that would have been so much more so much better if she's like
1040		"I'm in blah blah blah this country or this continent" /
1041		Like this could literally be a set /
1042	Taylor	It's just impoverished children
1043	Alex	Where ↑
1044	Pat	I think people are more inclined to help if they know who they are helping /
1045	Alex	Yeah if I could get like
1046	Pat	Help!
1047		I'd be more inclined to help if it said "Help this person"
1048	Sx	Like a piece of paper that says this is who you'll help
1049	Pat	Yeah
1050	Alex	Instead of theoretically helping African children
1051	T	[Interjects to tell students to be sure that they have a few statements about the subtext]

Constructing Perspectives and Rationality

1052	Taylor	So /
1053		if you give money you're a good person or something like that or you will have a heart
1054	Pat	If you have a heart
1055		you will give money

After the small groups had time to discuss the commercial, they reconvened in a whole class discussion. Ms. Nelson asked the students to report on what the groups had decided about the video's context. A brief bit of that conversation follows.

1101	Sam	There is no context at all about the country where this is /
1102		and where money goes /
1103	T	Does it matter ↑
1104	Sam	It makes it more accountable /
1105		You see /
1106		there were scandals with this organization [Christian Children's Fund] today regarding where the money goes /
1107	Denny	And woman as a central figure in commercial sends the message that we should have this maternal instinct /
1108	T	Let's consider context too /
1109		widespread famine in Ethiopia during this time
1110	Toby	Exploitation of the people in the commercial /
1111	T	So
1112		that makes things more complicated /
1113		there was an awareness of the need.
1114		And the people of Ethiopia needed help /
1115		So
1116		So how do you help ↑
1117		This ad is typical of the 1980s that asks us to get involved.

Other comments about the commercial in the whole class discussion included the following:

a. If you have a heart, you'll donate money.
b. It is the responsibility of the privileged to give money to help the poor.
c. You should feel guilty for the privilege in which you were born, so donate.

d. A little goes a long way.
e. It doesn't take much sacrifice to change a life.
f. The victims are to blame for their situation.
g. The parents are incapable of using given resources to help their children.

Near the end of their discussion, Ms. Nelson asked, "Again, these aren't necessary intentional. But would you agree they're there?"

During the next class session, Ms. Nelson played a song titled, "Do They Know It's Christmas?"[2] The lyrics to the song include the lines:

> But when you are having fun
> There's a world outside your window
> And it's a world of dread and fear
> Where the only water flowing
> Is the bitter sting of tears
> And the Christmas bells that ring there
> Are the clanging chimes of doom
> Well tonight thank God it's them
> Instead of you
> And there won't be snow in Africa this Christmas time
> The greatest gift they'll get this year is life
> Where nothing ever grows
> No rain or rivers flow
> Do they know it's Christmas time at all?

Ms. Nelson then asked the students to call out key phrases from the song. Their call-outs included the following:

h. "Thank God it's them instead of you."
i. "The greatest gift they'll get this year is life."
j. "There's no snow in Africa, do they know it's Christmas time at all?"

Ms. Nelson asked students to derive subtexts from the song. "Talk it out. I want subtext statements. What are the messages being sold through those lyrics?" Their call-outs, some of which were similar to their call-outs from the previous day, included the following:

k. "It's important to give thanks for stability because basic needs are met."
l. "Don't take positive things for granted."
m. "People in poverty don't have time to celebrate."
n. "The African population is oblivious."
o. "If you have a heart, you'll donate money."
p. "It is the responsibility of the privileged to give money to help the poor—the white man's burden."

Constructing Perspectives and Rationality 97

q. "You should feel guilt for the privilege in which you were born, so donate."
r. "A little goes a long way."

After three class sessions on the commercial and the song, Ms. Nelson and her students began reading and discussing *Things Fall Apart*. Ms. Nelson wrote the following about beginning to read the novel:

> As the question and answer session continues, I clarify that we will be working toward creating consensus rather than having to resort to taking a majority vote. This point is crucial because it dictates that students must see all arguments and viewpoints as potentially valid. Group members cannot simply dismiss an argument because it is in opposition to their own. They will have to find ways to honor the voices and viewpoints at the table in order to accomplish the task in a way that satisfies everyone involved. This will not be easy for them, but the previous classroom spaces have given them preparation to face this next step.
>
> (p. 10)

Given limited space, we will summarize a series of instructional moves by Ms. Nelson as she guided her students through reading *Things Fall Apart* and then writing a culminating essay, what she described as a "report":

> Each student will examine the evidence they gather from the "handbook" (the text of *Things Fall Apart*) to determine whether human rights are indeed being violated in Umuofia. Using this evidence to inform their position on intervention, they will prepare reports that make a recommendation for or against intervention into the village of Umuofia and supply plentiful evidence as support.

Table 4.1 captures some key features of the class sessions on *Things Fall Apart*. Across six class sessions on the novel, Ms. Nelson orchestrated a series of process drama activities (cf., Edmiston, 2013; Heathcote, 1991) that included role playing as ethnographers to describe what is familiar and what is strange about Igbo culture and role playing as members of Human Rights Watch International Intervention Review Board. The task of the Review Board was to consider if a letter of complaint from a (fictional) Igbo child indicates if human rights have been violated and if an intervention is needed and to write a report to Human Rights Watch making an argument for or against outsider intervention.

A final assignment asked the students (in their respective roles) to then revise their essay/report using warranting as a way to consider multiple perspectives in making their written arguments. The report was to be addressed to a fictional "Director of Human Rights Watch International"

Table 4.1 Key Features of Role Playing and Process Drama Sessions

Session	In Relation to Reading Things Fall Apart (TFA)	Materials Used	Instructional Activities/ Assignments	Composing Arguments
One	Before reading TFA	Copied passages from TFA	Individually predict character, setting, conflict, and theme, and then share and refine their predictions in a small group	Learning to provide autonomous analysis, predicting multiple possible outcomes, and collaboratively considering valid predictions
Two	After reading part I		Listing of the familiar and strange in TFA to explore what seems like reasonable practices	Understanding how a culture is analyzed by outsiders versus natives
Third	Before missionaries arrive in part II	Letter of complaint from young Igbo boy against Umuofia, memo addressed to Intervention Review Board	Three-days of role playing members of Human Rights Watch International Intervention Review Board	Prepare reports that make a recommendation for or against intervention into the village of Umuofia and supply plentiful evidence as support
Fourth	Before missionaries arrive in part II	The novel, TFA used as "a handbook on the village"	Explore the intersection where two oppositional perspectives meet, to concede or acknowledge that intersection, and then to make the case for the argument they want to make	"Determine whether human rights are being violated in Umuofia and make a recommendation for or against intervention"

Table 4.1 (Continued)

Session	In Relation to Reading Things Fall Apart (TFA)	Materials Used	Instructional Activities/ Assignments	Composing Arguments
Fifth	After reading part IV	The novel, TFA as "a handbook on the village"	Another informal board meeting	Students work together to see other points of view
Sixth	Reading the novel complete	Students' draft reports	Revise reports by warranting claims and evidence	Warrant claims and evidence with general beliefs and definitions upon which the whole group can agree

and based on "extensive research, prepared reports, discussion [to] present a recommendation for or against intervention." Two student essays are shown later in the chapter and are discussed in depth.

Framing Multiple Perspectives in a Dialectic of Rationalities

At the beginning of the chapter, we noted that the use of multiple perspectives in the teaching, learning, and reading of literature always involves an ideological contextualizing even if unacknowledged. Here, we focus on ideological contextualizing that involves a dialectic space and in particular because we are interested in the use of "arguing to learn" as part of the teaching, learning, and reading of literature, we focus on dialectical spaces in which there are diverse rationalities.[3]

Underlying every argument and every conversation involving argumentation is an underlying rationality (or rationalities), an ideology (or ideologies) about what is reasonable and what is not. As we discussed in Chapter 2, some people equate logic with rationality: a rational person is a logical person, an irrational person is an illogical one. But logic is only one component of rationality; rationality is a broader system of concepts, ideas, practices, ways of constructing narratives, definitions of personhood, ethics, what is the good and what is not, and ways of being in the world that all come together to distinguish between what counts as reasonable and acceptable and what is not, distinguishing between the rational and irrational. Perhaps one of the more compelling ways to understand this notion of rationality is to assume that rather than universal laws and axioms (what we have elsewhere called "decontextualized rationality," Newell et al., 2015, pp. 142–143), rationality is constructed locally and situationally within the interaction of teachers and students (what we have called "contextualized rationality," Newell et al., 2015, pp. 142–143).[4] Examining—analyzing, unpacking, and problematizing—the rationalities of the actions of people in their daily lives (or of characters in a literary text), of the social institutions within which people work, play, learn, express religious beliefs, and so forth, and of the broader cultural and societal groups in which they are located, provides insights into what it means to be human and into the human condition that might not be available otherwise.

Ms. Nelson's commitment to argumentation began with a concern with what we view as a growing skepticism about the value of decontextualized rationalities. In a chapter (in progress) she is writing for a book on teaching argumentative writing, Ms. Nelson described this shift that began when one of her students complained, "I'm sorry, but do you think the author was really thinking that when she wrote it? Maybe this just isn't that deep. How do you know the author wanted us to read it this way?" Ms. Nelson's response was to shift her curricular conversations from episodic stretches of textual analysis to a recasting of the conversation to focus on "arguing to learn."

> I was pleased that they felt empowered to challenge the validity of an interpretation, but I was pretty sure they were doing so for the wrong reasons. They were simply seeking to supplant me with a higher authority—the author—to validate a claim about a text. What I really wanted was for my students to see *each other* as authorities of a text and as valued stakeholders in the conversation. I wanted their push-back to be driven by a need to seek out the complexity of a text and the nuances of an argument, not by their need to be passively told *The* Truth, which they believed that only the author could impart. Their access to the skills of mature argumentation were being blocked, in part, by me. Fully considering any complex argument requires that we first be able to stand in the place from which the argument is given; in this way, we might truly hear what is being said. But I was allowing my students to stand still. If I wanted my students to seek out multiple and sophisticated ways of seeing a text and reading the world, I would have to create new spaces in my classroom—spaces that by design would help them discover on their own that they needed to reposition themselves into different viewpoints in order to unpack and build complex arguments.

Part of what Ms. Nelson's statement reveals about her use of multiple perspectives ("ways of seeing") is that it is framed by a commitment to problematize taken-for-granted interpretations of a literary text by unpacking the relationship of language, culture, and power, an eschewing of the search for correctness and Truth supplanted by a gradual building toward a new understanding of what it means to be rational.

Ms. Nelson set up the teaching of *Things Fall Apart* earlier with Plato's "Allegory of the Cave." As we noted earlier, she created a binary between ignorance and knowing (lines 833 to 838). She grounds the binary of ignorance and knowing in the experience of suffering (lines 825), which facilitates learning about oneself (lines 825 to 830). She positions the students, metaphorically, as currently not looking at the sun (being ignorant) to gradually turning to be able to look at the sun (gaining understanding, lines 844–849), which may be unpleasant (line 844). We can surmise, *post hoc*, that Ms. Nelson is referring to the students learning to read the "subtexts" (unpack the rationalities and ideologies) of the various texts that they will be reading and discussing in her class.

Ms. Nelson used the class sessions on the Christian Children's Fund commercial and the song "Do They Know It's Christmas?" to prepare her students for the reading of *Things Fall Apart*. Those class sessions allowed Ms. Nelson to give her students experience with identifying and analyzing subtexts and making them visible. The teaching, learning, and "reading" of the commercial and the song involved an ideological contextualization of economically privileged Americans and people living in poverty elsewhere (a context not dissimilar to that of many of the students). The small peer group discussion on the commercial reveals several ideologies that suggest that giving to the fund is, indeed, a highly rational choice. For instance, that 70 cents a day to save a child is not asking for much (lines 1002 to 1010), that the children appear as fragile and vulnerable (lines 1001, 1014, 1017, and 1042), that the setting for the children's home seems unlikely to support children's lives (line 1038, see also call-out g), and that people watching the video should have enough compassion to give generously (lines 1053 to 1055, see also call-outs a and e). Note that the students do not mention the fact the video does not include any reference to how the children and their families came to live in such awful conditions. Nor do the students in the small peer group discussion seem to reject the message of the video even though they identify some of the rhetorical moves made in the commercial to manipulate viewers' feelings (e.g., lines 1010, 1013 to 1014, 1016, 1017, 1021, 1032–1033, 1053).

When the class reassembles for a whole class discussion to report on their small group discussions, Ms. Nelson makes three moves: (a) she asks a question—does it matter? (line 1103), (b) offers some details about the context for the commercial (lines 1109 to 1114), and (c) then provides additional details regarding the larger socio-political context of the 1980s (line 1117). All of this was to explore the rationality behind the commercial, that is, how the ideology of the message is revealed by making inferences grounded in possible biased assumptions held by the commercial's consumer. When viewed within De Certeau's (1984) distinctions between strategies (belonging to institutions) and tactics (used by ordinary people to make sense of and navigate the world), Ms. Nelson's use of subtexts become clear: the seemingly rational reasons for sending money to the Christian Children's Fund is undermined by the tactic of considering subtexts as counter to the text of the commercial. What Ms. Nelson is asking her students to do is "read" the commercial's ideologies with particular attention to what seems to get normalized (rationalized) in the commercial as the charitable action in support of impoverished children around the world. Put another way, Ms. Nelson has asked her students to generate subtexts as a form of contextualized rationality that accounts for the strategies of the charitable institutions and the strategy of generating subtexts and this is how she wants her students to engage multiple perspectives within a dialectical space.

The classroom conversation initiated by reading the song "Do They Know It's Christmas?" also engaged the students in identifying and analyzing subtexts (see call-outs k through r). Of particular importance is the students call-out of "Thank God it's them instead of you" (call-out h). This call-out, a reference to the lyric in the song, "Well tonight thank God it's them/Instead of you," establishes the positionalities of "them" and "you" (which, given the rhetoric and playing of the song as part of the music of middle-class Western societies, is also an "us"). This binary of "them" versus "you/us" is reiterated in each of the call-outs k through q and characterizes the "you/us" as needing to be thankful, not taking positive things for granted, having a heart, being privileged, having responsibilities to others, and being white. The "them" is characterized as people in poverty, African, poor, and non-white.

The discussion of *Things Fall Apart* builds upon the binary of "them" versus "you/them." In session two (see Table 4.1), the students list familiar and strange practices framed by both insider and outsider perspectives. Then they role play and juxtapose diverse "characters" and situations in the novel. That is, Ms. Nelson asks the students to role play members of Human Rights Watch International, members of an Intervention Review Board, an imagined a young Igbo boy, and Umuofia from the novel. This sets the different positionalities in tension and conflict with each other. This dialectical space is then used to contextualize the students' task of determining whether human rights are being violated and then making a recommendation regarding intervention. The tension of the dialectical space is heightened (compressed) in the fifth session, after reading part IV of the novel, by role playing an informal board meeting of the International Intervention Review Board. Inasmuch as the Board needs to come to a consensus recommendation, students in their role playing must acknowledge, listen to, understand, and work with each other's points of view. Thereafter, the students have an opportunity to revise their individual reports on whether there should be an intervention (and if so, what kind of intervention it should be) informed by the discussion among diverse and conflicting perspectives. Given the class sessions on the two previous texts (the commercial and the song), the students are already embedded in a dialectical space that calls into question the naturalization, imposition, and rationality of a middle-class, white, Western perspective on the situation of other people. In brief, students are exploring multiple rationalities within a context of hierarchical power relations that have resulted in pain and suffering for "them." There is no easy, obvious, or unconflicted solution or perspective.

Rationality in Two Argumentative "Reports"

As we noted previously, Ms. Nelson assigned the task of writing a report to the director of Human Rights Watch International from an imagined "International Intervention Review Board" about whether there were human rights abuses in Umuofia and whether there should be an outside intervention. The task was intimately linked to classroom activities and to Ms. Nelson's efforts to have her students struggle with multiple rationalities within a dialectical context. Our analysis of the two essays (see student work samples in Diagrams 4.1 and 4.2) is focused on how the students addressed underlying rationalities (and not on the quality of their writing *per se*). Although both essays find human rights abuses against women, the first essay, MG's report, argues for an intervention, whereas CW's essay argues against an intervention. We are not focused on whether there was an argument for intervention but rather how the two essays differentially addressed the dynamic of rationality/rationalities as a context for multiple perspectives. We begin with MG's report.

MG's Essay/Report. MG's essay/report with teacher comments is shown in Diagram 4.1.

MG states her claim at the very beginning of the essay: "After visiting the villages and multiple interviews with the people of Umuofia, there is no doubt in my mind that Umuofia needs an intervention immediately." Although there is an effort to understand the local culture, the contextual issues are ignored in favor of a pre-conceived notion of rationality. In both the first sentence and the second sentence, MG uses various modifiers to increase the urgency and need for an intervention: "immediately," "unacceptable," and "disturbing." Each of these terms indexes a rationality (what constitutes the "good" and "ethical") that also provides a warrant for the imagined International Intervention Review Committee, representatives of Western culture, to view itself as superior of the culture of Umuofia and as legitimately using its power to change the culture of Umuofia.

MG uses the remainder of the first paragraph to provide evidence for her claim based on "visiting the villages and multiple interviews with the people of Umuofia." Looking across the essay, MG does not provide

104 *Constructing Perspectives and Rationality*

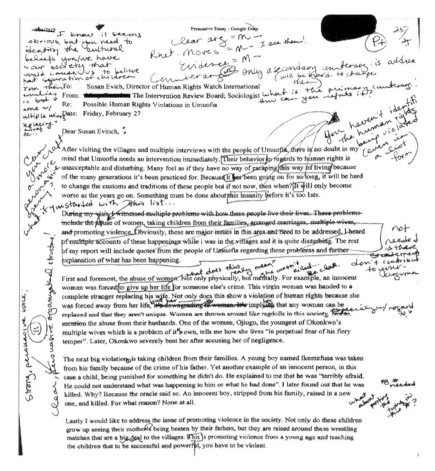

Diagram 4.1 Student Work Sample MG's Report

any commentary suggesting that what constitutes the "good" may be complex or conflicted. There are abuses, and intervention is needed to stop the abuse as "it will only become worse." We want to look at two levels of rationality in MG's essay: (a) the rationality MG projects on to the people of Umuofia and (b) the rationality warranting her advocacy of an intervention.

In MG's citing of evidence, grounded in her understanding of the context of the Umuofia village, she notes, "Many [Umuofians] feel as if they have no way of escaping this way of living because of the many generations it's been practiced for." Note the implied moral paradox: the desire of Umuofians to escape the abuses implies that they know the abuses are wrong and immoral. Yet they rationalized the continuation of the abuses because of tradition. MG further argues that "it will be hard to change" the way of life and its abuses because the people cling to their traditions. This implies that many Umuofians are incapable of adopting a rationality aligned with the moral good of stopping abuses, making them "insane" (see the end of MG's first paragraph). The intervention is thus aligned with the moral good and with rationality, and the continued way of life of the Umuofians is aligned with abuse and irrationality.

The rest of the essay, the last three paragraphs, include additional evidence in support of the intervention. Looking at the warranting in these three paragraphs we see that there is an implied warrant in the third paragraph of the essay that it is not reasonable for people to give up their lives, be abused by husbands, live in fear, or be beaten. In the fourth paragraph, MG argues that an innocent person should not be punished for what he didn't do. Implied here is that punishing someone for what they did not do is irrational, and that the young boy also thought it was irrational. MG highlights the irrationality of this way of living by writing, "For what reason? None at all." In the last paragraph, MG warrants the need for an intervention by noting that if someone grows up around violence (e.g., wrestling), then that child will grow up to be violent. Therefore, it is rational and moral to intervene to stop children from growing up in a context of violence and irrational to continue to let there be such a context of children's development. MG's argument is grounded in a decontextualized rationality. There is a singular rationality aligned with the moral good; alternatives are irrational and eschew the moral good.

Ms. Nelson's comments on the essay are mostly oriented to the clear, persuasive voice that MG uses: the need for a few better word choices and the need for a counter-argument so it can be refuted. However, Ms. Nelson also writes a comment that can be interpreted as positioning MG to reflect on and perhaps question her own values, perspectives, and rationality and her ethnocentricity. Ms. Nelson writes, "I know it seems obvious but you need to identify the cultural beliefs you/we have in our society that would cause us to believe that separation of children from their families is bad → same w/multiple wives, replacing wives, etc." The issue here is not whether one is in favor of or against violence against women and children, but rather "seeing" what happens in the novel from only one's own perspective as if it were the only perspective. For MG, the situation is simple and singular. Of course, what MG does not do in her essay is warrant an intervention. For the sake of argument, granting that the way of life in Umuofia is immoral and irrational, MG does not provide an argument (nor warrants or evidence) that an intervention will change the situation in a positive direction (nor does she define what a positive direction would be).

106 *Constructing Perspectives and Rationality*

> (M-)
>
> Clear arg = M
> Evidence } = P+E
> Rhet. moves = M-
> Counterarg. = M-
>
> 25/25

Human Rights Response Essay

Enlightened Oppression

    Societies have been shocked by the "uncivilized" actions and values of other cultures since the creation of civilization. When purportedly enlightened societies disapprove of those societal traits, they often make rash decisions that damage the values and traditions of other cultures. The cultural adjustments enforced by such enlightened oppressors, however benevolent in intention, are therefore harmful to the intricate and unique cultures of different societies. I believe that we should publicly express our disapproval of the abuse against women and children in Umuofia, however I do not think it is logical or acceptable to disrupt their otherwise flourishing society in an effort to change an integral part of their culture.

    In Umuofia, I have witnessed an institutional caste system based on age, achievement and gender. This system is an integral part of Umuofian culture. To truly address the problem of abuse against women in Umuofia, the caste system would have to be permanently changed to give men and women relatively equal social status and influence in society, as only then could women truly be safe from abuse. Destroying this caste system would be devastating to the Umuofian society and culture, as it has relied on this institutional hierarchy for thousands of years. This is similar to a situation in China during the 19th century, when European missionaries were shocked and appalled at the ancient Chinese practice of binding the feet of Chinese women; a painful process which involved snapping the foot at the arch. The response of these Europeans was to send more missionaries to China to adjust this undesirable aspect of their culture. This act served as catalyst for increased future foreign intervention and eventually culminated in the Opium War, the division of China into spheres of foreign influence, and the Boxer Revolution which killed millions of people and devastated Chinese culture. While it is unlikely that there would be devastation of this scale if we chose to intervene in Umuofia, there is genuine potential for the clash of cultures to result in a similar destruction of their culture and societal practices.

    While Umuofia is by no means a peaceful society, there are signs of positive change, specifically with regard to the rights of women in their culture. At a public court session, I witnessed a man being punished and threatened with castration after severely beating his wife. In 19th century China, native Chinese aristocrats began a campaign to stop the foot binding practice of their culture, however these efforts were drowned out by the flood of foreign missionaries and the accompanying chaos of cultural clashing. At the same time period, Japan began to modernize in the Meiji restoration, completely independent of foreign intervention, despite European qualms with their emphasis on the practice of suicide. Without any foreign cultural intervention, they were able to fully industrialize while preserving and modernizing their culture. Because they were given the opportunity to adjust their society without foreign intervention, Japan became as modern and sophisticated from a technological and cultural standpoint as any European country.

    I understand the desires of many to come to the aid of women and children in Umuofia, as no one should have to be raised or live in such a violent and brutal society, however we must recognize that there are significant cultural differences between their culture and ours. To clash our cultures in an attempt to "fix" Umuofian society not only poses a threat to damage their ancient culture, but risks an increase in violence in the area as a response to forced imposition of the rules deemed acceptable by our culture.

Diagram 4.2 Student Work Sample CW's Report

CW's Essay/Report. CW's essay/report with teacher comments is shown in Diagram 4.2.

CW titles his essay "Enlighted Oppression," capturing a tension within which he crafted his response to the writing task. This tension is expressed in the first paragraph which we analyze sentence by sentence.

The first sentence, "Societies have been shocked by the 'uncivilized' actions and values of other cultures since the creation of civilization," contains a binary between "civilized" and "uncivilized" and a categorical system of cultures each with the potential of "othering." Within a so-defined culture, people have used their own culturally derived standards to evaluate the actions of other cultures in a manner that is shocking (which appears to be synonymous with irrational). From the perspective of a so-defined culture, the evaluation of another culture takes on the characterization of a decontextualized rationality; that is, the people of a culture view their rationality (their system of evaluation) as the only definition of being rational.

But the first sentence is undermined by the second sentence: "When purportedly enlightened societies disapprove of those societal traits, they often make rash decisions that damage the values and traditions of other cultures." The word "purportedly" makes clear that those societies that view themselves as "enlightened" are not necessarily so and as such calls into question their definition of rationality. "Enlightened" can be understood here as a claim to superiority and perhaps also to a power relation among cultural groups/societies (as indicated by the word "damage"). This sentence also appears to be the beginning of culturally contextualizing rationalities. The third sentence continues and elaborates the critique of decontextualized rationalities and the power and presumed superiority of "enlightened societies": "The cultural adjustments made by such enlightened oppressors, however benevolent in intention, are therefore harmful to the intricate and unique cultures of different societies." The phrase "cultural adjustments" we assume refers to interventions by the "superior" culture into the other culture. Building on the previous culture, "cultural adjustments" are linked to the evaluation standards and rationality of the "superior" culture. The phrase "intricate and unique cultures of different societies" establishes cultures as discrete entities and as having their own ways of life and rationalities. The word "harmful" alludes to both a power relation among cultures and an evaluation that lies above the rationalities of the cultures noted. That is, the writer (CW) takes a view of looking at the relation of the "superior" and "other" culture and uses a rationality located in neither to evaluate that relationship. Part of that evaluation is the characterization of the "superior" culture as possibly being "benevolent in intention." This is an instantiation of a tension: desiring to do good and defining one's actions as good but in fact doing harm. The fourth sentence builds on the rationality that lies above those of the cultures referenced ("should" indexes a moral good which indicates a system of rationality):

> I believe that we should publicly express our disapproval of the abuse against women and children in Umuofia, however I do not think it is logical or acceptable to disrupt their otherwise flourishing society in an effort to change an integral part of their culture.

108   *Constructing Perspectives and Rationality*

This sentence compresses a tension between condemning and acting to stop "abuse against women and children" (with the word "abuse" indexing a rationality associated with the "superior" culture of the imagined "International Intervention Review Board," presumably a Western institution) and the "otherwise flourishing society" of Umuofia (and the rationality that is an "integral part of their culture," suggesting that the "disruption" is not just a cessation to abuse but a fundamental change in the rationality underlying what they do and value).

In this first paragraph, CW establishes a dialectical space in which there is the compressed opposition of two diverse rationalities: it is untenable to witness abuse of women and children and do nothing but it is also untenable to intervene in another culture in a way that destroys the essence (the rationality) of that culture. CW seeks to find a compromise—condemning the abuse but not intervening.

Considered holistically, CW argues against outside intervention in the Umuofia village by first contextualizing his claim with references to "enlightened societies" that "make rash decisions that damage the values and traditions of other cultures" and then warrants his argument by pointing out a history of efforts to impose "harmful adjustments" on complex and "intricate cultures of different societies." This leads to his claim (at the end of the first paragraph) that "I believe that we should publicly express our disapproval of the abuse against women and children in Umuofia, however I do not think it is logical or acceptable to disrupt their otherwise flourishing society in an effort to change an integral part of their culture." To marshal evidence for this claim, in the next two paragraphs, CW confronts abuse of women that he has "witnessed" in the Umuofian village. In the second paragraph, he admits that he has seen the effects of an institutional caste system but quickly points out that this is an "integral part of the Umuofian culture" that would have to permanently changed. But to do so would have devastating effects. In the third paragraph, CW offers an instance in which a man is punished for beating his wife, an event that CW regards as "signs of positive change." In a concluding paragraph, CW speaks directly to his audience/readers (presumably members of the imagined "International Intervention Review Board" who are representatives of Western culture) to warn against taking action to fix the Umuofian society that would lead to "a clash of cultures." Here, CW engages in contextualized rationalization in that he simultaneously recognizes the repugnancy of abuse against women and children and the dangers of outside interventions and "forced imposition of the rules deemed acceptable by our culture." This point is strengthened when CW reminds the reader of his evidence gleaned from his own observations and understanding of Umuofian cultural values of hierarchy and power.

Rather than relying on his own contextualized understanding of Umuofian cultural values, however, CW makes another move: he relies on the support of historical cases from 19th-century China and the implications of European missionaries that led to war and devastation. To make his argument against intervention, he describes a moment in 19th-century Japan in which the Japanese were able to adjust to modernization "because they were given the opportunity to adjust their society without foreign intervention." These references to historical cases are suggestive of abductive reasoning; that is, logical inferencing grounded in an observation or set of observations that seek to find the simplest and most likely explanation for the observations. CW's process, unlike deductive reasoning, offers a plausible conclusion, but he does not express this in absolute terms. CW qualifies his claim with "I do not think it is logical or acceptable to disrupt their otherwise flourishing society." His abductive conclusions are qualified as having a remnant of uncertainty or doubt, which is expressed in retreat terms such as "best available" or "most likely."

Final Comments on Multiple Perspectives and Rationalities

In a series of instructional conversations and activities, Ms. Nelson established how misunderstandings can occur about any one group of people when their behavior and cultural beliefs are approached from a stance of evaluation or judgment, that is, from a decontextualized or universal rationality grounded in the superiority of one culture over another culture. For instance, in one lesson, Ms. Nelson posed a series of questions linked to the theme of empathy that she had established earlier in the school year: "Is it possible that [as an outsider] it [a particular way to be human] could be true and real for them [people of a different culture] and not for you? You will encounter this again and again when reading this book [*Things Fall Apart*]. It's not your culture, but can it be real?" Accordingly, Ms. Nelson raised the questions of not only what counts as being human but also what counts as rational or "true and real," especially in contexts where cultural and linguistic differences between people are pronounced, obvious, and a source of tension and possible genocide.

We take it as axiomatic that in a diverse and complex society seeking an ethics of democracy and social justice that social, cultural, and philosophical differences will exist at many levels including both daily life, community life, and institutional life. As we see it, these differences create a series of dialectical spaces within which people in such societies live their lives, including how teachers and students in a high school literature class read, talk, and write. Rather than view such differences and tensions as obstacles whose resolution is a retreat to extreme relativism, we view such differences as a productive resource for learning, for reading literary texts, and for making arguments about them. As we define it, Dialogic Literary Argumentation invites teachers and students to incorporate and consider diverse perspectives and rationalities in the classroom in a substantive way that yields new insights despite being messy, controversial, unresolvable, and personal. Although difficult and potentially risky (risky in the sense of disrupting a taken-for-granted understanding/rationality replaced by a sense of uncertainty in what counts as rationality or rationalities), engaging students in a dialectical space in which a decontextualized rationality is challenged can elevate the ways in which students read, think, write, and argue by suspending judgment and superficial understanding and moving toward appreciating and seeking diverse viewpoints with a range of rationalities about what makes sense and how to take reasonable action.

We want to note one additional insight that we learned from observing Ms. Nelson's class and talking with her and her students. Ms. Nelson also relied on the theme of "empathy" to guide her curricular and instructional decisions as well as the conversations she had with students prompted by the literature they read. This included the teaching of critical literary theories and teaching students to consider issues from a variety of perspectives and contextualized rationalities "and ultimately, what they and others perceive to be true rather than seeing the world through absolutes." She wanted students to understand how seeking and challenging alternative perspectives can resist a single story about any one group of people or issue and ultimately increase awareness and foster empathy.

Notes

1. This quote is excerpted from an e-book chapter (currently in progress) by Ms. Nelson titled "A Journey in Perspective: Creating the Spaces to Explore Multiple Ways of Seeing in Argumentation."
2. "Do They Know It's Christmas?" is a song written in 1984 by Bob Geldof and Midge Ure in reaction to television reports of the 1983–1985 famine in Ethiopia. Lyrics to the song can be found at <https://genius.com/Band-aid-do-they-know-its-christmas-lyrics>
3. We assume that there many ways to ideologically contextualize the use of multiple perspectives. We do not discuss alternatives here but note that the contextualizing of multiple perspectives within a dialectical space involving diverse rationalities gets part of its meaningfulness through the existence of alternative ideological contextualizations.
4. Flyvbjerg (2000) points out that, in Western society, the term *rationality* has become synonymous with rule-governed analytical rationality, which looks for objective, general principles and uses deduction to break down a whole into its component parts. What gets argued is framed by and in service to the Truth. From this perspective, argumentation is a process of seeking and determining the Truth or at the very least moving toward the Truth. What one argues is not so much against another argument as it is advocacy that what is being represented by one's argument stands closer to the Truth than alternative arguments. By contrast, what we call contextualized definitions of rationality (see Newell et al., 2015; Ryu, 2016, 2017) assume that what counts as rational depends on the situation in which people are building and using knowledge (epistemic action), on how people are interactionally and

dialogically engaged with each other (pragmatic action), and on the goals and nature of the social institution within which knowledge is being constructed and used. For example, consider Gilligan's (1993) discussion of an ethics of care in contrast to the ethics of justice. An ethics of care suggests that morality depends on not only specific projected consequences of actions but also friendship and kinship relations among the individuals involved (cf., Simon, 2005). Consider lies. Following Kant's discussion of reason, morality, categorical imperatives, and rationality (Kant, 1997, 2009), lying would always be immoral and irrational, regardless of the individuals and the circumstances. By contrast, a view based on the ethics of care considers both the probable consequences of the lie and the underlying relationship between people in a particular situation (Simon, 2005). Contextualized definitions of rationality make clear that multiple rationalities can and do co-exist and that different people can employ differently framed arguments, arrive at different "whats" and "hows" and that it would be a non-sequitur for either to claim being closer to the Truth.

5 Constructing Intertextuality and Indexicality in Dialogic Literary Argumentation

In the previous chapters, we shared analyses of teachers and students engaged in Dialogic Literary Argumentation as they read, discussed, and wrote about particular novels. Those analyses mirrored part of the journey we took in conceptualizing a model of Dialogic Literary Argumentation. Another part of that journey involved looking across the instructional units in which teachers engaged their students. That is, the literature education that students experience in high school classrooms typically involves a series of literary works. For example, in Mr. Watson's 12th-grade class, there were instructional units that focused on the "Allegory of the Cave" (from Plato's *Republic* [Hamilton et al., 1961]), *Macbeth* (1606/2003), *Hamlet* (1603/2003), and *Heart of Darkness* (Conrad, 1988). Within each instructional unit, other literary texts were used to enhance the students' learning of literature and to enrich their use of literature to explore personhood and the human condition. Beyond the literary texts that teachers bring into their instruction are a series of other texts: narratives from popular culture; narratives students told about classroom events and their lives (both real and imagined); texts students composed in response to classroom assignments; and texts students received, produced, and shared through the electronic devices they had (e.g., iPhones, electronic tablets). In brief, no text, including literary texts, exists in isolation of an evolving and socially constructed universe of other texts. The questions to ask are:

- What are those other texts?
- How have they been juxtaposed?
- What is the meaning, social significance, and cultural import of the juxtaposition of those texts?

These questions recognize that any text, any conversation, and any utterance exist in relation to other texts, conversations, and utterances, both those co-present in time and space and those at a distance in time and space. They also recognize that any word or text is not whole in and of itself. In addition to and intimate with its relationship to other texts, a word and a text reference a universe of events and ideological contexts. In brief, a text-in-use is always intertextual and indexical. Thus, in addition to the previous questions, one needs to ask:

- What are events, contexts, and ideologies indexed by a text-in-use?
- How have they been indexed?
- What is the meaning, social significance, and cultural import of the indexicality of those texts?

There is an important caveat to these questions. We take the position that the intertextuality and indexicality of a text are functions of and situated within their social construction within social interaction. That social interaction can be face-to-face or otherwise, co-present or over time and space. (For more extended discussions about the nature of intertextuality and indexicality, see Hanks, 2000; Shuart-Faris & Bloome, 2004; Strauss & Feiz, 2014). In this chapter, we explore the aforementioned questions with specific regard to Mr. Watson's 12th-grade classroom as a way to explore intertextuality and indexicality as part of a model of Dialogic Literary Argumentation—Constructing Intertextuality and Indexicality in the Teaching, Learning, and Reading of Literature.

Teaching, Learning, and Reading Across Texts in a 12th-Grade College Preparation English Language Arts Classroom

Mr. Watson and his thirty 12th-grade students (17 female and 13 male; 15 white, eight Black, six Hispanic, and one Pacific Islander) participated in a college preparatory classroom located in a lower- to middle-class urban community. Students' academic backgrounds ranged from the highly successful to some who were also enrolled in "make-up" classes to erase previous failures. Mr. Watson had six years of high school English language arts teaching experience and a master's degree in education at the time of data collection. He describes himself as an innovative teacher who is continually developing his professional background. Indeed, it was for this reason that he joined the Argumentative Writing Project.

On the basis of interviews with Mr. Watson and with the students, the majority of students in this classroom were not academically motivated. Few were planning to pursue higher education. Many of the students worked after school, which limited the amount of homework that Mr. Watson believed he could or should assign. In spite of such challenges, students appreciated Mr. Watson's efforts to provide multiple ways of engaging in classroom argumentative practices. One student commented that he felt "comfortable talking and writing about [my] own argument without the anxiety of being judged."

Mr. Watson developed the theme of "learning about ourselves and the world" to guide his curriculum and instruction across the school year. He considered that despite the varied motivation level, interests, and needs of his students, Dialogic Literary Argumentation could be the "vehicle" to help students make sense of and communicate their own life experiences and make "connect[ions] between different types of texts." His overarching goal was to make the learning of literature "personally meaningful and valuable to every student."

At the beginning of the school year, Mr. Watson purposefully adopted a structural approach to argumentation—what we refer to as "learning to argue"—to establish a shared vocabulary for argumentation and to socialize his students into academic practices that he believed foundational for success in his classroom. For example, the first instructional unit was on Plato's "Allegory of the Cave" from *The Republic* (Hamilton et al., 1961). Students were informed that "the study of Plato will be a model for how we will analyze, discuss, and write about literature for the entire year." After Mr. Watson's mini-lecture on the historical context of Plato, the entire class read the short allegory together as Mr. Watson used his tablet PC wirelessly connected to an LCD projector to show a visual representation of the cave. A brief, whole class discussion of meanings of key symbols (e.g., light, shadow, shackles) in the Allegory followed. The following transcript captures a moment in which Mr. Watson elicited diverse meanings of "shackle."

1201	T	In our world /
1202		what are some of the things that shackle our minds ↑
1203		Or hold us back /
1204		thing that are chaining us down ↑
1205	Molly	Electronics
1206	T	Technology /
1207		cell PHONES
1208		Like it holds you back in classrooms /
1209		in education general /
1210		Charles↑
1211	Charles	Your background
1212	T	What do you mean↑

Constructing Intertextuality and Indexicality 115

1213	Charles	Like where you grew up
1214	T	OK /
1215		so your upbringing /
1216		your background /
1217		for sure /
1218		Your FAMILY
1219		What else↑
1220	Mia	School
1221	T	Schools↑
1222		In what ways can that be a shackle or a chain on your growth of knowledge ↑
1223		How can schools /
1224	Mia	Teachers //
1225		studying for the standardized testing not by
1226	T	Yeah /
1227		think about more like /
1228		like in our life itself /
1229		I think we are kinda focus on schools /
1230		What else /
1231		Tim ↑
1232	Tim	Really just any kind of authority figures
1233	T	Authority figures ↑
1234		OK /
1235		can shackle us /
1236		the government can do that
1237	Jena	Yourself ↑
1238	T	Yourself can do that /
1239		SURE
1240		Personal baggage and insecurity ↑
1241	Kayla	Religion /
1242	T	Religion can do THAT
1243	Jena	Other people
1244	T	It could be family /
1245		it could be people in your life in general //...
1246		The judgment you feel from the people can hold you back /

1247		your worry about those thing ↑
1248		So /
1249		we can see that out of ONE part of it /
1250		just that shackle part /
1251		can symbolize tons of things /
1252		Part of the charm of this

The exchange between students and Mr. Watson unfolded at a rapid pace. The conversation orchestrated by Mr. Watson solicited a series of responses to which "shackle" might refer. This previous bit of transcribed conversation was followed by a conversation about questions that included "How are the perspectives of the freed prisoners and the cave prisoners different?" "What does the prisoner's getting freedom suggest about intellectual freedom?" and "Do you agree or disagree with the assumption of the Allegory—there is a distinction between appearances and reality?"

To extend and explore their reading of *The Republic*, Mr. Watson introduced a poem, "Allegory of the Cave" (Dunn, 1990), and an essay, "In the Cave: Philosophy and Addiction" (O'Connor, 2012). Mr. Watson explicitly asked his students to connect these texts to the events of the original text and to fill out the "they say/I say" template to respond to the texts (see Diagram 5.1).

On the basis of our observations and conversations with Mr. Watson, how he engaged his students in reading, discussing, and writing about the "Allegory of the Cave" served as a model for the rest of their literature study in three ways: (a) students were expected to question the text, (b) to transfer knowledge and experiences across the literary texts studied in the class, and (c) to appreciate multiple perspectives in reflecting on the complex nature of personhood and the human condition (which can be characterized as advanced ontological and epistemological stances rather than absolutism).[1]

Over time, as Mr. Watson and his 12th-grade students shifted from "learning to argue" to "arguing to learn," their reading, discussion, and writing practices shifted to critiquing diverse perspectives and to making intertextual connections among literary texts. For example, Mr. Watson created a graphic organizer that asked students to summarize the common threads (e.g., man versus nature, evil, death) across the literary texts that they had read along with textual evidence. This task was done first individually and then as a whole class using the online classroom platform. Table 5.1 is the version of the chart created as a whole class.

> **They Say/ I Say Template--- Do not fill in the template. Write out your own paragraph using this formula!!**
>
> The general argument made by author X in her/his work, _____, is that _____. More specifically, X argues that _____. She/he writes "_____ _____." In this passage, X is suggesting that _____. In conclusion, X's belief is that _____.
>
>   In my view, X is wrong/right, because _____. More specifically, I believe that _____. For example, _____ _____. Although X might object that_____, I maintain that
>
> Therefore, I conclude that
> _____.

Diagram 5.1 Mr. Watson's "They Say/I Say" Template

    By having students work on the chart together, Mr. Watson assumed that they would negotiate and reconstruct meanings of the literary texts through the juxtaposition of multiple texts and their prior knowledge and cultural experiences. Student interviews revealed that they believed that this activity enhanced their retention of the key learning points and use of the texts and relevant themes.

    Toward the end of the school year, the class read and discussed Joseph Conrad's *Heart of Darkness* (1899/1988). Mr. Watson used small peer group discussion to engage his students in discussing the novel. However, prior to their small peer group discussions, Mr. Watson reminded his students of guidelines for group discussion including equal participation, sharing, and building on each other's ideas. He also provided a list of 14 discussion prompts for students to use as a guide. He was not verbally involved in the small peer group discussions but monitored the groups as he walked around the classroom, posing questions, and at times answering students' question. One of the small peer discussion groups engaged

Table 5.1 Mr. Watson's Literature Evidence Graphic Organizer

TEXT / THEME	Allegory of the Cave	Macbeth	Hamlet	Heart of Darkness
Man versus Nature	Everything has a bigger source to it, we as humans have to fight ourselves and get out of the cave to explore the world more to learn.		Sometimes, plotting revenge will fall on you too. Hamlet showed us that revenge only makes you stoop to not only to their level but also to a level below them.	Marlow had to fight the inner him, who was close to Kurtz. He felt as though he and Kurtz were similar and had to fight some of the same thoughts he had.
Man versus Society	The men in the cave did not have an actual idea of what society was.	Macbeth wanted to become powerful, and society saw him as crazy and greedy.	Society viewed Hamlet as crazy because of his father's death, but Hamlet just wanted to avenge his father.	Kurtz was worshiped in the society in the Congo. Everyone loved him.
Man versus Religion	When the man went into the light, it could be considered his death, and when he tried to return to the cave and get the others, he couldn't touch them because he wasn't actually there.	Fighting the higher power like the witches and his own will to kill the king and then his guilty conscious showing him everyone he had killed.	His urge to stop himself from killing the king during prayer to ensure that the king wouldn't get the chance to go to heaven and be spared of what he had done.	When Kurtz was dying and going to the light, he was seeing everyone he had killed and was being tortured one last time by the sight he saw while he was dying.
Punishment for crime/ sin/evil	The man that left the cave was punished by the people remaining in the cave when he came back to tell them about the world outside of the cave. It was as if leaving the cave and coming back with knowledge of the outside world was a sin to them and they shunned him for it.	Macbeth is killed in the end as a way to bring justice to him for the crimes he had committed. Not only is Macbeth punished but also is Lady Macbeth.	Hamlet was punished for who he killed in the end. He killed Polonius, Laertes, and Claudius, but ended up being killed himself.	Kurtz is punished by death for the evil he had done while working for the company in the Congo.

				Da Congo
Overcoming Adversity	Battle the transition from the cave to light	The people standing between him and the power of king	Killing Claudius with enough convincing evidence	
Sacrifice for Friendship	Sacrificing friendship to pursue knowledge	Macbeth betraying Banquo to keep his title	Horatio having full faith in his friend Hamlet. He risked it all to support him.	Kurtz was a motivation to Marlow.
Importance of Balance	Thinks with how enlightened he has become, things will become easier but it puts him at odds with others	Macbeth gained an imbalance of power and in turn lost everything	Kills the king as he intended but also loses his own life	Struggle between good and bad, light and dark, civilized and savage, Marlow and Kurtz, London and the Congo
What Is Love?	Baby don't hurt me	Don't hurt me	No more	
Death	Getting out of the cave is like an afterlife	Macbeth killing the king to become king	Hamlet killing literally everyone	Kurtz killing the natives while he was in the Congo

in a discussion of what it means to be civilized versus savage (see the following transcript).

1301	Hunter	OK,
1302		*what makes one culture civilized / and another savage in the eyes of the world* ↑ *Are these distinctions valid* ↑ [prompt provided by the teacher]
1303		So /
1304		this question really focuses on the theme of imperialism in the book
1305	Molly	whites sitting over there like /
1306		YES
1307		Like yes /
1308		LEARNING
1309		THEY DO PAY ATTENTION
1310	Hunter	Where /
1311		you know,
1312		people would kind of like /
1313		Well /
1314		obviously we know when and that's about it /
1315		But /
1316		what I put [in written response] /
1317		is that /
1318		the distinctions between civilized and savage /
1319	Molly	*What does it mean to act humanely* ↑ [prompt provided by the teacher]
1320	Hunter	I think it's very rare /
1321		Maybe to us /
1322		civilized means /
1323		we're sleeping in bed at night /
1324		we have technology we use every day /
1325		we go to school /
1326		we're educated /
1327		And then /
1328		I don't know /
1329		yeah /
1330		savage is like /

Constructing Intertextuality and Indexicality 121

1331		live out in the woods or whatever and just kinda fend for yourself /
1332		that's savage to us /
1333		But /
1334		maybe to other cultures /
1335		like the cultures in *Heart of Darkness* /
1336		maybe they don't completely understand what civilization is /
1337		to an extent /
1338		But /
1339		their civilization and their culture is their God /
1340		maybe /
1341		or whatever they worship /
1342		or their practices /
1343		and things like that
1344	Molly	Right /
1345	Hunter	So maybe /
1346		to them /
1347		We're savages because people try to go and steal that
1348	Molly	Right
1349	Hunter	You know what I mean ↑
1350	Molly	Yeah
1351	Mia	I think it's kind of like /
1352		It's funny because /
1353		I feel like those who appear more civilized are actually not really civilized at all /
1354		And it's like the white man in this book is conquering /
1355		or colonizing Africa /
1356		And the way they treat them /
1357		is almost savage itself
1358	Molly	Right /
1359	Mia	So it's kind of ironic /
1360	Hunter	Yeah /
1361		and there's several examples of that /
1362		even though the Spanish Inquisition /
1363		and things like that /
1364		It seems like the most civilized people were dark /

122 *Constructing Intertextuality and Indexicality*

1365		kind of like /
1366		screwed up /
1367	Molly	Right /
1368		That's a great /
1369	Adam	It goes back to ethics and things like that /
1370		If you have a stateless sense of morality /
1371		then you are civilized /
1372		whether or not you're being a savage /

The discussion began with Hunter posing a question provided by Mr. Watson: "What makes one culture civilized and another savage in the eyes of the world? Are these distinctions valid?" (line 1302). By asking whether the distinction is "valid," this question challenges the students' ontological and epistemological stances about civilization and savageness. Hunter connected (line 1303) this question to the theme of imperialism (line 1304), the central controversy raised by Mr. Watson earlier in the unit on *Heart of Darkness*. Molly then comments on how civilization might look on a surface level—white people's "educating" indigenous people (lines 1305 to 1309). She then posed another question provided by Mr. Watson —"what does it mean to act humanely?" (line 1319). As their small peer group conversation continues, the students examine and redefine what it means to be civilized and savage, contesting both the presumed definitions of those terms in the novel and more broadly accepted definitions of those terms in Western society (lines 1333 to 1358). Through the use of personal pronouns, such as "we" (lines 1323 to 1326) and "us" (e.g., line 1332) versus "they" (e.g., 1336) and "them" (e.g., 1346), the students locate their own cultural group membership but frame definitions and perspectives as relative (lines 1345 to 1347) and not absolute. The students' dialogue on "civilized" and "savage" results in their reconstruction of the notion of civilization (lines 1369 to 1371) and defenestration of the binary of civilized and savage (line 1372).

As the small peer group discussion continues, the students address the prompt "*Why does Heart of Darkness have two competing heroes? Make the case for either Marlow or Kurtz as the true hero of the book. How do you define hero for this book, and why doesn't Marlow kill Kurtz?*"(line 1401)

| 1401 | Hunter | (Reading aloud a prompt provided by the teacher): *Why does Heart of Darkness have two competing heroes* ↑ *Make the case for either Marlow or Kurtz as the true hero of the book. How do you define hero for this book, and why doesn't Marlow kill Kurtz* ↑ |

Constructing Intertextuality and Indexicality 123

1402		"Hero's" such a weird word to use in this /
1403	Adam	But if anybody's a hero it's going to be Marlow /
1404		I think /
1405	Molly	Right /
1406		Yeah /
1407		I would /
1408		He didn't
1409	Mia	He's kind of like an accomplice to a crime /
1410		He certainly doesn't do anything about it
1411	Molly	Right /
1412		He just leans back
1413		and he's not going to do anything
1414	Hunter	And really /
1415		he's involved in it /
1416		He's working for the company that is doing these things /
1417		so
1418	Molly	He's in the middle /
1418		He's the middleman
1419	Hunter	Yeah
1420		I don't think there's any argument for Kurtz being a hero /
1421		I think that's weird /
1422		I don't think so at least /
1423		because we've seen all these horrible things that Kurtz is doing and just kind of like /
1424		If anything Marlow's definitely the hero of the book /
1425		It said that Marlow goes through a lot of trouble to save Kurtz /
1426		and that's really the only reason that he could be considered a hero /
1427		So /
1428		that's the reason with why Marlow doesn't kill Kurtz
1429	Adam	Well he doesn't kill Kurtz /
1430		I just don't think he's in love with the man /
1431		He still really admires Kurtz even though he saw the
1432	Molly	There was a quote /
1433		it was like /
1434		he's still a remarkable man /
1435		it was like the end or something /

1436		Do you know where that is
1437		Mr. Watson ↑
1438	T	What ↑
1439	Molly	Where he's saying Kurtz is a remarkable man /
1440		in the end of the book
1441	T	One something
1442	Hunter	161 /
1443		*it is impossible to know him and not to admire him*
1444	Adam	Is Marlow saying that /
1445		or is the attendant saying that ↑
1446	Hunter	Marlow /
1447		Marlow said it /
1448		and then the attendant said it is impossible to know him and not to love him
1449	Adam	I don't know /
1450		something about the whole conversation between him and the attendant seems so shallow
1451	Molly	It really did
1452	Adam	Because the attendant is /
1453		that even shows how women are in a world of their own /
1454		just kind of doing /
1455		Because she's like /
1456		"oh/ he's such a great du+de he's so good/he's such a sweet man /"
1457		Like he might have been but he's not anymore /
1458		Marlow saw his true self /
1459		So /
1460		I feel like Marlow is just telling her what she wants to hear /
1461		So /
1462		Like with his last words /
1463		I honestly thought that he means that he admired him
1464		Because I wouldn't admire him
1465	Molly	He was with him all the time /
1466		He wanted to be near him all the time. /
1467		"Oh/where's Kurtz/OK/I'm there/Always /"
1468	Adam	So /
1469		it's like you want what you can't have /

Constructing Intertextuality and Indexicality 125

1470		or what you shouldn't have /
1471		Same kind of thing /
1472		he shouldn't become Kurtz /
1473		but he wants to spend time with him
1474	Mia	I think Kurtz was someone he wanted to embody so much that he couldn't actually love himself so he just
1475	Hunter	Why would he want to embody him though ↑
1476	Mia	Power ↑
1477	Molly	Right /
1478		because you remember he was /
1479		He got everything /
1480		he was the top //
1481		he got all the ivory for everything
1482	Hunter	But I think he also saw the cons of that
1483		obviously there's pros /
1484		because you're at the top of the food chain /
1485		but there's cons, because you go mad /
1486		and start killing people /
1487		and putting their heads on stakes /
1488		So /
1489		I still don't understand the admiration /
1490		If /
1491		this is probably a really stupid example /
1492		Hitler was super-powerful /
1493		but he was also a terrible person /
1494		You don't want to be that
1495	Molly	Some people loved him /
1496		That's why he had so many people followed him /
1497		Because at one point I guess they thought he made sense /
1498		but no /
1499		he was just using his words to get what he wanted
1500	Adam	They were following him like a god /
1501		and that's exactly what happened to Kurtz
1502		Because he was a god
1503	Molly	Like the chain /
1504		Just keep saying oh great blah blah blah

126 *Constructing Intertextuality and Indexicality*

1505	Adam	Like a false perception
1506	Molly	Right /
1507		They don't tell them "oh/hey/he's actually a madman" /
1508	Adam	They might have been blinded by everything that was told to them /
1509		they had the methods /
1510		and that's why they liked him so much
1511	Hunter	I think we do that too /
1512		Nowadays /
1513		If we get told something's so amazing and our expectations are set at such a high level /
1514		then actually /
1515		I mean
1516	Molly	Then you do it and you're like "wow, OK. . . "
1517		It's just how people perceive things /
1518		Again /
1519		it goes back to how you look at the character in each step /
1520		That's how you look at the darkness /
1521		you just look at it in different aspects

As soon as Hunter read out this prompt, he expressed his skepticism regarding the premise that there is a true "hero" in *Heart of Darkness* (line 1402). Other students agreed with him that Kurtz is obviously not a hero (lines 1403, 1409, 1413) for "all these horrible things that Kurtz is doing" (line 1423), but Marlow could tentatively be a hero (line 1424). The small peer group discussion migrates to questions of admiration (lines 1463 to 1489), the relationship of power and admiration (lines 1476 to 1494), sanity and insanity (line 1507), and the relationship of perception, expectations, and what actually happened (lines 1508 to 1521).

Intertextuality in Dialogic Literary Argumentation

As teachers and students engage in dialogue with each other about a literary text, focusing on "arguing to learn," that dialogue is bounded by the literary text itself. Other literary texts and texts from a broad range of other social spaces are brought into the dialogue. These include literary texts read previously in the class or in previous years, narratives of personal and community experience, texts from popular culture, and texts from a broad range of social institutions, among others. The question to ask about engagement in Dialogic Literary Argumentation is not whether intertextuality is present, but rather *how* it is present? And perhaps most important, how is intertextuality used in the social construction of meaning, social significance, and cultural import?[2]

One of the uses of the social construction of intertextuality (and indexicality) in the teaching, learning, and reading of literature is to contextualize the dialogue beyond the immediate literary text and beyond the immediate social event. Such expansion is a key aspect of the social construction of meaning, social significance, and cultural import both within the immediate event and across events.

We need to take an aside here to explain what we mean by the social construction of meaning, social significance, and cultural import *across events*. From the perspective of the teacher, one is always "seeing" students in at least two time scales. The first is that of the immediate event. As teachers, we attempt to orchestrate the immediate instructional event, how we and students will interact with each other, with a literary text(s), and with other texts. Teachers and students, in general, want the lesson (the social event of teaching and learning) to go well. What it means for a lesson to go well may vary from procedural display to substantive engagement (cf., Bloome et al., 1989). While there may be student resistance to the teacher's efforts to orchestrate a lesson and while how a lesson actually proceeds may differ from how it was planned, nonetheless, one way teachers "see" students is through that immediate social event (the lesson).

However, in general, teachers also "see" students across longer stretches of time, such as a school year. As nearly all of the teachers in our study told us, it takes at least a year for students to learn how to learn to argue, argue to learn, and to engage literature through Dialogic Argumentation. They plan the academic year to facilitate that growth. As we noted previously, Mr. Watson used the theme of "learning about ourselves and the world" to guide his curriculum and instruction across the school year. The theme provides not only one way in which there would be coherence across lessons, but also a sense of the student as a learner over time. As teachers engage students in a lesson, they may "see" the student within both time scales, orchestrating both the immediate social event while also considering how that event will fit into their students' long-term evolution and education. For example, consider Mr. Watson's comments when the students were reading and discussing the "Allegory of the Cave" at the beginning of the year. He told them, "The study of Plato will be a model for how we will analyze, discuss, and write about literature for the entire year." This statement reveals not only how Mr. Watson was viewing his students within two time scales (that instructional unit and across the year) but also how he was asking the students to "see" themselves as being in two time scales. Some of the comments students made in interviews with us confirmed that they did "see" themselves within these two time scales. However, not every student seemed to take up those two time scales. From informal conversations, some students in Mr. Watson's class viewed themselves only within the time scale of the immediate classroom event, getting through the class and then on to other events. These two time scales have implications for how the phrase "across events" can be viewed.[3] Across events can refer to the how previous events and events at a distance come to impact an immediate social event. For example, one could ask how previous events have influenced the small peer group discussion about *Heart of Darkness* in Mr. Watson's class. Alternatively, across events can refer to how a particular event is a part of a broader set (or sets) of social events. For example, one could ask how the small peer group discussion about *Heart of Darkness* is part of the entire instructional unit.

Intertextuality is one of the ways that people in interaction with each other connect events.[4] For example, consider the graphic organizer Mr. Watson prepared for his class that asked his students to compare four literary works: *Allegory of the Cave*, *Macbeth*, *Hamlet*, and *Heart of Darkness*. Table 5.1 shows that graphic organizer completed through a series of whole class discussions.[5] Overtly, this graphic organizer juxtaposes a set of literary texts along with a specified set of predetermined literary dimensions. Each literary text indexes a series of classroom events the students have experienced in Mr. Watson's classroom. Thus, part of what the graphic organizer does is propose a juxtaposition of classroom events over time (those events in which the students were engaged in discussing the literary texts noted).

With regard to this graphic organizer, we want to foreground two dynamics related to the teaching, learning, and reading of literature. The first concerns the dimensions (themes) selected. Each of the selected themes is a standard of literary analysis. As the students work on the graphic organizer at first individually and then with others, they have to take each dimension and apply it to a literary text. In effect, regardless of what the outcome is of applying any particular dimension (theme) to any particular book, the students are becoming familiar with and accepting as given that these dimensions (themes) are appropriate framing for analyzing and for comparing literary works. The second dynamic concerns applying the dimensions across literary works rather than applying them just to a particular novel. In effect, it is to say to students that they are not reading an individual literary text *per se* but rather they are reading a literary text to be understood as part of a particular universe of literary texts.

The intertextual issues at play in the teaching, learning, and reading of *Heart of Darkness* in Mr. Watson's 12th-grade class go beyond those evident in the graphic organizer he created. Consider the small peer group discussion. The students invoke numerous texts including the novel *(Heart of Darkness)*, the prompts located on a sheet distributed by Mr. Watson, and students' written responses to the prompts. Grand narratives are also brought into the conversation: the white man conquering or colonizing Africa (lines 1353 to 1355) and hero as savior (lines 1425 to 1426). The grand narratives invoked are often undermined by how the students take them up (juxtaposed with a counter-narrative). To the grand narrative of Western superiority, the students juxtapose the counter-narrative of Westerners stealing from the native people (lines 1345 to 1361), the Spanish inquisition as "screwed up" (lines 1362 to 1367), and to the grand narrative of hero as savior is the counter-narrative of Hitler ("this is probably a really stupid example | Hitler was super-powerful | but he was also a terrible person | You don't want to be that" lines 1491 to 1494).

There are also reported speech narratives. For example, when Adam reports an imagined utterance by the attendant ("oh/ he's such a great du+de he's so good/he's such a sweet man /," line 1456). Adam's use of imagined reported speech is two-sided; one side looks back to the novel and provides an evaluation of the characters (i.e., Marlowe and the attendant; see lines 1452 to 1460), whereas the other side contributes to the immediate dialogue among the interlocutors (the students) with an authority based on the verisimilitude of reported speech (even though it is not accurately report speech but imagined reported speech). There's also reported speech from imagined events intended to characterize typical events in the students' lives. For example, Hunter states that they (the students) are similar to the people conned by Marlow because "If we get told something's so amazing and our expectations are set at such a high level" (line 1513), which Molly builds upon, imagining a current event and reporting the speech therein, "Then you do it and you're like 'wow, OK. . . '" (line 1516). All of these aforementioned instances of reported speech and others in the small peer group conversation function to create what might be called an intertext. That is, the conversation the students have is a text made up of multiple texts—metaphorically, a quilt. While it might be claimed that every text is essentially an intertext (Hanks, 1989, 1999), a prominent feature of the conversation in the small peer group is that the intertext is overt and public. The universe of texts that have been visibly constructed and brought together in this conversational intertext connect texts and events over time and between the novel and events outside of it, including those experienced by students, those imagined by students, historical events, and others.

One of the consequences of the intertext constructed by the students is to bring the literary text *Heart of Darkness* into the students' world. In line 1304, Hunter locates *Heart of Darkness* in the past (in the time referenced in the novel; "obviously we know when" line 1314) but the prompt "*What does it mean to act humanely?*" (line 1319), which is contiguous with (and thus connected to) the distinction between civilized and savage (line 1318) and thus connected to the novel, is in the present tense. The ensuing conversation is located in the present and contextualized by "we" (both a general reference to people in the students' society and to the students themselves; see lines 1321 to 1332 and 1347). The prompt to consider how Marlow or Kurtz (the protagonists of *Heart of Darkness*) are "true" heroes relocates the conversation back into the book and its time period. The students maintain that time frame (lines 1403 to 1454) but then relocate the consideration of hero in a present time frame by imagining reported speech in a style located in their time frame ("Because the attendant is | that even shows how women are in a world of their own /," lines 1452 to 1453; " 'oh/ he's such a great du+de he's so good/he's such a sweet man /'," line 1456) and returning to the use of the first person (lines 1464, 1474, 1511, 1513) and second person (referring to a generalized "you," lines 1469, 1478, 1484, 1485, 1494, 1516, 1519, 1520, and 1521). When Hunter says, "You don't want to be that" (line 1494), he laminates the admiration of Kurtz with the story of Hitler and with their own situation (in which "you" can be interpreted as both a generalized "you" and as the other students in the small peer group).

In brief, one of the functions of intertextuality lies in its potential to reconfigure time and space by laminating different times and spaces, allowing, for example, the students to bring their dialogue about *Heart of Darkness* into their time and space. It is in this sense that we view intertextuality as a resource for engagement in Dialogic Literary Argumentation: the use of dialoguing and arguing about literature to explore personhood and the human condition not at a distance but intimately.

Indexicality in Dialogic Literary Argumentation

Agha (2007) writes:

> The social effects mediated by speech are highly context-bound or **indexical** [original emphasis] in character: they are evaluated in relation to the context or situation at hand. . . . Either an utterance is felt to be appropriate to the situation already understood, or it alters the context in some recognizable way, transforming it into a situation of an entirely different kind.
>
> (p. 14)

What is at issue in any conversation is what is being indexed and how. Although recognizing that utterances index a broad range of social dynamics, here we are specifically interested in the indexing of social and cultural ideologies (hereafter "ideologies"). As we see it, Dialogic Literary Argumentation asks teachers and students to engage, examine, unpack, critique, call into question, and reconstruct both taken-for-granted and overt ideologies as they explore personhood, the human condition, and the permutations and possibilities of both.

Mr. Watson set a framework for examining ideologies at the beginning of the year when he and the students were reading "Allegory of the Cave." Their discussion of "shackle" (lines 1201 to 1252) makes visible that a word can act indexically to invoke diverse ideologies ("so I we can see that out of ONE part of it I just that shackle part I can symbolize tons of things I part of the charm of this"; lines 1248 to 1252). The ideologies raised by students can be viewed as having the syntax of "_____ constrains human actualization"; for example, "electronics/technology (lines 1205 and 1206) constrains human actualization," "your background (line 1211) constrains human actualization," "authority figures (line 1233) constrains human actualization." In our view, what is at issue in Mr. Watson's framing of literature discussions as investigating ideologies is not a particular syntax but recognizing that discussions of literature—as he is framing them—requires exploration of ideology(ies).

When Mr. Watson's class begins dialoguing about *Heart of Darkness*, they address the ideological formation of civilization (lines 1302 to 1372), which was initiated by his prompt (line 1302). Over the course of their conversation, the small instructional peer group addresses the binary of civilized versus savage (lines 1318 to 1333), places that binary in a relativistic context (lines 1334 to 1347), and then undermines and defenestrates the binary (lines 1352 to 1372). The undermining and defenestration of the binary is the result of placing the two opposing concepts ("civilized" and "savage") into a dialectical space and compressing that opposition, yielding a new definition of "civilized" ("It goes back to ethics and things like that I If you have a stateless sense of morality I then you are civilized"; lines 1369 to 1372) and a rejection of the binary ("then you are civilized I whether or not you're being a savage"; lines 1371 and 1372). Later the class engages in dialogue about the ideologies of heroism (lines 1401 to 1442), sanity (lines 1485 to 1488, 1507), and leadership/following (lines 1460 to 1518). Each of these ideologies is interrogated in the conversation among the students.

Dialogic Literary Argumentation and Locating Readers/Students Across Social Events, Time, and Spaces

When we began the Argumentative Writing Project some 11 years ago, the teachers with whom we were working told us that the teaching and learning was a year-long if not years-long process. At that time, and subsequently, we interpreted what they were telling us was that learning argumentation took a long time, especially learning warranting, and that learning the social practices for how to engage in arguing to learn also took a long time. And indeed, we found this to be so. Yet as we began to conceptualize Dialogic Literary Argumentation, it became clear that extended time was also needed for teacher and students to build up a series of events that could build on each other and that could be laminated. What we mean by "events that could build on each other" is exemplified by Mr. Watson's graphic organizer. Over time, Mr. Watson was able to orchestrate iterations of classroom conversations about literature that engaged the students in considering a series of themes (as listed in Diagram 5.2) and that gave them experiences using the novel to explore their own lives and the worlds in which they lived. All of the teachers with whom we worked planned the academic year to build learning over time. For some of them, this meant beginning with learning to argue so that students could acquire a "language" with which to talk about argumentation and about literature and then taking up learning to argue as a framework for teaching and learning literary texts. Some of them made the juncture between learning to argue and arguing to learn overt and explicit (e.g., Ms. Field in Chapter 2 and Mr. Mosley in Chapter 3). Others just jumped into arguing to learn from the beginning of the year (Ms. McClure in Chapter 6). Regardless, each planned the year to provide recursive iterations of Dialogic Literary Argumentation, introducing new expectations for the depth and quality of the classroom dialogues as the year progressed.

While it could be argued that any utterance is inherently intertextual (cf., Hanks, 2000) and indexical (cf., Agha, 2007; Hanks, 1989), we are concerned here with the acquisition of social practices for constructing intertextuality and indexicality. Not only is extended time required to acquire the knowledge and competency for engaging in the particular social practices of intertextuality and indexicality, but also extended time is needed to learn how to recontextualize the social practices acquired within a particular set of social events to another social context and set of social events. Further, extended time is needed to accumulate a series of social events involving Dialogic Literary Argumentation that can be laminated, that is, constitute a set of social events that students can look at in order to get beyond dialogues prompted and framed by any particular literary work. That is, it provides teachers and students opportunities to look across the dialogues that they have had and build a broader and deeper dialogue through intertextuality and indexicality. It is this broader and deeper dialogue that elevates the teaching, learning, and reading of literature beyond learning about literary works in-and-of themselves to refocusing on personhood and the nature of the human condition. We take this up in the next chapter.

Notes

1. Dialogic Literary Argumentation, as we have defined it, involves critical exploration and reflection on the nature of human being and the social world. However, taking this stance runs against the human disposition to simplify complex issues and look for intuitive and absolute answers (Kahneman,

2011; Kahneman, Slovic, & Tversky, 1982). Dialogic Literary Argumentation requires a shift in epistemological and ontological beliefs, moving from seeing knowing as a one-way street toward absolute reality or truth, to regarding knowledge as an entity that is constantly developing and knowing as a dialogic, iterative process of questioning and justifying the known and the unknown. The field of personal epistemology suggests that a person's epistemological beliefs progress from a dualistic, absolutistic view of knowledge as either "right" or "wrong" set by the authority to more complex understanding of knowledge as relativistic, justifiable, and socially constructed (Hofer, 2000; Kuhn, 1991; Perry, 1970; Schraw, 2001).
2. Intertextuality among texts can be socially constructed at multiple levels, including at levels of words, syntax, text structure, and genre (see Bloome & Egan-Robertson, 1993).
3. Here, we are focusing on two time scales; we recognize that there are multiple time scales at play (for a discussion of time scales, see Lemke, 2000).
4. Intertextuality juxtaposes texts as well as the social events within which those texts have been experienced by interlocutors or are otherwise linked. Thus, in socially constructing intertextual connections among texts, people are also constructing intercontextuality.
5. There are a few humorous items in the chart that should be discussed. The theme "What is Love?" is followed by a lyric from a song by that title: "Baby don't hurt me | don't hurt me | No more." In the square at the intersection of "Overcoming Adversity" and *Heart of Darkness*, is written "Da Congo." These two humorous items involve a juxtaposition of texts that violate what Bloome and Egan-Robertson (1993) call intertextual substance (the universe of texts that can legitimately be juxtaposed according to the standards held by the people in the social event). It is this violation of intertextual substance that makes them humorous.

6 Constructing Personhood in the Teaching, Learning, and Reading of Literature

The word "person," like any word (concept), is a socially and culturally constructed artifice to encapsulate a complex set of ideas that stands in relation to other such artifices (words) both constituting and indexing a social and cultural ideology. As we noted in Chapter 2, we build on Egan-Robertson's (1998) definition of personhood as "a dynamic, cultural construct about who is and what is considered a person, what attributes and rights are constructed as inherent to being a person, and what social positions are available within the construct of being a person" (p. 453).

Although people take for granted what a "person" is, what constitutes a "person" is not given but socially constructed and is often contested. What is included in the word (concept) "person" varies across cultural groups, across social institutions, and across social situations. Included in any definition of "person" is both what constitutes a person (and what is not a person) as well as the various types of "persons" and the qualities and characteristics of a "person." Personhood, as we use it, refers to all of the social dynamics involved in the situated defining and use of "person." This includes those dynamics within the social interaction of an immediate social event, of an institutional context, of a broader cultural and social ideological context, and of historical contexts.

There are diverse approaches to theorizing and exploring personhood (e.g., Butler, 1990/2007; Fowler, 2004; Geertz, 1973, 1979; Gergen & Davis, 1985). The approach we take can be called "Languaging Personhood" (cf., Bloome & Beauchemin, 2016). In brief, as people interact with each other, their uses of language construct shared definitions of personhood. The definitions of personhood (including teachers and students) may not be overt, nonetheless every exchange of utterances involves a languaging of personhood.

In Dialogic Literary Argumentation, teachers and students approach the languaging of personhood at two levels. The first level is overt. As they read and dialogue about a literary text, they explicitly consider the implications for how personhood might be defined (or redefined). For example, consider a classroom discussion in which the students have been reading *Inside the Hotel Rwanda* (Kayihura & Zukus, 2014).[1] In response to a teacher question about the effects of experience with genocide, Helen says, "So it is something that you could learn but | I think that your brain automatically after time is going to try and heal itself |." Helen is explicitly defining a quality of a person (that the brain tries to heal itself). The second level lies just below the level of consciousness. As teachers and students dialogue with one another, every utterance involves an implied definition of personhood (or aspect thereof). For example, consider a brief bit of conversation that occurred during a whole class discussion. The teacher was orchestrating the discussion to generate so-called essential questions that could later be investigated. She asked, "So if we are going to talk about the judicial system, how could we frame a question where we would be learning more about it?" Denise responded, "How did it improve?" On the surface, this conversational exchange is not about personhood, it is about the institution of law. However, embedded in the conversational exchange are assumptions about personhood: that a person is capable of engaging in moral and legal actions and that they are motivated to do so by the nature of the justice system and the power it has to punish (an assumption based on a more basic assumption that a person reacts to both punishment and the threat of punishment). Also implied is that people make decisions to act in particular ways aligned with being just and that such decision-making is rational and thus people are accountable for their actions.

In this chapter, we look closely at the conversation Ms. McClure and her students had prompted by their reading of *Inside the Hotel Rwanda*. In addition to reading *Inside the Hotel Rwanda*, the students had attended a talk by Edouard Kayihura about the Rwandan genocide and the book, read excerpts from Philip Gourevitch's *We Wish to Inform You That Tomorrow We Will Be Killed With Our Families: Stories From Rwanda* (1999), and searched for related information on the internet. Our purpose is to gain insight into how Dialogic Literary Argumentation can lead students to interrogate conceptions of personhood.

Teaching, Learning, and Reading *Inside the Hotel Rwanda* in a 10th-Grade Honors Class

Midtown High is located in an urban area of a major Midwestern city and hosts around 1,300 students whose demographics are racially and ethnically diverse: white, Black, Hispanic, Asian, Somalian, Appalachian, and multi-racial. The school has a higher poverty rate than most schools in the surrounding area, and Midtown High performs below the state average in academic achievement. While the school and neighborhood may not be highly regarded by these traditional measures, its teachers and students give a different impression. In our observations, we were impressed with how collaborative the teachers seemed to be and how involved they were with the school and local community.

136 *Constructing Personhood*

The teacher cooperating in this study, Ms. McClure, has been teaching English language arts for over 15 years and has worked with our research team and the Argumentative Writing Project as a teacher participant in years past. After becoming involved with the Argumentative Writing Project, she continued to pursue new and innovative approaches to the teaching of writing and literature and has been actively involved in professional development programs such as the area's local Writing Project. In a conversation with Ms. McClure, she explained that one of the reasons she has engaged so much with the students and community at Midtown High is that she is treated as a valued professional and could teach writing and books that actually reflected the students and their experiences of the world. Similar to the respect Ms. McClure feels at Midtown, students have reported feeling valued and respected during her class and often enthusiastically remark that time goes by quickly when they are there.

Generating Essential Questions from *Inside the Hotel Rwanda*

Toward the end of the school year, the class began reading and discussing *Inside the Hotel Rwanda*. As they had done in previous instructional units, after reading a literary work, Ms. McClure led the class in generating a series of essential questions. The students would then take one of the essential questions, explore it and then report back to the class. The reporting back often took the form of writing an argumentative essay and making a presentation (often with PowerPoint) to the class. However, for the instructional unit on *Inside the Hotel Rwanda*, the assigned task was to work in a small group on one of the essential questions and make a presentation to the class. No formal paper was assigned.

The following is a transcript of the conversation Ms. McClure had with her students to generate essential questions after reading *Inside the Hotel Rwanda*. It was not unusual for students in Ms. McClure's other classes to sit in on another one of Ms. McClure's classes, and occasionally another teacher would join the class. Indeed, during the following transcribed event, Mr. Baldwin, a social studies teacher, participated in the conversation (no students from other classes were there at that time). The movable tables in the class were organized in a big square with students and teachers spaced around the square. The transcribed conversation begins with the teacher discussing their goal to generate essential questions.

| 1601 | T | When we do our questions on essential questions I want them to focus on argument |
| 1602 | | So we don't want to focus on the what and wheres we really want to focus on the whys and the hows |

1603	Mary	(undecipherable) XXXXXXXX
1604	T	So if we are going to talk about the judicial system, how could we frame a question where we would be learning more about it ↑
1605	Denise	How did it improve ↑
1606	T	OK So how (typing on computer showing on smartboard)
1607		oops
1608		So you can see all my mistakes now
1609		(ten-second pause while T is typing on to the smartboard)
1610		How do you spell judicial ↑
1611	Baldwin	i-c-i-a-l
1612	Ss	*(Several students talk at once)*
1613	T	OK so how did the judicial
1614		I know
1615		How did the judicial system improve
1616		ummmm
1617		So in order to know that we would have to have background information right ↑
1618	S	How it was before and how it was after
1619	T	OK
1620	Baldwin	Like what was the process
1621		like constitution
1622		XXXXXXXX (undecipherable)
1623	Idil	They don't have
1624		They don't have a constitution

As they generated essential questions such as "How did the judicial system improve?" Ms. McClure wrote them on her computer and projected them on a screen for all to see. Essential questions had to probe for more than description, they had to "focus on the whys and the hows" (line 1602). Denise offers such a framing for a question about the judicial system ("How did [the judicial system] improve?" line 1605), which is validated by Ms. McClure (line 1615) and expanded by an unidentified student ("How it was before and how was it after?" line 1618). One thing to note about this bit of conversation is that questions must be framed to elicit narratives ("How was it before and how was it after?" line 1618). Also of note is that the generation and framing of essential questions is a task shared between the teacher and the students.

138 *Constructing Personhood*

As the conversation continues, Ms. McClure explains how they will respond to the essential questions.

1651	T	The judicial system can definitely be one thing that we look at
1652		I think we can move away from
1653		Remember we are going to talk about groupings and how we want to do our
1654		How we want to
1655		We'll do research first
1656		We'll talk about how you want to put your research information together
1657		But we want to figure out what it is that you are interested in
1658		We have this umbrella of the Rwandan genocide
1659		so far
1660		we have him come in
1661		how have we looked at *Hotel Rwanda*
1662		we've read pieces from Paul's book
1663		His autobiography
1664		And then we will look at
1665		pieces from the book *We Wish to Inform You That Tomorrow We Will Be Killed With Our Families*
1666		And these will be individual stories as well

The students will work in groups (line 1653) and engage in a process that begins with doing research (line 1655) and then putting the research together (line 1656). From our year-long observations in the class, we know that "put the research together" refers to creating a coherent narrative rather than reporting a simple list of facts about the topic. Ms. McClure makes clear that in generating the essential questions, students have to create questions that will provide them with opportunities to explore the Rwandan genocide in a way that allows the students to research something that they are interested in (line 1657 and line 1658).

One of the keys to how *Inside the Hotel Rwanda* is framed is in Ms. McClure's characterization of the various sources they are reading as "stories" (line 1666). Ms. McClure had made clear that the story in *Inside the Hotel Rwanda* would be different from the story told in the movie about the Rwandan genocide, *Hotel Rwanda*. One of their tasks would be to reconcile the different stories being told.

In Chapter 4, we introduced the notion of abductive reasoning; that is, logical inferencing grounded in an observation or set of observations that seeks to find the simplest and most likely explanation for the observations. One way to understand a concept such as forgiveness is to consider how a series of stories explores how it is described, experienced, and examined. In the following transcript, Baldwin, a visiting teacher, reconstructs a story of forgiveness from a news story in an Amish community in 2006—the emphasis on forgiveness and reconciliation in the Amish community's response was widely discussed in the national media. This moment captures how stories as well as canonical literary texts can become props for developing an idea, in this case forgiveness.

1701	Baldwin	You guys will probably be finished
1702		I remember a story a few years ago where a man ran into an Amish community
1703		an Amish school or something like that
1704		he opened fire
1705		You know
1706		It was like a big story
1707		That the Amish community forgave that guy
1708		xxxxxx
1709		I mean you guys just talked about
1710		because they all needed to forgive the situation
1711		like
1712		The question I have is
1713		How do you learn to do that ↑
1714		You guys are high school sophomores
1715		I don't know that I could do it
1716		xxxxxx
1717		xxxxxx
1718		How did you learn that ↑
1719		What does that look like
1720		How do you change the entire mindset of a whole group of people ↑
1721	Helen	like Amish community they're taught
1722		xxxxxx
1723		They can't have pain
1724		They [can't] have malice
1725		They have to be helpful and kind natured and that
1726		xxxxxx
1727	Idil	What's their religion

1728		Uhhh
1729	Helen	Christian I think
1730		They are set off from the mainstream

As the discussion continues, Mr. Baldwin, the social studies teacher who joined the class for this discussion, raises a question about forgiveness (line 1711) not just for an individual but for "a whole group of people" (line 1721). Idil raises the question of religion (line 1728). We know from past observations in the classroom and an interview with Idil that her religion, Islam, is very important to her as is her identity as Somali. The students continue to discuss forgiveness.

1762	Helen	XXXXXX (undecipherable)
1763		forgive them over the years
1764		then to feel that feel over something that happen that you can't change
1765		the anger that I have I can't live with this
1766		XXXXXX (undecipherable)
1767		So it is something you could learn but
1768		I think that your brain automatically after time is going to try and heal itself
1769		something else and you just have to get over this
1770		XXXXX (undecipherable)
1771	T	So our essential question is
1772		If we want to talk about that
1773		What is
1774		Is it possible to forgive

Helen defines forgiveness as both something learned (line 1767) and as something biological (line 1768) and juxtaposes forgiveness and anger (line 1765). In brief, Helen articulates a dialectical space that frames the ongoing discussion of forgiveness.

1801	Helen	it's like say
1802		say you're going to break up over some things that are small ridiculous
1803		You don't like what was done but you forget it because it was irrelevant
1804		like you have to get over it and move on
1805	Barbara	I don't know I just felt like

Constructing Personhood 141

1806		he
1807		I mean like
1808	Helen	*(begins to talk)*
1809		I'm sorry
1810	Barbara	Go ahead
1811	Idil	like XXXXXX (undecipherable) and you feed him
1812		at do you do you still hate them ↑
1813	Ss	*(Many students talk at once)*
1814	Chloe	OK
1815		let's say you hate someone
1816		You don't have to talk to them
1817		You don't
1818		Just because you hate them
1819		If I hate someone I am not going to
1820		gonna talk to them or anything
1821		I feel like you don't have to communicate or
1822	Idil	About doing XXXXXXX (undecipherable)
1823	Helen	XXXXXXX (undecipherable)

Helen compares the issue of forgiveness after the Rwandan genocide to a break up among friends (lines 1802 to 1804). Barbara disagrees but does so in a way that does not directly confront Helen (lines 1805 to 1807). When Helen jumps into the conversation to respond (line 1808), she interrupts Idil who has also bid for a turn at talk. Helen and Barbara back off, a move that is not insignificant given that in classroom conversations earlier in the year they would not have done so and given that there had been some antagonism among them. It may be the case that Helen and Barbara's backing off and willingness to listen to what Idil has to say (lines 1811 and 1812) is in part a response to Ms. McClure's attempts to get students to listen to each other as part of their engagement in Dialogic Literary Argumentation. Chloe offers a story from her life (perhaps an imagined story) that parallels the earlier story that Helen told.

As the conversation continues, Mr. Baldwin returns to the question of how a whole group of people might be moved to forgive (line 1721 earlier and line 1824 in the following transcript).

1824	Baldwin	How do you get an entire mass of people thinking about
1825		And with that
1826		The other side of that

142 *Constructing Personhood*

1827		How do you get a group of people to decide
1828		we're going to kill all those people who
1829		whatever
1830		How do you get that many people to agree ↑
1831		I mean
1832	Denise	XXXXXXX (undecipherable)
1833	T	OK
1834		That that could be one of our essential questions too

The question of how a group of people decides to forgive is expanded by Mr. Baldwin to include how they might decide to kill (line 1828). Ms. McClure brings the issue of how one gets a group of people to forgive or to kill to a close by making it one of the essential questions. However, one of the students, Sagal, had wanted to contribute to the discussion but had not yet had a turn at talk. The conversation continues with Sagal finally getting a turn at talk and Ms. McClure apologizing for not having recognized her (lines 1851 and 1852).

1851	Sagal	I want to say that
1852	T	I'm sorry honey
1853	Sagal	XXXXXXXX (undecipherable) minds and over and over again you have like
1854		if you keep saying the Tutus and the Tutus are the Tutus are
1855	Ss	*(Many students talking)*
1856	Helen	They condition you they condition you
1857		They condition you to get ready for war
1858		They desensitize yourself against killing
1859	Idil	Cause like you will hear it over and over again

Helen responds by revoicing Sagal's contribution with the term "condition" (lines 1856 and 1857); Idil follows Helen but uses some of Sagal's own words ("over and over again" lines 1853 and 1859), which can be taken as support of Sagal's ideas and of her voice.

Constructing Personhood

Nominalizations of Personhood

One of the ways that Ms. McClure and her class (including Mr. Baldwin) construct personhood is through nominalization: naming kinds of

Constructing Personhood 143

persons and naming qualities that a person has. We have listed some of the nominalizations in Table 6.1.

The nominalizations of kinds of people, the components of people, and the qualities of people are being discussed and negotiated by the students; for the class, they are not settled definitions of personhood.

In some cases, the nominalizations reflect taken-for-granted definitions of personhood (e.g., gendered categories of personhood, such as man, line 1702). In other cases, personhood is a function of membership in a group (e.g., Tutsi, Amish) or of a relationship (e.g., students and teacher). What is at issue is, in part, what kinds of people are nominalized, and in part what is of issue is the acceptance of the categories, components, and qualities offered. That Ms. McClure places the quality of forgiveness as an essential question—"Is it possible to forgive?"—locates that quality of personhood in a dialectical space (existing in the compressed opposition between an inherent and universal quality of a person, a learned quality, or a quality of being students).

Table 6.1 Select Nominalizations of Personhood

Nominalization	Line #	Comment
man	1702	A person has a gender
Amish	1702, 1722	Category of people
You guys	1709	Refers to students as a group distinct of persons
High school sophomore	1714	Label for a group of persons defined in terms of institutional age
I	1715	Person as individual; here individual as adult
Can't have pain	1723	Quality of a particular kind of person defined by membership in an ethnic/religious group
Can't have malice	1724	Quality of a particular kind of person defined by membership in an ethnic/religious group
you can't change	1764	Universalized quality of a person
anger	1765	Emotion a person might have
brain	1768	Component of a person
forgiveness	1774	Quality of a person
hate	1812, 1818, 1819	Emotion person might have
Tutu [Tutsi]	1854	Category of people
Conditioning	1856, 1857	A quality of a person
Desensitize	1858	A quality of a person

144 *Constructing Personhood*

Narrativizing Personhood

Even in the brief segment of classroom conversation transcribed earlier, Ms. McClure and her students construct a series of narratives that provide definitions of personhood (see Table 6.2).

Table 6.2 Narratives of Personhood

Lines	Narrative	Comments
1617	Responding to an essential question has a first step of acquiring background knowledge	Narrative projected onto the students
1618 to 1620	The story of how the judicial system evolved	Institutional narrative
1653 to 1666	A narrative about the students' processes for completing their work on essential questions	Narrative projected onto the students
1702 to 1714 and 1721 to 1729	A narrative about Amish forgiveness	Narrative illustrating personhood quality of forgiveness and locating it in a kind of persons (Amish)
1714 to 1720	A narrative about the students having the quality of forgiveness	Assignment of forgiveness as a quality of the students' personhood
1730	Narrative about the relationship of the Amish from the mainstream	Relationship quality of Amish as "set off from the mainstream"
1768	Narrative about the brain healing	Locating forgiveness as a biological quality
1802 to 1804	Narrative about a student break-up	Quality of forgiveness as a person's decision
1811 to 1812	Narrative about relationship of people who hate each other but feed them	Narrative of forgiveness in a context of hate
1815 to 1821	Narrative about relationship of people who hate each other and therefore do not talk	Narrative of hate and communication (implicitly contrasted with killing narrative)
1824 to 1831	Soliciting narrative about getting a group of people to decide to forgive or to kill	Quality of a person as a member of a group
1851 to 1859	Narrative about conditioning	Response to solicitation of a narrative to explain how a group of people decide to hate and kill

Constructing Personhood 145

These narratives serve several functions including defining and illustrating a quality of personhood, projecting a quality of personhood onto a group, constructing social relationships that implicitly define personhood, and assigning personhood as a function of membership in a group.

Narrative, Time, and Personhood

Personhood is promulgated not only in nominalizations and in narratives explicitly focused on types of persons and components and qualities of personhood but also through the chronotopes of the narratives constructed. Bakhtin (1981) defines chronotope as follows:

> We will give the name *chronotope* (literally "time space") to the intrinsic connectedness of temporal and spatial relationships that are artistically expressed in literature (p. 84). . . . The chronotope as a formally constitutive category determines to a significant degree the image of man *[sic]* in literature as well. The image of man *[sic]* is always intrinsically chronotopic.
>
> (p. 85)

Since the implications of a chronotope for defining a person—the hero in Bakhtinian terms (see Bakhtin, 1984)—has been discussed at length elsewhere (e.g., Halasek, 1999; Schuster, 1985) we only briefly discuss it here. In brief, any narrative implies a movement of people through time and space. This movement through time and space is fashioned. Consider the chronotope implied in the narrative Ms. McClure tells about how the students will respond to the essential questions being generated.

1654	T	How we want to
1655		We'll do research first
1656		We'll talk about how you want to put your research information together
1657		But we want to figure out what it is that you are interested in
1658		We have this umbrella of the Rwandan genocide
1659		so far
1660		we have him come in
1661		how have we looked at *Hotel Rwanda*
1662		we've read pieces from Paul's book
1663		His autobiography
1664		And then we will look at

| 1665 | | pieces from the book *We Wish to Inform You That Tomorrow We Will Be Killed With Our Families* |
| 1666 | | And these will be individual stories as well |

The narrative of responding to the essential questions lists a series of events that the students will experience as a group (line 1654)—researching (line 1655), putting information together (1656), looking at a series of sources each of which tells "individual stories," and then (from earlier conversations) making a presentation to the class. We note that the narrative does not include a climax, a point at which the protagonist (in this case, the student) can fail. In effect, the movement through time and space eschews the binary of success and failure and thereby defines the students (the protagonists of the narrative) as being successful. It is a narrativized quality of their personhood implicit in the chronotope of the narrative.

The chronotopes of the multiple narratives related to forgiveness vary in the qualities assigned to a protagonist: a horrid event occurs (e.g., a murder(s), a genocide) and then the survivors have to decide whether and how to forgive. In some of the forgiveness narratives, the protagonist makes the journey to forgiving by changing herself or himself, whereas other narratives suggest that there is no change *per se* as forgiveness is a function of the brain (rather than of learning or of needing to continue without the burden of hate). That forgiveness becomes an essential question can be viewed as asking the students to complete the narrative of forgiveness and in so doing define, at least in part, personhood. As such, the conversation the students have in the classroom about forgiveness (the transcribed conversation) can be viewed as the juxtaposition of various potential narratives in a dialectical space (in the compressed tension of what is taken to be a natural, innate, feeling of hate versus the innate or learned quality of forgiveness). The exchange of narratives regarding forgiveness, with their implied chronotopes, can be viewed as an initial dialogue in which the students are arguing to learn about the nature of forgiveness and how it may be a quality of personhood.

Framing Essential Questions as Arguments About the Human Condition

As we consider Ms. McClure's efforts to generate researchable and arguable essential questions for research that would eventually lead students to presentations, we also take stock of the essential questions that were proposed with particular interest in how they suggested issues related to personhood. Across the transcribed discussions included in this chapter, we note four essential questions:

1. How did it [judicial system] improve?
2. How do you change the entire mindset of people?
3. Is it possible to forgive?
4. How do you get that many people to agree?

These four questions consider personhood from various perspectives: as institutions (judicial system), as cultural and political (mindset), as human relationships (forgiveness), and as rhetorical (to agree). Each of these four domains prompts students to explore the human condition as something significant but perhaps even more important is what Ms. McClure includes in deciding what counts as significant and what is worth researching, discussing, and sharing in presentations with one another.

As it turns out, organizing instruction around big ideas and essential questions is not new (see Burke, 1972; Wiggins & McTighe, 2008) but has proven challenging to enact (Applebee, Burroughs, & Stevens, 2000). The manner in which Ms. McClure positions herself as a collaborator who respects and values her students' ideas and experiences has her approach essential questions as shaped by her notion of her students who are autonomous thinkers. For example, Ms. McClure's approach to *Inside the Hotel Rwanda* was to begin with broad questions that invite discussion and debate about issues from the book and across a broad domain of students' own experiences. Note too that she framed her approach not as information collecting and report but as arguable: "When we do our questions on essential questions I want them to focus on argument" (line 1601). So we don't want to focus on the what and wheres we really want to focus on the whys and the hows" (line 1602). In lines 1604 and 1605, she asks, "So if we are going to talk about the judicial system, how could we frame a question where we would be learning more about it?" Denise responds with an essential question, "How did it improve?" Ms. McClure's move here is an interesting instance of assuming Denise's personhood in that she not only welcomes the student's suggestion but recommends it as an essential question for Denise's peers to consider.

Final Comments—Personhood in Dialogic Literary Argumentation

What we have suggested in this chapter is that personhood in Dialogic Literary Argumentation is both explicit and implicit. Prompted by the literary works they read, teachers and students may explicitly engage in conversations about what it means to be human (personhood). Not only in Ms. McClure's class but in all of the classrooms described in this book (and in all of the classrooms of all of the teachers who participated in the research), teachers and students explored the question of what it means to be human and the nature of the human condition.

In Ms. Hill's class, she and her students explicitly asked questions about the doctor and the degree to which the doctor assigned personhood to the "Indians" and to women, and what a failure to do so would say about the personhood of white people like the doctor. Ms. Field's class explicitly encouraged her students to explore personhood in *To Kill a Mockingbird*, juxtaposing two essays with opposing views of Atticus Finch as hero. Those two opposing views assigned to Atticus different chronotopes, different ways of moving through time and space, each view assessing what Atticus did with a different set of criteria based on different definitions of personhood. Marsha, a student in the class, raised questions about the personhood Harper Lee differentially assigned to Atticus Finch, Boo Radley, and Tom Robinson. She reconstructed the personhood of Tom Robinson as equivalent to that of the others in the novel, a move that made public her disagreement with what she argued was Harper Lee's differential assignment of personhood. Mr. Mosley foregrounded Daisy Buchanan's decision to choose Tom Buchanan or Jay Gatsby as a way to raise questions about who counts as a person (versus being an object for others to compete over). Ms. Nelson, in her teaching of *Things Fall Apart*, asked her students to explore rationality as a quality of personhood. That is, she asked students to explore definitions of rationality and who and how people took up what definitions of rationality with what consequences for whom. The binary of rational and irrational as a framing for personhood needed to be interrogated, and power relations needed to be considered as an aspect of rationality. In Mr. Watson's classroom, conversations prompted by the reading of *Heart of Darkness* were juxtaposed with conversations earlier in the year prompted by the reading of other literary works, in particular the "Allegory of the Cave." In such a juxtaposition, Mr. Watson's students were able to "get above" the construction of personhood implied in any one literary work and consider personhood both within *Heart of Darkness* and across the set of literary works they had read.

In each iteration of Dialogic Literary Argumentation that we have shared in this book, whether explicitly named or not, personhood was a central dimension of the teacher's and students' making of meaning, social significance, and cultural import. It was similarly so in the classrooms of those teachers who collaborated with us in the study but who are not mentioned here. In Chapter 1, we noted the ubiquity of race, class, gender, sexuality, and other forms of oppression in the teaching, learning, and reading of literature in high school classrooms in the United States. In the classrooms we observed in our study of Dialogic Literary Argumentation, race, class, gender, sexuality, and other forms of oppression were often explicit topics of conversation and often focused on the construction of personhood and its differential defining of what definitions of person applied to which human beings, when, where, and how. We also observed that conversations of personhood in the classrooms we observed took place on multiple levels and in ways that allowed students to reconstruct (as part of their contesting) the personhood of characters in the literary works and of the people those literary works were reflecting. The reconstruction of personhood in and through Dialogic Literary Argumentation also occurred among teachers and students in the classroom. As such, the frameworks within which students defined themselves and each other evolved through their engagement in Dialogic Literary Argumentation.

Note

1. Although Kayihura and Zukus's *Inside the Hotel Rwanda* (2014) is classified as non-fiction, except for the first chapter, which is a history that frames the racial divide between people who are Hutu and those who are Tutsi, the book is written as a memoir, a narrative story. Thus, we would still classify the book as "literature" although we recognize that some scholars and educators would not. In part, we decided to use the dialogues in Ms. McClure's classroom around *Inside the Hotel Rwanda* because Ms. McClure viewed the book as part of her teaching of literature; and in part because the classroom conversations exemplified the emphasis in Dialogic Literary Argumentation on the use of a literary text as a prop to engage in dialogues about personhood.

7 Final Comments

The Possibilities of Dialogic Literary Argumentation in English Language Arts Classrooms

In the summer of 2014 as a new iteration of the Argumentative Writing Project began, we initiated a second project grounded in collaborations with high school English language arts teachers on the teaching and learning of what we originally referred to as "literature-related argumentative writing." At that time, we had also begun writing our first book titled, *Teaching and Learning Argumentative Writing in High School English Language Arts Classrooms* (Newell et al., 2015) in which we conceptualized argumentation as a social practice.

> In our view, the teaching of argumentative writing involves not only a concern for effectively teaching a written genre, acquiring argument schema, and specific tactics and strategies, but learning how to engage in the social practices associated the academic domain of the language arts and literature. These social practices—particular ways of using spoken and written language and other semiotic systems within particular social situations—involve ways of reasoning, sharing ideas, expressing opinions, exploring perspectives, inquiring into the human condition, constructing texts, generating insights, establishing social relationships, expressing social identities, and using spoken and written language. These practices are essentially social in at least two ways. The teaching and learning of argumentative writing are social because argumentative writing is essentially and by definition communication and engagement with others; and it is social because teaching and learning are essentially social as teachers and students interacting with each other constructing new knowledge and new understandings.
>
> (Newell et al., 2015, pp. 17–18)

This social practice framework proved to be a powerful heuristic for taking our next step: a reconceptualization of the relationship between argumentation, argumentative writing and literature with its long history as the central disciplinary content of English language arts (Applebee, 1974). In our Institute of Education Sciences proposal, we had described our possible contribution to the field as "a fundamental reconceptualization of teaching argumentation and argumentative writing that provides principles and practices from which a successful constellation of activities can be generated." We think that we have accomplished nothing less and something more: a new vision that we named Dialogic Literary Argumentation. As we complete this research monograph, our gaze has already begun to turn to yet another book, but this time we will write specifically for English language arts teachers describing a new approach to the teaching of literature that asks teachers and students to consider argumentation and argumentative writing as ways to learn, communicate, and explore ideas and experiences.

A Few Surprises Along the Way: Taking an Ethnographic Perspective

Any long-term effort has twists and turns along the way, and we had a few surprises. For instance, long before our second research began in 2014, many of the teachers with whom we collaborated had begun to rethink their teaching and their students' learning by relying on the principles of Dialogic Literary Argumentation. Of course, these teachers were largely unaware of the value of their work and the promises it held for our collaboration with them. The issues and concerns of the teachers' practices helped us shape what counted as interesting and important, honing our own notions of what to pay attention to in the classrooms we observed. We hope what we learned will provide practitioners (and researchers) new questions to ask and new ways to consider their approaches to English language arts. Put another way, our project has been fundamentally grounded in what is happening in classrooms in order to construct a new model. In generating dimensions of Dialogic Literary Argumentation, we have moved between theorizing and detailed, thick microethnographic discourse analytic descriptions (cf., Bloome et al., 2005) of actual and particular social events in which teachers and students were engaged in Dialogic Literary Argumentation.

Literature provides an interesting and, in some ways, an unusual ground for the study of interactions between teachers and students—the ways of passing on cultural wisdom as well as fostering the development of new ideas. These imply very different ways of participating in the study of literature as well as differing roles for teachers and students. As we realized that there have been few new ideas about literature instruction and, as Applebee (1993) has pointed out, that classrooms often reflect a mishmash of approaches ranging from the New Criticism to personal response, we saw the need for a new model. Accordingly, another possible surprise—this time for the reader—is that this book is not so much about reporting research findings as it is about theory construction.

Because our theorizing involved constant movement back and forth between theories and classrooms, constantly revising our understanding and ways of articulating what we learned from being in classrooms and how we are theorizing Dialogic Literary Argumentation, a great deal of the "data" in this book are brief descriptions of classroom literature lessons. Our use of an "ethnographic perspective" (Blommaert & Jie, 2010) was more than a way of doing fieldwork and collecting data, for "ethnography can as well be seen as a 'full' intellectual programme far richer than just a matter of description" (Blommaert & Jie, 2010, p. 5). To clarify, our project was anchored in ethnographic data that included language as discourse-in-use to study classroom life. The ethnographic and languaging data were not employed as evidence that Dialogic Literary Argumentation "works" to improve students' learning to think, talk or write, but to describe the messy and complex work of teachers and students and not reducing the complexity, but to explore and explain it. Perhaps another surprise was that as we employed an ethnographic perspective, we have had a "democratic" relationship with teachers that has changed us as researchers. How it has changed the teachers is much harder to say, but we have had moments when they have described our collaborations as moments of reflective consideration of their practices.

A Theoretical Framework for Research and Teaching

As the research team met and as we collaborated with teachers in classrooms, summer workshops, and monthly teacher meetings, we constantly engaged in conversations to interrogate the theoretical frames we brought with us and new frames we studied at the time. In these research contexts, our theoretical framings of the teaching, learning, reading, and writing about literature were indeed emergent as well as constantly challenged and constantly evolving. In general terms, we view our intellectual and theoretical approach to the teaching, learning, reading, and writing about literature in high school classrooms as social practices reflective and projective of social, cultural, and political ideologies associated with social institutions, such as schools, and of more widespread social contexts. But more than abstractions, they directed our gaze as researchers, shaped our conversations among the researchers and teachers, distinguished our work from other research endeavors, and deepened our understanding of what and how we were researching.

As we discussed in Chapter 1, there are four key theoretical framings that have guided our articulation of Dialogic Literary Argumentation. We briefly reiterate them as follows.

The Centrality of the Social

The study of social processes and practices in classrooms theorizes and focuses on the work of teachers and students as they interactionally construct everyday life in classrooms. A contribution of empirical work on the social practice of knowledge construction is the shift in focus from the individual student to that of the social. This shift suggests the need to examine the social processes shaping what counts as knowledge, to consider a communal understanding of meaning, to evaluate ideas set in historical and public contexts, and to recognize the importance of the assessment of knowledge claims by relevant groups.

Learning as a Social Construction

As researchers studying academic life in classrooms, we take as a given that teachers and students jointly construct what they know and believe, including what they know and believe of themselves and of social relationships through the languaging of their activities and experiences. Accordingly, in our research, we employed a microethnographic approach to discourse analysis (Bloome et al., 2005), identifying key events, transcribing them from video recordings, and analyzing each line (utterance) with regard to how it builds upon previous utterances, implies social relations among people including the reader and the author, indexes particular kinds of evidence, constructs opportunities for engagement with others, shifts between the substance of an argument (content) and the structure of an argument (form), references previous and future events, and links to various social contexts.

Race, Class, Gender, and Sexuality, as Defining Social Constructions

Unlike the profile Applebee (1993) presented over 25 years ago, the literature instruction that we observed in our case study classrooms included a range of traditions beyond that of white, Anglo-European males. Many of the literary texts taught, learned, and read in the high school classrooms we observed involved issues of race, class, gender, and/or sexuality. Issues of race, class, gender, and sexuality, however, were not limited to the literary texts selected for study in those classrooms, but were issues that permeated nearly all aspects of the English language arts classroom including who the students were in each class, how students related to each other (and to the teacher), the arguments made, and the nature of the classroom discussions.

Approaching Literature as Props to Foster Dialogue about the Human Condition

Without rejecting the importance of the text, the reader, or the interpretive community, we have positioned the literary text as a prop. By arguing for the dialogic that is socially constructed within instructional conversations, we prioritized a shift from the meaning making process from the text itself and from the transaction of reader and text to the social construction of meaning that unfolds during talk and social interactions around literary texts. An implication of this shift is that the role of the reader and text change regarding what counts as "text." "Text" is not just the print text but also the social practices of discussion. Metaphorically, the literary text becomes a prop to foster dialogue that brings together multiple texts and engages people (teachers and students) in ongoing dialogue and conversation about the human condition.

Four Dimensions of Dialogic Literary Argumentation

The four aforementioned theoretical frames (that were described in greater detail in Chapter 1) were the theoretical context within which we developed a "model" of Dialogic Literary Argumentation. Chapters 3, 4, 5, and 6 each take up one of the dimensions. Here, we briefly reiterate the four dimensions.

Constructing Dialogue and Dialectics in Arguing to Learn in the Teaching, Learning, and Reading of Literature

Most obvious across the classrooms was that there was a lot of student engagement in dialogue with each other and the teacher. Whether the teachers used Socratic Circles, small group discussion, whole group discussion, or some other conversational structure, the teachers focused students on responding to each other (not necessarily to contradict but also to complement, clarify, offer potential alternatives, etc.). They sought to create dialogue among the students and between themselves and the students, and on occasion imagined dialogues between the students and the author or a literary character. Across the classrooms, prompted by the literature that they had been reading, the teachers orchestrated classroom conversations to create what we have called a dialectical space. By dialectical space, we are referring to social events in which interlocutors can explore how the tensions between opposing views can provide additional insight and depth in the complexities of the human condition and personhood.

Constructing Multiple Perspectives and Rationality in the Teaching, Learning, and Reading of Literature

As we define it, a multiple perspectives framing of the teaching, learning, and reading of literature involves a complex, dynamic, and evolving dialectic, a chronotopic complexity with implications for the social construction of meaning, cultural import, and social significance over time and space. That is, we eschew the relativism that often frames the envisionment and enactment of multiple perspectives and foreground the construction of and wrestling with tensions among the perspectives in producing new insights, conceptions and understandings of what it means to be human.

Constructing Intertextuality and Indexicality in the Teaching, Learning, and Reading of Literature

Simply stated, intertextuality is the juxtaposition of two or more texts. The texts may be co-present or located in different events, locations, times, and social contexts; they may be juxtaposed at various levels from the level of words to genres. Indexicality can be defined as a sign that connects an event to something outside of the event. The power of these two constructs lies in what texts and what contexts are juxtaposed, how, when, where, by whom, and how taken up. We are especially interested in those juxtapositions of texts and events that create dialogic and dialectic spaces that allow students and teachers to explore tensions; unpack taken-for-granted concepts; envision new ideas, theses, and perspectives; and take on and create new ways of languaging their own worlds as well as imagined worlds.

Constructing Personhood in the Teaching, Learning, and Reading of Literature

Both in their conversations about a literary text (or more accurately, a set of texts and contexts) and in the literary text(s) itself, teachers and students together are always negotiating what it means be human, when, where, how, and with what consequences. This dimension of our model of Dialogic Literary Argumentation is a key component in that it is through and with the notion of personhood as way not only to understand the fears, dilemmas, and joys of literary characters but also to connect with others. It is in this sense that Dialogic Literary Argumentation offers a different perspective on teaching, learning, and reading literature, rather than conceptualize the teaching, learning, and reading of literature as a way to prompt a personal response or as a way to belong to an interpretive community, but as a way to deeply explore what it means to be human while recognizing the complexity, diversity, uncertainty, situated nature, and lack of closure engaging in asking and dialoguing about such a question.

Looking Across Chapters

In this chapter, we also consider our examination of the potentialities of Dialogic Literary Argumentation as a construct for researching and teaching literature by looking across the previous chapters and identifying what we see as some major takeaways from those chapters. While doing so, we are mindful of a key point made in Chapter 1: this book is a starting point, not a final commentary, on Dialogic Literary Argumentation, and on what we believe it offers to the teaching and learning of literature and argumentative writing in secondary school English language arts classrooms. The teaching and learning possibilities revealed in our descriptions and analyses of Dialogic Literary Argumentation in action across several specific classroom settings constitute opening and exploratory moves in an ongoing conversation about Dialogic Literary Argumentation that we have attempted to initiate. We envision rich possibilities for Dialogic Literary Argumentation and secondary school English language arts pedagogy as we move forward in this work.

This chapter will not simply repeat points made in the earlier chapters, especially the first and second chapters, where we defined Dialogic Literary Argumentation and highlighted what we see as it core components. Instead, the chapter continues our effort to move Dialogic Literary Argumentation forward in conversations about literature instruction and argumentative writing by putting forth some perspectives that emerge from the previous chapters.

Literature Is Not Devalued or Diminished in Dialogic Literary Argumentation

As we pointed out earlier, literature continues to be the central disciplinary content of English language arts (Applebee, 1974), and as we discussed in Chapters 1 and 2, how literature might be selected, taught, discussed, understood, and written about has been the object of intense debate among English language arts educators for decades. Thus, it occupies a special but contested place in the field. For many, perhaps most, teachers, literature is something to be learned about as a subject with its own inherent value. This is a difficult stance to move teachers away from, and against this backdrop, we recognize that our notion of the literary text as a prop and what that framework suggests for literature instruction, especially in conjunction with argumentative writing, may be perceived as threatening or at least disquieting. Thus, as we close this book, we want to make clear where we stand with the teaching, learning, reading, and writing about literature.

We have explained that within the Dialogic Literary Argumentation framework, literary texts do not sit on pedestals to be gazed upon and admired and treated as objects to be studied in their own right so that students may acquire various kinds of literary information that is deemed to be important in teaching and learning standards, in curricula, and in textbooks. Nor do we assume that the reader is the final arbiter of what counts as meaning. Once again, we view literary texts as props that, when talked about with other readers and written about argumentatively with other writers, foster invaluable opportunities for dialogic interactions that allow students to connect literary texts meaningfully with the human condition and their own experiences. While reader response theory is often proffered as a way to foster student involvement and New Criticism approaches as providing techniques for the study of individual texts, these two traditions often produce tensions and inconsistencies within the classroom rather than a coherent and integrated approach to the teaching and learning of literature (Applebee, 1993). However, our efforts reside not in dismissing any perspective but to offer teachers another way of conceptualizing and enacting the teaching and learning in English language arts classrooms.

For us, this does not make literature less important nor does it suggest disrespect for the literary text itself, for the reader or for the traditions of criticism that shape literary studies. Echoing the concept of literature as a prop, Leki (1993) notes that "a [literary] text is not a puzzle or a dictator; it is a partner in a dialogue, in a negotiation" (p. 21). This is how many of the teachers with whom we have collaborated with over 12 years approached the literary texts with which they elected to work. The texts were selected not strictly for their literary properties but also because of the possibilities they presented for the creation, consideration, and exploration of multiple perspectives within a dialectical space that would foster student learning about themselves and lead to participation in what can be called "responsive argumentation" in ways that prepare students for the worlds they live in both in and out of school.

For those concerned about Dialogic Literary Argumentation as a set of frameworks that limit the value of the literary text, the dialogically grounded model we have demonstrated values the text and literature instruction but in new and different ways. What we problematize are standard ways of treating literary texts that limit what students can gain from encounters with them. We assume that students can still learn about and appreciate literature. We do not reject the value of literary knowledge, the vocabulary of the discipline, or a range of theoretical perspectives; rather, we seek to integrate such sources of understanding with what we believe to be more important experiences and insights to be gleaned by students from dialogically grounded literary encounters that are negotiated and expressed through argumentation. Hence, as students use the tools of argumentation (and especially that approach to argumentation we call "arguing to learn") to interact jointly with texts and each other in Dialogic Literary Argumentation, new possibilities for literature instruction emerge. For example, by reframing "Indian Camp" as a case of dominance, Ms. Hill brought her students into new ways of seeing and experiencing that text as well as into new relationships with one another. It was not merely a text to be learned for literary purposes but rather a context for meaningful dialogue that, as the students exchanged perspectives on that theme, brought them into deeper engagement with themselves and their situatedness with the human condition. We saw similar

158   *Final Comments*

outcomes in the other chapters in this book. Using *The Great Gatsby* as a prop, Mr. Mosley took the role as facilitator and recorder of students' debates over Daisy's choice between two men offering two different futures for her and her children. Here, we see how both the dialogic and dialectics work in tandem as students were released into encounters with Daisy, and with each other, that brought into consideration of their own places in the world in relation to the human condition.

Dialogic Literary Argumentation Offers New Opportunities for Teaching and Learning Warranting

We knew from our own experience and from the research literature that teachers tend to rely on the Toulmin model of argumentation and that, as Smith, Wilhelm, and Fredricksen (2012) maintain, "warrants are the least understood element of Toulmin's model" (p. 14).[1] Hillocks (2011, p. 101) notes "the complexity of warrants." And, as noted earlier, we had compiled ample evidence of problems with warranting in students' writing. Thus, a topic of particular interest to us was how warranting would play out in the classrooms of the teachers we observed.

Something that has stood out to us during the past decade as we have observed argumentative writing instruction in numerous classrooms are the challenges teachers and students encounter with warranting. We saw this same issue in hundreds of pre-, post-, and delayed post-test essays student participants in our studies wrote (for details, see Newell et al., 2015). Even in many essays where we rated students highly in their use of claims and evidence, there was frequently a drop-off when we looked at their attempts at warranting. This was also a point that emerged during our summer workshops with teachers. They had their own uncertainties about warranting and how to teach it. As such, one of the most interesting developments we observed in the study reported in this book is how the collaborating teachers were able to work with warranting as they engaged in the social processes and practices that are central to Dialogic Literary Argumentation. However, warranting a literary argument did not become an issue until we began to witness its significance in instructional conversations: how students might read and understand a text are shaped by the teacher's willingness to explore the warrants and backing for the interpretations proffered during instructional conversations that are not just text based or grounded in canonical literary interpretations but in the students' and teacher's own lived experiences and in their engagement with each other.

An illustration of this was seen in Ms. Hill's classroom in Chapter 1 as she pressed her students to warrant their claims and evidence concerning the theme of dominance in a short story that she had introduced. Because the students had to sort through their own understandings of and experiences with dominance, rather than relying solely on the text, they were able to establish stronger ties between their claims and evidence. Warranting became a more personal and social process of reasoning than in traditional literature lessons, in which students engage only in close, and possibly decontextualized and disengaged, reading of and writing about the assigned literary text. Ms. Nelson's 11th-grade students began a unit on *Things Fall Apart* considering what she called "subtexts" to see beneath the surface of a text to the ideologies of what counts as successful versus failed cultures. Warranting became especially significant as Ms. Nelson shifted attention to the novel that she repurposed as a guidebook to understand the Umuofian culture. Perhaps as one of the more compelling uses of warranting, she asked students to role play members of a Human Rights agency who simultaneously took perspectives of a bureaucracy and their own personal views (as 11th graders) to weigh the affordances and limitation of intervening to "save" the Umuofian village from itself.

Rethinking the Relationship Between Writing and Literature

Part of our motivation for the research we discuss in this book was to examine argumentative writing differently to how we did in our earlier work (Newell et al., 2015) that was not specifically interested in literature instruction. We recognized a paradox: while researchers have focused on writing in and out of school on a range of personal, social, and political topics, much of the writing secondary school students do is about literature. Surely the nature of students' interpretation of literature needs to be considered concomitantly with writing. Accordingly, we saw an enticing opportunity to link our previous work in argumentative writing as a social practice with literature instruction as social construction of meaning in the text, in the interactions about the text, and in the connections between literary events and events from life as we know it.

On the one hand, there are technical challenges associated with warranting: understanding how it operates within and contributes to the Toulmin model and how to express warrants clearly and effectively. Then, too, daily discourse often lacks warranting, as Hillocks (2011) observes in his comment that "people make judgments all the time without questioning them or thinking them through" (p. 102). However, as we saw Dialogic Literary Argumentation evolving over the course of a school year, there were indicators of the kind Ms. Hill experienced, showing that the multiple perspectives, the construction of dialectical spaces, intertextuality, indexicality, and the social practices of the Dialogic Literary Argumentation–framed lessons enabled many students to move beyond this kind of problem articulated by Hillocks. That is, as the students sorted through their own thoughts and experiences and had to construct warrants, they experienced warranting more meaningfully and purposefully. On the whole, the social, interactional, and communicative practices and processes at the heart of Dialogic Literary Argumentation afforded teachers new and productive opportunities to work with warranting, to help demystify its definition and application in argumentative writing.

We see rich possibilities for further conceptualization and development of warranting in literature-based instruction within the context of Dialogic Literary Argumentation. For example, when Ms. Nelson assigned writing about *Things Fall Apart*, she did so after a series of instructional conversations and activities that allowed her students to unpack their underlying assumptions or warrants about how to respond to another cultural context quite alien to their own. Rather than simply mandating the inclusion of warrants into the structure of their essays, Ms. Nelson's writing assignment was contextualized as an inquiry into the question asking if a human rights organization should intervene in a Umuofian village. Her students were required to ground their arguments in explorations of both contextualized and decontextualized rationalities over a series of lessons that were quite intentionally oriented to clarifying and sharing the grounds for those arguments. Rather than one more feature of a structural requirement in an argumentative essay, warranting was part and parcel of the sense making as well as necessary for considering of the underlying rationalities of the students' arguments.

Dialogic Literary Argumentation Requires Sustained, Long-Term Effort and Commitment

As we explained in Chapter 1, Dialogic Literary Argumentation provides for the kinds of extended experiences with literary texts and argumentative writing that make literature-based argumentation a richer and more substantial experience for both teachers and students. Dialogic Literary Argumentation is not intended as the goal of a single instructional unit or a relatively brief encounter with literature that, for example, enables students to practice the ability to form a productive claim or to search for evidence in effective ways. In other words, it is not an isolated or short-term attempt to facilitate learning about argumentation and about literature. Instead, Dialogic Literary Argumentation is a much deeper commitment to ways of teaching, learning, reading, thinking, talking, and writing about literature that release students into the full potential for literary texts to shed light on personhood and the human condition.

This kind of learning does not happen in a sprint. Establishing the core features of a Dialogical Literary Argumentation classroom is an ongoing process that will be multi-faceted and not always smooth and linear. Dialogic Literary Argumentation requires teachers and students to view learning itself in different ways, ways that necessitate building a certain kind of classroom community in which students come to see each other as partners in social practices of learning. Thus, Dialogic Literary

Argumentation is a journey, and like many journeys, it needs time to evolve and to settle into productive instructional dynamics. In other words, Dialogic Literary Argumentation will not be instantiated through engagement with one literary text or over a short period of time.

Although the cases presented in this book focused on the teaching, learning, and reading of individual literary texts, those were successes embedded in year-long (and in some cases, multiple years) instructional plans and efforts. As was described in Chapter 5, Mr. Watson had planned his students' engagement with Dialogic Literary Argumentation across the year beginning with "Learning to Argue," and the "Allegory of the Cave" followed months later with a shift to "Arguing to Learn" and engagement with other literary works. During the latter part of the school year, Mr. Watson shared authority with his students as they worked in small groups. His approach, what we have called "Arguing to Learn," was to explore how their understandings of *Heart of Darkness* might inform their understanding of their own worlds. More simply stated, how the students engaged with *Heart of Darkness* near the end of the school year was presaged by all that they and Mr. Watson did previously starting at the very beginning of the school year.

As another example, consider Ms. Nelson and her students (Chapter 4). About midway through the school year, she and her students engaged with the novel *Things Fall Apart*. Committed to helping students view literary texts and the events they depict through multiple as well as multicultural and critical points of view, Ms. Nelson had begun the school year by introducing the students to her core notion of "ways of seeing" that she applied throughout the school year. By the time the curricular conversation focused on *Things Fall Apart* in the spring of that school year, the students had had numerous experiences with ways of seeing located within dialectical spaces. As we demonstrated in Chapter 4, Ms. Nelson problematized the standard approaches to the use of multiple perspectives and introduced "ways of seeing" as an alternative framing of such perspectives. Thus, important groundwork had been laid steadily as the school year progressed, so that the students were prepared for deeper engagement with "ways of seeing" and links to argumentation as well as literature.

This is the essence of Dialogic Literary Argumentation as we theorize it. Ms. Nelson, Mr. Watson, Ms. Hill, Mr. Mosley, Ms. McClure, and all of the teachers involved in the Argumentative Writing Project had a long-range view of what they wished to accomplish with literature and argumentation and thus were prepared for the extended engagement with the elements of Dialogic Literary Argumentation that we argue are necessary for meaningful application of the frameworks and techniques of Dialogic Literary Argumentation. Hence, another important takeaway from this book is that teachers wishing to adopt Dialogic Literary Argumentation frameworks must be prepared for a year-long journey through their curriculum and their instructional practices.

Dialogic Literary Argumentation will be new to students (and teachers), and they will need time to be acculturated into its nuances, perspectives, and priorities. This process of acculturation will unfold over experiences with multiple literary texts during the course of a school year. The elements of this long-term process are delineated in a companion text to this volume to focus in-depth on specific pedagogical aspects: *Teaching Literature Using Dialogic Literary Argumentation in Secondary Schools*. Meanwhile, in this book we are, as stated in the first chapter, introducing the elements of Dialogic Literary Argumentation as we currently understand it. That is, we are unveiling the frameworks that constitute Dialogic Literary Argumentation: the what and the why of Dialogic Literary Argumentation. The companion volume delves into the how, that is, how Dialogic Literary Argumentation can be employed by educators for the teaching of literature and writing. That volume will shed further light on the extended engagement with Dialogic Literary Argumentation shown in this book.

Dialogic Literary Argumentation Fosters a Non-Adversarial Classroom Ecology

Argument scholars have presented and debated approaches to argumentation since the work of Aristotle in ancient Greece. These debates have been important in our research on argumentation over the past decade, and they have continued to play a role in the work presented here. As we observed the teachers in this study and saw traces of Dialogic Literary Argumentation emerging from their instructional choices and practices, we were struck by how they tended to avoid the kinds of classroom exchanges that pit students against each other and foster a competitive atmosphere. Instead, students tended to be engaged in non-adversarial as opposed to adversarial exchanges (Belcher, 1997) that enable students to see the text, and themselves, in deeper ways because they eschew an approach to argumentation that leads to victory and defeat. The non-adversarial approach, derived from feminist theory (Annas & Tenney, 1996), proposes a treatment of argumentation where there are no winners or losers but instead partners in dialogue and the construction of knowledge, and this was how the teachers presented in this book operated.

Berrill (1996) asserts that "it may be that we are approaching our teaching of argument in ways that hinder its development" (p. 176) by framing argument as a competitive act in which the writer needs to emerge as the winner. What she and others refer to as the "argument as war" metaphor may "restrict reasoning processes" (p. 177). This line of reasoning might even be applied to the dominant "Toulmin model" that permeates English language arts classrooms and that we have long observed in our research. Gilbert (1997), for example, maintains that "Toulmin's greatest weakness, from one point of view, lies in the inherently adversarial nature of his approach. . . . There will be one winner and one loser" (p. 10). The teachers we presented in this book moved in the opposite direction because they approached literary texts as occasions for learning about what it means to be human and used argumentative resources in ways that generate collaborative communities inside the classroom, communities that sought mutual respect. Learning to speak and write about literature in non-adversarial ways where the purpose is not to "silence the opposition" (Berrill, 1996, p. 185) but rather to learn from different points of view in the process of generating well-reasoned arguments allows more beneficial learning about oneself and the human condition in addition to argumentation itself.

Ms. Nelson in Chapter 4 exemplified this non-adversarial approach in her commitment to what she called "creating consensus" instead of an adversarial atmosphere as group and class discussions and presentations occurred. She helped the students become mutual stakeholders in their dialogic interactions, so that there was shared understanding, instead of oppositional dynamics, as the class discussed and responded to *Things Fall Apart*. The kinds of dialogic exchanges and interactions we see as central to Dialogic Literary Argumentation mesh well with, and help promote, this non-adversarial framing of argumentation. This was not something we encouraged the participating teachers to adopt; instead, it emerged organically for them as they ventured into instructional practices that reflected frameworks at the heart of Dialogic Literary Argumentation.

Teaching and Learning Literature as an Exploration of Personhood

In their conversations about a literary text (or more accurately, a set of texts) and in the literary text(s) itself, teachers and students together are always negotiating what it means be human, when, where, how, and with what consequences. This idea permeates the case studies of teaching and learning Dialogic Literary Argumentation that we have described at some length in this book. Specifically, the classrooms we have observed provide robust and powerful instances of how and when personhood is socially constructed. Whether discussing characters in a post–World War II southern town or human rights in a Umuofian village or considering Daisy's dilemma as she decides whom to spend her life with, these are all examples—we might say "storied cases"—of what it means to be a person. That is, how do we see others, imagined or real, as human with all the rights and privileges that we might want for ourselves, whether in the domains of family, bureaucratic institutions, politics, religion, and so forth. Personhood as a construct was most visibly captured in Ms. McClure's classroom as she asked her students to generate essential questions to explore ethical issues and moral complexity prompted by

164 *Final Comments*

their reading of *Inside the Hotel Rwanda*. Our analysis of the nominalizations of personhood in the whole class discussion revealed two interrelated kinds of moves the teacher made to humanize characters: (a) what kinds of people are nominalized and (b) the acceptance of the categories, components, and qualities offered. But it is important to understand that Ms. McClure's efforts to examine the quality of forgiveness was a way she supported her students as human beings with their own experiences and agency to develop essential questions for their own interpretations. Worth noting is the manner in which she fosters an arguable question by locating the quality of personhood in a dialectical space by suggesting the opposition between an inherent and universal quality of a person, a learned quality, or a quality of being human.

The Role of Teacher Agency and Expertise in Enacting Dialogic Literary Argumentation

A point we stressed early in this book and at later points is that the study we report on did not begin with us handing participating teachers a preset or scripted approach to literature instruction called Dialogic Literary Argumentation. When the teachers were recruited for the study and took part in our summer workshop before the school year in which data gathering occurred, we orchestrated discussions of literature and argumentation that were open ended and presented no boundaries on how the teachers were to teach literature in the particular classes we would observe. Nor did we impose a particular approach to argumentation or argumentative writing; instead, we explored different approaches to argumentative writing based on the principled practices that we had begun to articulate in a concept paper that we shared with the collaborating teachers.[2]

As researchers, during the summer workshops and monthly teacher meetings, we provided the principles of Dialogic Literary Argumentation, but it was the teachers who took charge of making curricular plans for and enacting the principles within their classrooms. We saw and discussed, as a group, initial or working drafts of those plans as the workshop ended and we moved toward the beginning of the school year, but in the final analysis, it was the teachers who initiated and enacted the principles into their practices leaving traces of what we eventually came to call Dialogic Literary Argumentation. This was true during the summer workshop, in their classrooms throughout the school year, and when we held teacher meetings. Thus, an important takeaway from this book is the recognition and understanding of the teachers and their engagement with the instructional dynamics through which Dialogic Literary Argumentation emerged.

What was intriguing and exciting for us was seeing how the teachers themselves began to tease out what eventually became important elements of Dialogic Literary Argumentation. What was equally meaningful for us was seeing the agency the teachers exercised as they embraced the opportunity to link argumentation and literature instruction in new ways. Here, we see a connection to teacher cognition research, which, as Borg (2003) says, has found that teachers who are highly engaged in their profession "are active, thinking decision-makers who make instructional choices by drawing on complex, practically-oriented, personalized, and context-sensitive networks of knowledge, thoughts and beliefs" (p. 81). In other words, they have agency when they think and act in such ways. Instead of staying within the boundaries of what Hatano and Inagaki (1986) call "routine expertise," where experts "learn merely to perform a skill faster and more accurately, without constructing or enriching their conceptual knowledge" (p. 266), the teachers presented in this book were agentic. Where routine experts stay within the comfort zone of instructional actions that have worked to some extent over a long period of time, the teachers we observed willingly and actively stepped out of their comfort zones. As Kayi-Adyar (2015) explains, "When individuals take on agentic positions, they have the capacity or willingness to act" (p. 95). This is what we saw in the teachers shown in the previous chapters. And this agentic attitude and activity was necessary to the construction of Dialogic Literary Argumentation.

To cite a few examples from earlier chapters, Ms. Hill eschewed the traditional approach of teaching "Indian Camp" as a story of initiation by introducing the topic of dominance and having her students explore, from different directions (using claims, evidence, and warrants), the application of that possible theme. In doing so, she went out on an instructional limb, not knowing how well that approach would work. Her classroom became a place where students were engaged in a process of reasoning in which, as we have previously articulated, the literary text served as a prop instead of the focus of the inquiry taking shape. This was an agentive act on her part. She chose to teach "Indian Camp" not as an exemplar of certain literary techniques students should learn in a literature lesson or course, but rather as what we earlier called a "storied case" that helped foster dialogic interactions that had personal value and relevance for the students.

We saw similar agentive behavior on the part of Ms. Field, who moved from the previous school year's focus on the three-prong essay that treated argument as structure to an emphasis on arguing to learn via interaction with a literary text. The three-prong essay structure was one she knew well and that many of her students were also quite familiar with, having been in her class the previous school year. Now she took them in a new direction by raising the possibility that the beloved main character of *To Kill a Mockingbird*, Atticus Finch, was not necessarily a hero. The more conventional learning to argue approach would have been to ask the students to search the text for evidence in support of the long-standing claim that Atticus was a hero. In asking the students to read and discuss two essays presenting contrasting views on the issue of Atticus as hero and leaving open the question of whether Atticus was a hero, Ms. Field introduced a more complex dynamic into the treatment of the novel, one where the notion of hero was interrogated from different vantage points. This was something she *chose* to do in an effort to make writing argumentatively about literature more meaningful for her students as well as to make a literary text more than a set of literary features to be learned. This process began with her own agency as a teacher of literature and writing.

Why does this issue of agency matter in our examination of Dialogic Literary Argumentation? There are two answers to this question. One is that implementation of the core features of Dialogic Literary Argumentation that our work has theorized requires agentive teachers like those presented in this book. These are the teachers Hatano and Inagaki (1986) would call "adaptive experts," that is, those who are willing to acquire and to experiment with new conceptual knowledge and are prepared to treat the literary text as a prop toward students' deeper understanding, not of literature only as a subject, but of themselves while they collectively explore issues like dominance and the true meaning of hero, as in the classes taught by Ms. Hill and Ms. Field, respectively (also see Newell et al., 2017). Our hope is that adoption of a pedagogy rooted in Dialogical Literary Argumentation will help promote the kind of agentive behavior we saw in the classrooms we observed.

The second reason agency matters is that Dialogic Literary Argumentation not only has the capacity to facilitate teacher agency, but also that teacher agency, in part, defines Dialogic Literary Argumentation. This was true not just in the class sessions we observed but also in the summer workshops and in the teacher meetings we held. Put another way, the teachers who took risks and reflected on and revised their approaches to using argumentation for literature learning did much more than adapt a program for teaching; they reflected a set of principles and understandings and refracted them in anticipation of their classroom community's needs, histories, and goals and in doing so shaped what it meant to use and take up Dialogic Literary Argumentation.

The teacher agency dimension of Dialogic Literary Argumentation is also important because of its implications for broadening understanding of teacher expertise, which we have been interested in throughout our research on argumentation. We have been guided in particular by the routine-adaptive expertise distinction noted earlier and address that topic in Newell et al. (2015). There, as also shown in Newell et al. (2017), we continued to explore aspects of teacher expertise as we moved to our research on Dialogic Literary Argumentation. However, where early teacher expertise scholarship focused on the novice–expert distinction (Berliner, 1986; Shulman, 1986), we have been guided by the work of

Bereiter and Scardamalia (1993) as well as Hatano and Inagaki. Observing the limitations of the novice–expert dichotomy during their research on composition, Bereiter and Scardamalia (1993) proposed that the emphasis in expertise research should be placed on "the process of expertise" (p. 82) instead of expertise as a state delineated by the amount of experience a teacher has (little or none for the novice; a great deal for the expert). The agentive teachers we have shown in this book have helped us better understand this "process of expertise" and what it entails as we observed the teachers navigating the dynamics of what became Dialogic Literary Argumentation. As we continue our work with Dialogic Literary Argumentation, we intend to learn more about the expertise domains associated with Dialogic Literary Argumentation pedagogy.

Dialogic Literary Argumentation Helps Teachers and Students Shift From the Common Emphasis on "Learning to Argue" to the Less Explored But No Less Important Territory of "Arguing to Learn"

One of the most important takeaways from this book is what it shows regarding the elusive but significant "arguing to learn" dimension of argumentation. In the book based on our previous study (Newell et al., 2015), we explored in depth the limitations of an "argument as structure" approach to pedagogy. This heavily structural orientation, we said, is one where "argumentative writing is conceptualized as a particular type of writing with a preset form, and what students need to learn are the components, structures, and qualities of that form" (p. 7). This is the essence of learning to argue, and while that is part of the equation involved in learning how to write argumentatively, we wanted to move to the other side of the equation: arguing to learn.

Teaching and Learning Literature as an Exploration of the Human Condition

Since the Report of the Committee of Ten in 1894 when "English" became a school subject area until the present moment, literature teaching and learning has been framed as life skills, as an academic discipline, as key to personal growth, and as a path to cultural literacy. Various curricular models have been proffered to ensure basic skills, cultural heritage, and self-understanding through literary experience. We do not deny the value of this long conversation about the teaching of literature as a necessary consideration for what role literature might have not only in the curriculum but also in the lives of students. However, Dialogic Literary Argumentation offers a somewhat different and unique contribution shaped by a concern that Rosenblatt voiced in the first paragraph of *Literature as Exploration* (1999):

168 *Final Comments*

> In a turbulent age, our schools and colleges must prepare the student to meet unprecedented and unpredictable problems. He *(sic)* needs to understand himself *(sic)*; he *(sic)* needs to work out harmonious relationships with other people. He *(sic)* must achieve a philosophy, an inner center from which to view in perspective the shifting society about him *(sic)*; he *(sic)* will influence for good or ill its future development. Any knowledge about humankind and society that school can give him *(sic)* should be assimilated into the stream of his *(sic)* actual life.
>
> (p. 3)

Although Rosenblatt's assumption of the masculine identity of "student" is jarring, her introductory statement has significant import for our concept of Dialogic Literary Argumentation. We have argued for the use of literature as a prop to examine the human condition or what Rosenblatt describes as "knowledge about humankind and society." In subsequent pages of *Literature as Exploration*, Rosenblatt first indicates that "Teachers of literature have been too modest about their possible contributions to these demands" (p. 4). And then she warns that she is not proposing a return "to the horrors of the didactic, moralistic approach to literature" (p. 4). Her alternative is for "the teacher of literature will be the first to admit that he *(sic)* inevitably deals with the experience of human beings in their diverse personal and social relations" (p. 5).

We reference Rosenblatt's argument not to agree or disagree with her central contribution to conceptualize the centrality of the transactional experience of the reader with a literary text but to point out that we now recognize some of her unfinished business that became the central theme of our project. We understand that literary meaning does not begin and end with the individual reader. We argue that "both in their conversations about a literary text (or more accurately, a set of texts) and in the literary text(s) itself, teachers and students together are always negotiating what it means be human, when, where, how, and with what consequences" (p. 26). This suggests the significance of literature teaching and learning as a way of coming to a deeper understanding of "the other" in a heterogenous society that aspires to foster democratic and humane principles. Perhaps what was not so surprising is that in classroom discussions concern about what it means to be human—what we have called personhood—students were strikingly and oftentimes passionately interested in both discussing and writing about literature. As one student in our study described, "It's like the stakes are really high and I am trying to figure out if I should say something or just sit still for a while and just listen to what is going on." This student's pause to "just listen to what is going on" is maybe one of the more important dimensions of Dialogic Literary Argumentation.

Notes

1. A thorough reading of Toulmin's writings on argument and argumentation reveals a more complex, situated, varied, and nuanced approach than many teachers attribute to him (see Toulmin, 2003). Many of the teachers we have encountered at professional conferences and elsewhere are referring only to terminology and definitions when they reference the Toulmin model of argumentation.
2. Principled practice, suggested by Applebee (1986), proposes that a relationship between research and practice in that research on teaching "should focus on . . . using the skills of the researcher to articulate and sharpen the intuition of the skilled practitioner. . . . Models of principled practice would rely on the expertise of the practicing teacher to transform those principles into realistic approaches for the particular context of schooling" (pp. 6–7).

References

Agha, A. (2007). *Language and social relations*. New York: Cambridge University Press.

Agha, A., & Wortham, S. (2005). Discourse across speech-events: Intertextuality and interdiscursivity in social life. *Journal of Linguistic Anthropology, 15*(1), 1–5.

Alsup, J. (2015). *A case for teaching literature in the secondary school: Why reading fiction matters in an age of scientific objectivity and standardization*. New York: Routledge.

Althusser, L. (1970). *Lenin and philosophy and other essays*. New York: Verso.

Anderson, K. T. (2009). Applying positioning theory to the analysis of classroom interactions: Mediating micro-identities, macro-kinds, and ideologies of knowing. *Linguistics and Education, 20*(4), 291–310.

Annas, P. J., & Tenney, D. (1996). Positioning oneself: A feminist perspective on argument. In B. Emmell, P. Resch, & D. Tenney (Eds.), *Argument revisited; Argument redefined* (pp. 127–152). Thousand Oaks, CA: Sage.

Applebee, A. N. (1974). *Tradition and reform in the teaching of English: A history*. Urbana, IL: National Council of Teachers of English.

Applebee, A. N. (1986). Musings . . . principled practice. *Research in the Teaching of English, 20*(1), 5–7.

Applebee, A. N. (1993). *Literature in the secondary school: Studies of curriculum and instruction in the United States*. Urbana, IL: National Council of Teachers of English.

Applebee, A. N. (1996). *Curriculum as conversation: Transforming traditions of teaching and learning*. Chicago: University of Chicago Press.

Applebee, A. N., Burroughs, R., & Stevens, A. S. (2000). Creating continuity and coherence in high school literature curricula. *Research in the Teaching of English, 34*(3), 396–429.

Appleman, D. (2015). *Critical encounters in secondary English: Teaching literary theory to adolescents* (3rd ed.). New York: Teachers College Press.

Arendt, H. (1959). *The human condition*. New York: Doubleday.

Arendt, H. (1977/2000). *Eichmann in Jerusalem: A report on the banality of evil*. New York: Penguin Publishing Group.

Bakhtin, M. M. (1981). *The dialogic imagination* (C. Emerson & M. Holquist, Trans.). Austin, TX: University of Texas Press.

Bakhtin, M. M. (1935/1984). *Problems of Dostoevsky's poetics* (C. Emerson, Trans.). Minneapolis: University of Minnesota Press.

Bakhtin, M. M. (1953/1986). *Speech genres and other late essays.* Austin, TX: University of Texas Press.

Barnes, D. R. (1976). *From communication to curriculum.* Harmondsworth: Penguin Education.

Baynham, M., & Prinsloo, M. (Ed.). (2009). *The future of literacy studies.* New York: Palgrave Macmillan.

Bazerman, C. (2004a). Intertextuality: How texts rely on other texts. In P. Prior & C. Bazerman (Eds.), *What writing does and how it does it: An introduction to analyzing texts and textual practices* (pp. 83–96). New York: Routledge.

Bazerman, C. (2004b). Intertextualities: Volosinov, Bakhtin, literary theory, and literacy studies. In A. Ball & S. W. Freedman (Eds.), *Bakhtinian perspectives on languages, literacy, and learning* (pp. 53–65). Cambridge: Cambridge University Press.

Bazerman, C. (2008). Theories of the middle range in historical studies of writing practice. *Written Communication, 25*(3), 298–318.

Beach, R., & Beauchemin, F. (2019). *Teaching language as action in the ELA classroom.* New York: Taylor & Francis.

Beach, R., & Bloome, D. (Eds.). (2019). *Languaging relations for transforming the literacy and language arts classroom.* New York: Routledge.

Beach, R., & Swiss, T. (2011). Literary theories and teaching of English language arts. In D. Lapp & D. Fisher (Eds.), *Handbook of research on teaching the English language arts* (3rd ed., pp. 145–151). New York: Routledge.

Beauchemin, F. (2019). Reconceptualizing classroom life as relational-key. In R. Beach & D. Bloome (Eds.), *Languaging relations for transforming the literacy and language arts classroom* (pp. 49–68). New York: Routledge.

Becker, A. (1991). Language and languaging. *Language & Communication, 11*(1–2), 33–35.

Belcher, D. D. (1997). An argument for non-adversarial argument: On the relevance of the feminist critique of academic discourse to L2 writing pedagogy. *Journal of Second Language Writing, 6,* 1–21.

Benedict, R. (2005 [orig. 1946]). *The chrysanthemum and the sword: Patterns of Japanese culture.* Boston, MA: Houghton Mifflin Harcourt.

Bereiter, C., & Scardamalia, M. (1993). *Surpassing ourselves: An inquiry into the nature and implications of expertise.* Chicago and La Salle, IL: Open Court.

Berger, P. L., & Luckman, T. (1991). *The social construction of reality: A treatise in the sociology of knowledge.* London: Penguin.

Berliner, D. C. (1986). In pursuit of the expert pedagogue. *Educational Researcher, 15*(7), 5–13.

Bernstein, B. (1975). *Class and pedagogies: Visible and invisible.* London: Routledge.

Bernstein, B. (1990). *The structuring of pedagogic discourse.* London: Routledge.

Berrill, D. P. (1996). Reframing argument from the metaphor of war. In D. P. Berrill (Ed.), *Perspectives on written argument* (pp. 171–187). Cresskill, NJ: Hampton Press.

Bertau, M-C. (2014). Introduction: The self within the space-time of language performance. *Theory & Psychology, 24*(4), 433–441.

Bewley, M. (1954). Scott Fitzgerald's criticism of America. *The Sewanee Review, 62*(2), 223–246.

Biemann, A. D. (2002). Introduction. In A. D. Biemann (Ed.), *The Martin Buber reader: Essential writings* (pp. 1–20). New York: Palgrave Macmillan.

Blackburn, M. (2019). Literacy teaching and learning in school as polyphonic: A close examination of a lesson focused on *Fun Home*, the graphic memoir and musical. In D. Bloome, M. L. Castanheira, C. Leung, & J. Rowsell (Eds.), *Re-theorizing literacy practices: Complex social and cultural contexts* (pp. 115–125). New York: Routledge.

Blackburn, M. V., & Schultz, K. (2015). *Interrupting hate: Homophobia in schools and what literacy can do about it*. New York: Teachers College Press.

Bleich, D. (1975). The subjective character of critical interpretation. *College English, 36*(7), 739–755.

Blommaert, J., & Jie, D. (2010). *Ethnographic fieldwork*. Bristol, UK: Multilingual Matters.

Bloome, D., & Beauchemin, F. (2016). Languaging everyday life in classrooms. *Literacy Research: Theory, Method, and Practice, 65*, 152–165.

Bloome, D., Beierle, M., Grigorenko, M., & Goldman, S. (2009). Learning over time: Uses of intercontextuality, collective memories, and classroom chronotopes in the construction of learning opportunities in a ninth-grade language arts classroom. *Language and Education, 23*(4), 313–334.

Bloome, D., Carter, S. P., Christian, B., Otto, S., & Shuart-Faris, N. (2005). *Discourse analysis and the study of classroom language and literacy events: A microethnographic perspective*. New York: Routledge.

Bloome, D., Castanheira, M., Leung, C., & Rowsell, J. (Eds.). (2019). *Re-theorizing literacy practices*. New York: Routledge.

Bloome, D., & Egan-Robertson, A. (1993). The social construction of intertextuality and classroom reading and writing. *Reading Research Quarterly, 28*(4), 303–333.

Bloome, D., Puro, P., & Theodorou, E. (1989). Procedural display and classroom lessons. *Curriculum Inquiry, 19*, 265–291.

Borg, S. (2003). Teacher cognition in language teaching: A review of research on what language teachers think, know, believe, and do. *Language Teaching, 36*, 81–109.

Bourdieu, P. (1977). *Outline of a theory of practice*. New York: Cambridge University Press.

Bowles, S., & Gintis, H. (1986). *Democracy and capitalism*. New York: Basic Books.

Brooks, C. (1947). *The well wrought urn: Studies in the structure of poetry*. Boston, MA: Houghton Mifflin Harcourt.

Brooks, C., & Warren, R. P. (1938). *Understanding poetry*. New York: Harcourt Brace Jovanovich College Publishers.

Buber, M. (1966). *The way of response* (N. N. Glatzer, Ed.). New York: Schocken Books.

Buber, M. (1976). *I and thou* (2nd ed.). New York: Charles Scribner's Sons.

Burke, K. (1972). *The philosophy of literary form*. Berkeley, CA: University of California Press.

Butler, J. (1990/2007). *Gender trouble: Feminism and the subversion of identity*. New York: Routledge Classics.

Callahan, J. F. (1996). F. Scott Fitzgerald's evolving American dream: The "pursuit of happiness" in Gatsby, tender is the night, and the last tycoon. *Twentieth Century Literature, 42*(3), 374–395.

References 173

Carter, S. P. (2007). "Reading All that White Crazy Stuff": Black young women unpacking whiteness in a high school British literature classroom. *The Journal of Classroom Interaction*, 41/42(2–1), 42–54.

Castanheira, M., Crawford, T., Green, J., & Dixon, C. (2001). Interactional ethnography: An approach to studying the social construction of literate practices. *Linguistics and Education*, 11(4), 353–400.

Caughlan, S. (2007). Competing cultural models of literature in state content standards. In D. W. Rowe et al. (Eds.), *The fifty-sixth yearbook of the national reading conference* (pp. 178–190). Oak Creek, WI: National Reading Conference.

Chotiner, I. (2009, August 2). What is Malcolm Gladwell talking about? *The New Republic*. Retrieved from https://newrepublic.com/article/51326/what-malcolm-gladwell-talking-about

Cook-Gumperz, J. (Ed.). (1986). *The social construction of literacy*. Cambridge, England: Cambridge University Press.

Dafermos, M. (2018). Relating dialogue and dialectics: A philosophical perspective. *Dialogic Pedagogy: An International Online Journal*, 6. Retrieved May 22, 2019, from https://files.eric.ed.gov/fulltext/EJ1166855.pdf

Davies, B., & Harré, R. (1990). Positioning: The discursive production of selves. *Journal for the Theory of Social Behaviour*, 20(1), 43–63.

De Certeau, M. (1984). *The practice of everyday life*. Berkeley, CA: University of California Press.

Defalco, J. (1963). *The hero in Hemingway's short stories*. Pittsburgh: University of Pittsburgh Press.

Derrida, J. (1967/2016). *Of grammatology*. Baltimore, MD: John Hopkins University Press.

Dillard, C. B. (2012). *On spiritual strivings: Transforming an African American woman's academic life*. Albany, NY: State University of New York Press.

Dussel, E. (2013). *Ethics of liberation*. Durham, NC: Duke University Press.

Eagleton, T. (2003). *Marxism and literary criticism*. New York: Routledge.

Edmiston, B. (2013). *Transforming teaching and learning with active and dramatic approaches: Engaging students across the curriculum*. New York: Routledge.

Egan-Robertson, A. (1998). Learning about culture, language, and power: Understanding relationships among personhood, literacy practices, and intertextuality. *Journal of Literacy Research*, 30(4), 449–487.

Erickson, F., & Shultz, J. (1977). When is a context? *Newsletter of the Laboratory for Comparative Human Cognition*, 1(2), 5–12.

Fish, S. E. (1980). *Is there a text in this class? The authority of interpretive communities*. Cambridge, MA: Harvard University Press.

Fetterley, J. (1978). *The resisting reader: A feminist approach to American fiction*. Bloomington, IN: Indiana University Press.

Flyvbjerg, B. (2000). Ideal theory, real rationality: Habermas versus Foucault and Nietzsche. In *Papers for the political studies association's 50th annual conference, the challenges for democracy in the 21st century* (pp. 1–20). London: London School of Economics and Political Science.

Foucault, M. (1961/2013). *History of madness*. New York: Routledge.

Fowler, C. (2004). *The archaeology of personhood: An anthropological approach*. New York: Routledge.

Freire, P. (1970). *Pedagogy of the oppressed* (M. B. Ramos, Trans.). New York: Continuum.

Friedman, M. S. (2003). *Martin Buber: The life of dialogue*. New York: Routledge.
Fuentes, C. (2007). *This I believe: An a to z of a life*. New York: Random House.
Gadamer, H-G. (1976). *Philosophical hermeneutics*. Berkeley, CA: University of California Press.
Gadamer, H. G. (1989). *Truth and method* (2nd ed., J. Weimsheimer & D. Marshall, Trans.). London: Sheed & Ward (Original work published in 1960 as Wahrheit und Methode).
Gates, H. L., Jr. (2014). *The signifying monkey: A theory of African American literary criticism*. New York: Oxford University Press.
Geertz, C. (1973). *The interpretation of cultures: Selected essays*. New York: Basic Books.
Geertz, C. (1979). "From the native's point of view": On the nature of anthropological understanding. In K. Basso & H. Shelby (Eds.), *Meaning in anthropology* (pp. 225–241). Albuquerque, NM: University of New Mexico Press.
Geertz, C. (1983). *Local knowledge: Further essays in interpretive anthropology*. New York: Basic Books.
Gergen, K. J. (1999). *An invitation to social construction*. Thousand Oaks, CA: Sage.
Gergen, K. J. (2001). *Social construction in context*. Thousand Oaks, CA: Sage.
Gergen, K. J., & Davis, K. E. (Eds.). (1985). *The social construction of the person*. New York: Springer-Verlag.
Gilbert, M. A. (1997). *Coalescent argumentation*. Mahwah, NJ: Lawrence Erlbaum.
Gilligan, C. (1993). *In a different voice: Psychological theory and women's development*. Cambridge, MA: Harvard University.
Giroux, H. (2011). *Zombie politics and culture in the age of casino capitalism*. New York: Peter Lang.
Gladwell, M. (2009). The courthouse ring: Atticus Finch and the limits of Southern liberalism. *The New Yorker*. Retrieved from www.newyorker.com/magazine/2009/08/10/the-courthouse-ring.
Goffman, E. (1963). *Behavior in public places*. New York: The Free Press.
Goldman, S. R., Britt, M. A., Brown, W., Cribb, G., George, M., Greenleaf, C., ... Project READI. (2016). Disciplinary literacies and learning to read for understanding: A conceptual framework for disciplinary literacy. *Educational Psychologist, 51*(2), 219–246.
Gourevitch, P. (1999). *We wish to inform you that tomorrow we will be killed with our families: Stories from Rwanda*. New York: Farrar, Strauss, and Giroux.
Graff, G. (1979). *Literature against itself: Literary ideas in modern society*. Chicago: University of Chicago Press.
Graff, G. (2001). Hidden intellectualism. *Pedagogy, 1*(1), 21–36.
Graff, G., & Birkenstein, C. (2018). *They say/I say: The moves that matter in academic writing*. (4th ed.). New York: W. W. Norton & Company, Inc.
Green, J. L., & Dixon, C. N. (1993). Talking knowledge into being: Discursive and social practices in classrooms. *Linguistics and Education, 5*(3–4), 231–239.
Green, J. L., & Wallat, C. (1981). Mapping instructional conversations: A sociolinguistic ethnography. In J. Green & C. Wallat (Eds.), *Ethnography and

language in educational settings (pp. 161–207). Norwood, NJ: Ablex Publishing Corporation.
Greene, M. (1968). Literature and human understanding. *Journal of Aesthetic Education*, 2(4), 11–21.
Greene, S., & Abt-Perkins, D. (Eds.). (2003). *Making race visible: Literacy research for cultural understanding*. New York: Teachers College Press.
Gumperz, J. J. (1982). *Discourse strategies*. Cambridge: Cambridge University Press.
Habermas, J. (1984). *The theory of communicative action* (Vol. I). Boston, MA: Beacon.
Halasek, K. (1999). *A pedagogy of possibility: Bakhtinian perspectives on composition studies*. Carbondale, IL: Southern Illinois University Press.
Halliday, M. A. K. (1998). Language and knowledge: The unpacking of text. In D. Allison, L. Wee, B. Zhiming, & S. A. Abraham (Eds.), *Text in education and society* (pp. 157–178). Singapore: Singapore University Press.
Hanks, W. F. (1989). Text and textuality. *Annual Review of Anthropology, 18*, 95–127.
Hanks, W. F. (1999). Indexicality. *Journal of Linguistic Anthropology, 9*, 124–126.
Hanks, W. F. (2000). *Intertexts: Writings on language, utterance, and context*. Lanham, MD: Rowman & Littlefield.
Hatano, G., & Inagaki, K. (1986). Two courses of expertise. In H. Stevenson, H. Azuma, & K. Hakuta (Eds.), *Child development and education in Japan* (pp. 262–272). New York: Freeman.
Heath, S., & Branscombe, A. (1986). The book as narrative prop in language acquisition. In B. Schieffelin & P. Gilmore (Eds.), *The acquisition of literacy: Ethnographic perspectives* (pp. 16–34). Norwood, NJ: Ablex Publishing Corporation.
Heath, S., & Street, B. (2008). *On ethnography: Approaches to language and literacy research*. New York: Teachers College Press.
Heathcote, D. (1991). *Collected writings on education and drama*. Evanston, IL: Northwestern University Press.
Hegel, G. W. F. (1812/2010). *The science of logic* (G. Di Giovanni, Trans and Ed.). Cambridge: Cambridge University Press.
Hillocks, G., Jr. (2011). *Teaching argument writing, grades 6–12: Supporting claims with relevant evidence and clear reasoning*. Portsmouth, NH: Heinemann.
Hodges, A. (2018). Intertextuality in discourse. In D. Tannen, H. Hamilton, & D. Schiffrin (Eds.), *The handbook of discourse analysis* (2nd ed., pp. 42–60). Oxford: Wiley Blackwell.
Hofer, B. K. (2000). Dimensionality and disciplinary differences in personal epistemology. *Contemporary Educational Psychology, 25*, 378–405.
Holland, D., & Leander, K. (2004). Ethnographic studies of positioning and subjectivity: An introduction. *Ethos, 32*(2), 127–139.
Holland, N. (1975). *The dynamics of literary response*. New York: W. W. Norton & Company Inc.
Holloway, K. F. (2013). *Legal fictions: Constituting race, composing literature*. Durham, NC: Duke University Press.

Hymes, D. (1974). *The foundations of sociolinguistics: Sociolinguistic ethnography*. Philadelphia, PA: University of Pennsylvania Press.

Hymes, D. (1980). *Language in education: Ethnolinguistic essays*. Washington, DC: Center for Applied Linguistics.

Isenberg, N. (2016). *White trash: The 400-year untold history of class in America*. New York: Viking.

Ivanič. R. (1998). *Writing and identity: The discoursal construction of identity in academic writing*. Amsterdam: John Benjamins Publishing Co.

Jago, C. (2013). What English classes should look like in the Common Core era. *Washington Post*. Retrieved from www.washingtonpost.com/news/answer-sheet/wp/2013/01/10/what-english-classes-should-look-like-in-common-core-era/?utm_term=.9ac0012a4312

Johnson, T. S., Thompson, L., Smagorinsky, P., & Fry, P. G. (2003). Learning to teach the five-paragraph theme. *Research in the Teaching of English*, 136–176.

Jorgensen, J. N. (2004). Languaging and languagers. In *Languaging and language practices* (pp. 5–23). Copenhagen: University of Copenhagen.

Kahneman, D. (2011). *Thinking, fast and slow*. New York: Farrar, Straus and Giroux.

Kahneman, D., Slovic, P., & Tversky, A. (Eds.). (1982). *Judgment under uncertainty: Heuristics and biases*. New York: Cambridge University Press.

Kant, I. (1997). *Critique of practical reason*. New York: Oxford University Press.

Kant, I. (2009). *Groundwork of the metaphysic of morals*. New York: Harper Collins.

Kayi-Adyar, H. (2015). Teacher agency, positioning, and English language learners: Voices of pre-service classroom teachers. *Teaching and Teacher Education*, 45, 94–103.

Kayihura, E., & Zukus, K. (2014). *Inside the Hotel Rwanda*. Dallas, TX: Benbella Books.

Ketter, J., & Lewis, C. (2004). Learning as social interaction: Interdiscursivity in a teacher and researcher study group. In R. Rogers (Ed.), *An introduction to critical discourse analysis in education* (pp. 147–176). New York: Routledge.

Kim, M. Y. (2018). *Theorizing languaging thinking as ways of reading: A microethnographic study in an English language arts classroom* (Doctoral dissertation), The Ohio State University.

Kintsch, W., & van Dijk, T. (1978). Toward a model of text comprehension and production. *Psychological Review*, 85(5), 363–394.

Kriesberg, S. (1991). *Transforming power: Domination, empowerment, and education*. Albany, NY: State University of New York Press.

Kristeva, J. (1986). *The Kristeva reader*. New York: Columbia University Press.

Kuhn, D. (1991). *The skills of argument*. New York: Cambridge University Press.

Kuhn, D., Hemberger, L., & Khait, V. (2016). *Argue with me: Argument as a path to developing students' thinking and writing* (2nd ed.). New York: Routledge.

Langer, J. A. (1995). Literature and learning to think. *Journal of Curriculum and Supervision*, 10(3), 207–226.

Langer, J. A. (2011). *Envisioning literature: Literary understanding and literature instruction*. New York: Teachers College Press.

Latour, B. (2005). *Reassembling the social: An introduction to actor-network theory*. New York: Oxford University Press.

Layton, L. (2012, December 2). Common Core State standards in English spark war over words. *Washington Post*. Retrieved March 27, 2019, from www.washingtonpost.com/local/education/common-core-state-standards-in-english-spark-war-over-words/2012/12/02/4a9701b0-38e1–11e2–8a97–363b0f9a0ab3_story.html?utm_term=.2fae6621f8e7

Lee, C. D. (1993). *Signifying as a scaffold for literary interpretation: The pedagogical implications of an African American discourse genre*. Urbana, IL: National Council of Teachers of English.

Lee, C. D. (2007). *Culture, literacy, and learning: Taking bloom in the midst of the whirlwind*. New York: Teachers College Press.

Leki, I. (1993). Reciprocal themes in ESL reading and writing. In. J. G. Carson & I. Leki (Eds.), *Reading in the composition classroom: Second language perspectives* (pp. 9–32). Boston, MA: Heinle & Heinle.

Lemke, J. L. (2000). Across the scales of time: Artifacts, activities, and meanings in ecosocial systems. *Mind, Culture, and Activity, 7*(4), 273–290.

Levine, S., & Horton, W. S. (2013). Using affective appraisal to help readers construct literary interpretations. *Scientific Study of Literature, 3*(1), 105–136.

Lewis, W. E., & Ferretti, R. P. (2011). Topoi and literary interpretation: The effects of a critical reading and writing intervention on high school students' analytic literary essays. *Contemporary Educational Psychology, 36*(4), 334–354.

Lloyd-Jones, R., & Lunsford, A. A. (Eds.). (1989). *The English coalition conference: Democracy through Language*. Urbana, IL: National Council of Teachers of English.

Lunsford, A. A., Ruszkiewicz, J. J., & Walters, K. (2004). *Everything's an argument*. Boston, MA: Bedford/St. Martin's.

Lysaker, J., & Wessel-Powell, C. (2019). Comprehending as a manner of living. In R. Beach, & D. Bloome (Eds.), *Languaging relations for transforming the literacy and language arts classroom* (pp. 172–192). New York: Routledge.

Macaluso, M. (2017). Teaching to kill a mockingbird today: Coming to terms with race, racism, and America's novel. *Journal of Adolescent & Adult Literacy, 61*(3), 279–287.

Madsen, L. M., Karrebæk, M. S., & Møller, J. S. (Eds.). (2015). *Everyday languaging: Collaborative research on the language use of children and youth*. Berlin: Walter de Gruyter.

Mailloux, S. (1982). *Interpretive conventions: The reader in the study of American literature*. Ithaca, NY: Cornell University Press.

Mandell, B. (1980). *Three language arts curriculum models: Pre-kindergarten through college*. Retrieved from www.library.illinois.edu/archives/archon

Marx, K. (1868/2004). *Capital: A critique of political economy*. New York: Penguin.

McEwan, I. (2005). Literature, science, and human nature. In J. Gottschall & D. S. Wilson (Eds.), *The literary animal: Evolution and the nature of narrative* (pp. 5–19). Evanston, IL: Northwestern University Press.

Mellor, B., O'Neill, M., & Patterson, A. (1991). *Reading fictions*. Perth, Australia: Chalkface Press.

Merriam-Webster Dictionary. (2019). Retrieved May 3, from www.merriam-webster.com/dictionary/dialectic

Miall, D. S., & Kuiken, D. (1994). Foregrounding, defamiliarization, and affect: Response to literary stories. *Poetics, 22*(5), 389–407.

Morrison, T. (1992). *Playing in the dark: Whiteness and the literary imagination*. Cambridge, MA: Harvard University Press.

Mulligan, R. (1962). *To kill a mockingbird* [movie].

Newell, G., Bloome, D., & Hirvela, A. (2015). *Teaching and learning argumentative writing in high school English language arts classrooms*. New York: Routledge.

Newell, G. E., Beach, R., Smith, J., & VanDerHeide, J. (2011). Teaching and learning argumentative reading and writing: A review of research. *Reading Research Quarterly, 46*(3), 273–304.

Newell, G. E., Goff, B., Buescher, E., Weyand, L., Thanos, T., & Kwak, S. (2017). Adaptive expertise in teaching and learning of literary argumentation in high school English language arts classroom. In R. K. Durst, G. E. Newell, & J. D. Marshall (Eds.), *English language arts research and teaching: Revisiting and expanding Arthur Applebee's contributions* (pp. 157–171). New York: Routledge.

Noddings, N. (1992). *The challenge to care in schools—an alternative approach to education*. New York: Teacher College Press.

Nystrand, M., & Gamoran, A. (1991). Student engagement: When recitation becomes conversation. In H. Waxman & H. Walberg (Eds.), *Effective teaching: Current research*. Berkeley, CA: McCutchan.

Nystrand, M., & Gamoran, A. (1997). *Opening dialogue: Understanding the dynamics of language and learning in the English classroom*. New York: Teachers College Press.

O'Connor, P. (2012, January 8). In the cave: Philosophy and addiction. *The New York Times*. Retrieved from https://opinionator.blogs.nytimes.com/2012/01/08/out-of-the-cave-philosophy-and-addiction

Painter, N. I. (2010). *The history of white people*. New York: W. W. Norton & Company Inc.

Pearson, R. L. (1970). Gatsby: False prophet of the American dream. *The English Journal, 59*(5), 638–645.

Perry, W. G. (1970). *Forms of intellectual and ethical development in the college years: A scheme*. New York: Holt, Rinehart and Winston.

Popova, Y. B. (2019). Participatory sense-making in narrative experience. In R. Beach & D. Bloome (Eds.), *Languaging relations for transforming the literacy and language arts classroom* (pp. 153–171). New York: Routledge.

Prior, P. (2001). Voices in text, mind, and society: Sociohistoric accounts of discourse acquisition and use. *Journal of Second Language Writing, 10*(1–2), 55–81.

Prior, P., & Olinger, A. R. (2019). Academic literacies as laminated assemblage and embodied semiotic becoming. In D. Bloome, M. L. Castanheira, C. Leung, & J. Rowsell (Eds.), *Re-theorizing literacy practices: Complex social and cultural contexts* (pp. 126–140). New York: Routledge.

Probst, R. E. (2004). *Response and analysis: Teaching literature in secondary school*. Portsmouth, NH: Heinemann.

Purves, A. (1992). Testing literature. In J. Langer (Ed.), *Literature instruction: A focus on student response* (pp. 19–34). Urbana, IL: National Council of Teachers of English.

Rainey, E. C. (2017). Disciplinary literacy in English language arts: Exploring the social and problem-based nature of literary reading and reasoning. *Reading Research Quarterly, 52*(1), 53–71.

Rejan, A. (2017). Reconciling Rosenblatt and the new critics: The quest for an "Experienced Understanding" of literature. *English Education*, 50(1), 10–41.
Richardson, K. (1987). Critical linguistics and textual diagnosis. *Text—Interdisciplinary Journal for the Study of Discourse*, 7(2), 145–164.
Roberts, M. (2006). Scarface, the great Gatsby, and the American dream. *Literature/Film Quarterly*, 34(1), 71–78.
Rogers, R. (2004). *An introduction to critical discourse analysis in education.* New York: Routledge.
Rogers, T., & Soter, A. O. (1997). *Reading across cultures: Teaching literature in a diverse society.* New York: Teachers College Press,
Rorty, R. (1992). *The linguistic turn: Essays in philosophical method.* Chicago: University of Chicago Press.
Rosenblatt, L. M. (1976). *Literature as exploration.* New York: Modern Language Association.
Rosenblatt, L. M. (1978). *The reader, the text, the poem: The transactional theory of the literary work.* Carbondale, IL and Edwardsville: Southern Illinois University Press.
Rosenblatt, L. M. (1999). *Literature as exploration.* New York: Modern Language Association.
Ryu, S. (2016). *Teaching and learning of sophisticated argumentative writing based on dialogic views of rationality in high school language arts classrooms: A formative and design experiment* (Doctoral dissertation), The Ohio State University.
Ryu, S. (2017). A study on the conceptualization of rationality for the teaching and learning of argumentation. *Journal of Reading Research*, 44, 203–238.
Schatzki, T. R. (1996). *Social practices: A Wittgensteinian approach to human activity and the social.* New York: Cambridge University Press.
Schmoker, M., & Jago, C. (2013). Simplifying the ELA common core: Demystifying curriculum. *Kappa Delta Pi Record*, 49(2), 59–63.
Scholes, R. E. (1985). *Textual power: Literary theory and the teaching of English.* New Haven, CT: Yale University Press.
Schraw, G. (2001). Current themes and future directions in epistemological research: A commentary. *Educational Psychology Review*, 13, 451–465.
Schrijvers, M., Janssen, T., Fiahlo, O., & Rijlaarsdam, G. (2018). Gaining insight into human nature: A review of literature classroom intervention studies. *Review of Educational Research*, 20, 1–43.
Schuster, C. I. (1985). Mikhail Bakhtin as rhetorical theorist. *College English*, 47(6), 594–607.
Shuart-Faris, N., & Bloome, D. (Eds.). (2004). *Uses of intertextuality in classroom and educational research.* Greenwich, CT: Information Age Press.
Shulman, L. (1986). Those who understand: Knowledge growth in teaching. *Educational Researcher*, 15(2), 4–14.
Simon, R. S. (2005). Feminine thinking. *Social Theory and Practice*, 31, 1–26.
Smagorinsky, P. (2001). If meaning is constructed, what is it made from? Toward a cultural theory of reading. *Review of Educational Research*, 71(1), 133–169.
Smith, D. V. (1938). The contributions of research to teaching and curriculum-making in English July, 1934, to July, 1937: I. Composition, Grammar, and the Mechanics of English. *The English Journal*, 27(4), 295–311.
Smith, D. V. (1941). Today's challenge to teachers of English. *The English Journal*, 30(2), 101–113.

Smith, M. W., Wilhelm, J. D., & Fredricksen, J. E. (2012). *Oh, yeah? Putting argument to work both in school and out*. Portsmouth, NH: Heinemann.

Stacy, R. H. (1977). *Defamiliarization in language and literature*. Syracuse, NY: Syracuse University Press.

Strauss, S., & Feiz, P. (2014). *Discourse analysis: Putting our worlds into words*. New York: Routledge.

Street, B. (1985). Lit*eracy in theory and practice*. New York: Cambridge University Press.

Street, B. V. (Ed.). (1993). *Cross-cultural approaches to literacy*. Cambridge: Cambridge University Press.

Street, B. V. (1995). *Social literacies: Critical perspectives on literacy in development, ethnography and education*. London: Longman.

Strychacz, T. F. (2003). *Hemingway's theaters of masculinity*. Baton Rouge, LA: LSU Press.

Tannen, D. (1993). *Framing in discourse*. New York: Oxford University Press.

Tannen, D. (2006). Intertextuality in interaction. *Text & Talk*, 26(6), 567–617.

Tanselle, G. T. (1983). Hemingway's Indian camp. *Explicator*, 20(6).

Thomas, E. E. (2015). "We always talk about race": Navigating race talk dilemmas in the teaching of literature. *Research in the Teaching of English*, 154–175.

Toulmin, S. E. (2003). *The uses of argument*. Cambridge: Cambridge University Press.

van Eemeren, F. H., & Houtlosser, P. (Eds.). (2013). *Dialectic and rhetoric: The warp and woof of argumentation analysis*. Berlin: Springer Science & Business Media.

Van Leeuwen, T. (2008). *Discourse and practice: New tools for critical discourse analysis*. Oxford: Oxford University Press.

Volosinov, V. (1929/1973). *Marxism and the philosophy of language* (L. Matejka & I. Titunik, Trans.). Cambridge, MA: Harvard University Press.

Wiggins, G., & McTighe, J. (2008). Put understanding first. *Educational Leadership*, 65(8), 36–41.

Wilder, L., & Wolfe, J. (2009). Sharing the tacit rhetorical knowledge of the literary scholar: The effects of making disciplinary conventions explicit in undergraduate writing about literature courses. *Research in the Teaching of English*, 44(2), 170–209.

Williams, R. (1977). *Marxism and literature*. Oxford: Oxford University Press.

Wooten, D. (2015). *The invention of science: A new history of the scientific revolution*. New York: Harper.

Wynhoff Olsen, A. (2018). How language defines "learning": A classroom view. *No. Acta Paedagogica Vilnensia*, 41, 58–71.

Wynhoff Olsen, A., VanDerHeide, J., Goff, B., & Dunn, M. (2018). A study of student writing as social participation and response. *Written Communication*, 35(1), 58–88.

Literary Works Cited

Achebe, C. (1958/1994). *Things fall apart*. New York: Penguin Publishing Group.

Conrad, J. (1899/1988). *Heart of darkness* (R. Kimbrough, Ed., 3rd ed.). New York: W. W. Norton & Company Inc.

Dickens, C. (1854/2004). *Hard times*. New York: Barnes & Noble, Inc.

Dunn, S. (1990). Allegory of the Cave. In S. Dunn (Ed.), *Landscape at the end of the century: Poems* (pp. 15–16). New York: W. W. Norton & Company Inc.

Fitzgerald, F. S. (1925/2004). *The great Gatsby*. New York: Scribner.

Geldof, B., & Ure, M. (1984). *Do they know it's Christmas? Lyrics and recording*. Retrieved May 11, 2019, from https://genius.com/Band-aid-do-they-know-its-christmas-lyrics

Golding, W. (1954). *Lord of the flies*. New York: Penguin Publishing Group.

Green, J. (2006). *Looking for Alaska*. New York: Penguin New Readers Group.

Hamilton, E., Cairns, H., & Cooper, L. (Eds.). (1961). *The collected dialogues of Plato*. Princeton, NJ: Princeton University Press.

Hemingway, E. (1925). Indian camp. In E. Hemingway (Ed.), *In our time* (pp. 15–19). New York: Charles Scribner's Sons.

Hodges, A. (2015). Intertextuality in discourse. In D. Tannen, H. Hamilton, & D. Schiffrin (Eds.), *The handbook of discourse analysis* (pp. 42–60). Hoboken, NJ: Wiley Blackwell.

Lee, H. (1960/1988). *To kill a mockingbird*. New York: Grand Central Publishing.

Shakespeare, W. (1603/2003). *Hamlet*. New York: Simon & Schuster.

Shakespeare, W. (1606/2003). *Macbeth*. New York: Simon & Schuster.

Steinbeck, J. (1937/1993). *Of mice and men*. New York: Penguin Publishing Group.

Index

abductive reasoning 109, 138
academic socialization 15
Achebe, C. 87, 88–109, 148, 159–163
adapting 30; *see also* refracting
African-American 48; Black 56–57, 113, 136
agency 22, 84; teacher agency 164–167
Agha, A. 20, 28, 47, 131, 132
"Allegory of the Cave" by Plato 90, 101, 112, 114–119, 127, 128, 131, 148, 161
"Allegory of the Cave" poem by Dunn 116
Alsup, J. 1
Althusser, L. 62n10
Anderson, K. T. 21
Annas, P. J. 162
Applebee, A. N. 10, 12–15, 24, 29n7, 147, 150, 151, 153, 156, 157, 169n2
Appleman, D. 3, 12, 37, 52, 62n5
Arendt, H. 22
arguing: arguing to learn 16, 24, 27, 31, 35, 36–41, 56, 59–60, 63–85, 99, 100, 116, 126, 131, 132, 146, 154, 157, 161, 165, 167; five paragraph essay (three-prong essay) 31, 36, 38, 52, 53, 60, 61; learning to argue 36, 65, 66, 114, 116, 132, 161, 165, 167; responsive argumentation 16, 157
Argumentative Writing Project viii, 65, 66, 89, 113, 131, 135, 150, 161
Aristotle 162
audience 89, 92, 93, 108
authority for meaning *see* meaning

Bakhtin, M. M. 22, 37, 38, 41, 55, 59, 145
banality of everyday life 22

Barnes, D. R. 27, 81
Baynham, M. 20
Bazerman, C. 31, 47
Beach, R. 10, 20, 22, 29n7
Beauchemin, F. 25, 63, 134
Becker, A. 63
Belcher, D. D. 162
Benedict, R. 62n8
Bereiter, C. 167
Berger, P. L. 20
Berliner, D. C. 166
Bernstein, B. 58
Berrill, D. P. 162, 163
Bertau, M-C. 78
Bewley, M. 66
Biemann, A. D. 22
Blackburn, M. 3, 23
Black people *see* African-American
Bleich, D. 11
Blommaert, J. 152
Bloome, D. 20, 22, 23, 28n4, 31, 34, 35, 43, 47, 49, 55, 62n10, 127, 133n5, 134, 151, 153
Borg, S. 165
Bourdieu, P. 20
Bowles, S. 19
Brooks, C. 10, 37
Buber, M. 21–22, 37, 38
Burke, K. 147
Butler, J. 55, 134

Callahan, J. F. 66
Carter, S. P. *see* Power-Carter, S.
Castanheira, M. 20
Caughlan, S. 29n7
Chotiner, I. 32, 33, 38, 40, 43, 44–45, 48–53, 62n9
chronotope *see* time
civilization 106, 121–122, 131

class (socioeconomic class) 3, 19, 23–27, 84, 92, 93, 102, 103, 148, 153
classroom conversations *see* classroom discourse
classroom discourse 1, 3, 14, 23, 25, 33, 38, 48–52, 57, 59, 63–65, 68, 78–80, 83–84, 88, 102, 132, 134, 141, 144, 148, 153–154, 162, 168
classroom ethnography *see* ethnographic research
classroom interactions *see* classroom discourse
classroom lessons 4, 7–8, 14, 31, 32, 40, 60, 68–76, 81, 109, 127, 152, 159, 165; procedural display 49, 127
common core state standards (CCSS) 15
complexity 16, 41, 61, 88, 100, 152, 154, 155, 158, 163
Conrad, J. 112, 117
contextualization 44–46, 101
Cook-Gumperz, J. 20
counternarrative *see* narrative
critical awareness 90
critical race theory 86, 89
critical theory 37, 52
culture 61, 89, 97, 101, 103, 107, 109, 122, 126, 159; cultural import 30, 41, 42, 47, 48, 50, 60, 63, 78, 79, 84, 86, 112, 113, 127, 148, 154
curriculum 12, 13, 14, 17, 41, 58, 65, 66, 89, 114, 127, 161, 167

Dafermos, M. 84
Davies, B. 21
De Certeau, M. 102
Defalco, J. 4
definitions of knowledge *see* knowledge
democracy 13, 109
Derrida, J. 63
dialectic 1, 35, 38, 40, 41, 64, 65, 81–85, 99–103, 109, 154, 155, 157, 159, 161, 164
dialogic rationality *see* rationality
Dickens, C. 1
Dillard, C. B. 22
discourse 16, 152, 159; authoritative discourse 59; internally persuasive discourse 59, 60
discourse analysis 22, 25, 31, 34, 63, 151, 153
discussion *see* instruction
dominance 3–9, 14, 18, 20, 21, 24–27, 157, 158, 165, 166

"Do They Know It's Christmas?" 92, 96, 101–102, 110n2
drama 97
Dunn, S. 116
Dussel, E. 22

Eagleton, T. 54
Edmiston, B. 97
Egan-Robertson, A. 2, 23, 55, 133n2, 133n5, 134
emic perspective 48
empathy 90, 109, 110
epistemology(ies) *see* knowledge
erasure 57, 59
Erickson, F. 23
essential questions *see* instruction
ethics 62n7, 99, 109, 111n4, 131
ethnographic research 2, 16, 17, 19, 34, 35, 48, 60, 151, 152; classroom ethnography 40, 60
ethnography *see* ethnographic research
expertise 167; adaptive expertise 166; teacher expertise 164–167, 169n2
exploratory talk 3, 27, 81
evidence 4–9, 13 16, 18, 21–25, 31–33, 36, 38–44, 48–59, 60, 65, 78, 81–83, 108, 152, 158, 163, 165; textual evidence 1, 15. 59, 66–67, 70–74, 97–99, 103–105, 116, 118–119, 165

feminism 41, 77, 78, 86, 89, 162
Fetterley, J. 11, 24
Fish, S. E. 11, 12
Fitzgerald, F. S. 65, 66, 76
five paragraph essay *see* arguing
Flyvbjerg, B. 41, 110n4
Foucault, M. 63
Fowler, C. 55, 134
framing 18–26, 41, 43, 49, 52, 58, 78, 84, 87, 90, 91, 99–103, 128, 131, 137, 146, 148, 154, 161–163
Freire, P. 22
Friedman, M. S. 22
Fuentes, C. 54

Gadamer, H-G. 41, 88
Gates, H. L., Jr. 11, 24, 54
Geertz, C. 31, 42, 55, 134
Geldof, B. 110n2
Gender 3, 11, 15, 19, 23–27, 81, 84, 86, 89, 90, 92, 143, 148, 153

genre study 12, 14, 38, 150
Gergen, K. J. 20, 55, 134
Gilbert, M. A. 162
Giroux, H. 19
Gladwell, M. 32, 33, 38, 40, 43, 44, 48, 49, 50, 51, 53, 61, 62n9
Goldman, S. R. 15
Gourevitch, P. 135
The Great Gatsby 65–84, 86, 158
Green, J. L. 20, 28n4, 43, 60
Gumperz, J. J. 22

Habermas, J. 41
Halasek, K. 145
Halliday, M. A. K. 63
Hamilton, E. 64
Hamlet 112, 118–119, 128
Hanks, W. F. 47, 113, 129, 132
Hard Times 1
Hatano, G. 165, 166, 167
Heart of Darkness 112, 117, 118, 121–131, 133n5, 148, 161
Heath, S. 2, 20, 26
Heathcote, D. 97
Hegel, G. W. F. 64
Hemingway, E. 6–7, 64, 78
hierarchy 3, 25, 27, 38, 64, 108
Hillocks, G., Jr. 158, 159
Hodges, A. 2, 62n11
Hofer, B. K. 133n1
Holland, D. 21
Holland, N. 11
Holloway, K. F.
human condition 1, 2, 13, 16, 19, 22, 23, 26–27, 54–55, 65, 83, 88, 99, 100, 112, 116, 130, 132, 146, 147, 150, 153–154, 157, 158, 160, 163, 167–168
human rights 97, 102–103, 159, 160, 163
Hymes, D. 20, 22

ideology(ies) 15, 19, 24, 54, 59–61, 62n5, 62n6, 62n7, 63, 66, 87, 99, 101, 102, 113, 130–131, 134, 152, 159
"in-between" spaces 78–80
indexicality 35, 47–54, 62n6, 112–133, 155, 159
"Indian Camp" 19–26, 157, 165
Inside the Hotel Rwanda 134–149, 164
instruction 12–14, 17, 18, 88, 112, 114, 127, 147, 151, 153, 156–160, 164–165; essential questions 135, 136–147, 163–164; Socratic circles 37, 154; "ways of seeing" 87–110, 157, 161
instructional conversations *see* classroom discourse
intercontextuality *see* intertextuality
interdiscursivity *see* intertextuality
interpellation *see* intertextuality
interpretive community(ies) 10, 12, 52
intersubjectivity 42
intertextuality 2, 20, 48–52, 62n12, 62n11, 112–133, 133n4, 133n5; reported speech 129–130
Isenberg, N. 23
Ivanic. R. 20

Jago, C. 1
Johnson, T. S. 31
Jorgensen, J. N. 63

Kahneman, D. 132n1
Kant, I. 111n4
Kayi-Adyar, H. 165
Kayihura, E. 134, 135, 149n1
Ketter, J. 62n10
Kim, M. Y. 83
Kintsch, W. 28n5
knowledge 14, 15, 18, 20, 29, 29n7, 48, 61, 65, 110n4, 116, 117–119, 133n1, 150, 153, 162, 165–168; definition of 9, 52, 54; epistemology(ies) 2, 9, 18, 20–21, 59, 116, 122, 132n1; literary knowledge 2, 11, 14, 16, 26, 157; ontology(ies) 21, 27, 116, 122, 132n1
Kriesberg, S. 78
Kristeva, J. 55
Kuhn, D. 8, 22, 133n1

Langer, J. A. 11, 54
language and power *see* power
languaging 2, 21, 22, 27, 28n5, 30, 35, 63–64, 83, 134, 152, 153, 155
languaging thinking 83
Latour, B. 20
Layton, L. 1
learning opportunities 61
Lee, C. D. 3, 11
Lee, H. 148
Leki, I. 157
Lemke, J. L. 133n3
Levine, S. 37
Lewis, W. E. 37
literacy 167; ideological model of literacy 58, 59; literacy education 47; literacy event 26

literary text 1–3, 7, 11, 16, 18, 23, 26–27, 28n5, 30–32, 37, 40, 41, 48, 52–55, 64, 78, 86, 87, 100, 109, 112, 116–117, 126–129, 134, 139, 153–157, 159–163, 165, 168
literary theories: critical literary theories 37, 52, 110; interpretive communities 12, 52, 153, 155; new criticism 10–11, 14, 26, 29n7, 37, 52, 78, 86, 151, 157; reader response 11, 12, 37, 45, 49, 52, 53, 78, 86, 157
literature as a prop 2, 26, 149n1, 153–154, 156, 157, 165–168
literature education 3, 13, 112; critical encounters 29n8; cultural modeling 29n8; history of 13
Lloyd-Jones, R. 13
Looking for Alaska 60
love 22, 83
Lunsford, A. A. 13, 22
Lysaker, J. 29n5

Macaluso, M. 31
Macbeth 112, 118–119, 128
Madsen, L. M. 63
Mailloux, S. 11
Mandell, B. 13
Marx, K. 64
Marxism 41, 89
McEwan, I. 54
meaning: authority for meaning/interpretation 76, 78, 79; constructing meaning 60, 78, 86, 88, 127, 154, 159; definition of 30, 156
Mellor, B. 37
Miall, D. S. 63
microethnographic discourse analysis *see* discourse analysis
mid-level theory 31
morality 105, 111n4
Morrison, T. 24
Mulligan, R. 48
multiple perspectives 9, 32, 35, 41–47, 49, 62n5, 79, 86–111, 116, 154–155, 157, 159, 161

narrative 129, 138; counternarrative 129; grand narrative 129; of personhood 144–146
new criticism *see* literary theories
Newell, G. 9, 16, 17, 21, 22, 31, 36, 37, 56, 59, 60, 61, 65, 87, 100, 110n4, 150, 158, 159, 166, 167

Noddings, N. 78
nominalization 142–143
Nystrand, M. 14

O'Connor, P. 116
Of Mice and Men 60
ontology *see* knowledge
othering 107

Painter, N. I. 23
particularity 25
Pearson, R. L. 66
Perry, W. G. 133
personhood 16, 30, 35, 37, 38, 41, 54–61, 65, 82, 83, 88, 99, 112, 116, 130, 132, 134–150, 154–155, 160, 163–164, 168
Plato 64, 114, 127
Popova, Y. B. 29n5
positioning *see* social positioning
power 15, 20, 24–25, 37–38, 52, 54, 62n7, 84, 89, 92, 101, 103, 107–108, 126, 135, 148; power over 78, 84; power with 78
Power-Carter, S. 28n4, 63
Prior, P. 20, 47
problematizing 63, 86, 88, 100
Probst, R. E. 37
process drama *see* drama
Purves, A. 14

race 3, 11, 19, 21, 23–27, 89, 90, 92, 148, 153
Rainey, E. C. 15
rationality 35, 41, 42–46, 62n7, 78, 86–111, 148, 154–155; contextualized rationality 42, 100, 102, 111; decontextualized rationality 42, 100, 107; dialogic rationality 42
reader response *see* literary theories
recontextualization 20, 28
refracting 2, 20, 28, 30, 43, 55, 64, 166
Rejan, A. 11
relativism 1, 11, 28n5, 41, 109, 154
reported speech *see* intertextuality
responsive argumentation *see* arguing, responsive argumentation
revoicing *see* voice
rhetoric 22, 89, 102
Richardson, K. 63
Roberts, M. 66
Rogers, R. 63
Rogers, T. 24
role playing *see* drama

186   Index

Rorty, R. 55
Rosenblatt, L. M. 11, 167, 168
Ryu, S. 62n6, 110n4

Schatzki, T. R. 20
Schmoker, M. 1
Scholes, R. E. 11
Schraw, G. 133n1
Schrijvers, M. 54
Schuster, C. I. 145
semiotic 2, 20, 21, 26, 150
sexuality 3, 19, 23, 24, 25, 27, 92, 148, 153
Shakespeare, W. 60
Shuart-Faris, N. 47, 113
Shulman, L. 166
Simon, R. S. 111
Smagorinsky, P. 11, 31
Smith, D. V. 13, 14
Smith, M. W. 158
social construction 2, 7, 19, 21–22, 113, 127, 153–154, 159
social identity 47, 51, 59, 140, 168
social inequalities 84
social positioning 21, 30, 47, 49, 53, 54, 55, 59, 105
social practices 9, 13, 16, 20, 25, 31, 40, 58, 59, 61, 150, 153, 159
social relationships 9, 21, 22, 52, 59, 145, 150, 153
social significance 30, 41, 42, 47, 48, 59, 60, 63, 78, 79, 84, 86, 88, 112, 113, 127, 148, 154, 158
socioeconomic class *see* class
Socratic circles *see* instruction
spirituality 22
Stacy, R. H. 63
Steinbeck, J. 60
Strauss, S. 113
Street, B. 20, 29n5, 58
Strychacz, T. F. 4
subjectivity 45
subtext *see* text

Tanselle, G. T. 4
teacher(s): Ms. Field 31–62, 77, 132, 165, 166; Ms. Hill 3–9, 15, 20–27, 157, 159, 161, 166; Ms. McClure 132, 135–149, 161; Mr. Mosley 65–85, 132, 148, 158, 161; Ms. Nelson 87–110, 148, 159, 160–163; Mr. Watson 113–132, 161
teacher agency *see* agency
teacher expertise *see* expertise
tension 26, 64, 66, 68, 73–74, 80–83, 102, 106–108, 109, 146
text 6, 8, 10, 12, 14, 21, 26, 42, 47, 55, 59, 100, 102, 112, 113, 116, 126, 129, 153–159; subtext 92, 94, 96; *see also* literary text
Things Fall Apart 87–109, 148, 159–161, 163
Thomas, E. E. 3
three-prong essay *see* arguing
time 18, 20, 23, 25, 27, 30, 41, 54–55, 60–61, 112, 113, 127–132, 133n3, 145–148, 154; chronotope 41, 61, 145–146
To Kill a Mockingbird 31–35, 48–49, 77–78, 148, 165
Toulmin, S. E. 36, 65, 158, 159, 162, 169

uncertainty 88, 109, 110, 155
unpacking 63, 64, 76, 83, 84, 86, 88, 100, 101

van Eemeren, F. H. 64
Van Leeuwen, T. 20
voice 21, 22, 89, 105, 142; revoicing 4, 81, 82
Volosinov, V. 20, 22, 41, 55

warrant 4–9, 16, 21, 24–27, 32, 43–58, 60, 65–66, 78, 80–83, 97, 99, 103–105, 108, 131, 158–160, 165
"ways of seeing" *see* instruction
Wiggins, G. 147
Wilder, L. 15
Williams, R. 63, 64
Wooten, D. 42
Wynhoff Olsen, A. 62n6

Printed in the United States
By Bookmasters